DEEP IN THE HEART
OF THE ROCKIES

DEEP IN THE HEART
OF THE ROCKIES

*Selected Columns
from The Denver Post 1985-98*

Ed Quillen

Foreword by
Richard Lamm

Edited by
Mary Jean Porter

WESTERN OPINION SERIES

MUSIC MOUNTAIN PRESS
WESTCLIFFE, COLORADO

Western Opinion Series

DEEP IN THE HEART OF THE ROCKIES

Published by
Music Mountain Press
Box 899 • Westcliffe, Colorado 81252
Voice and Fax: 719 783-9012
Email: mmp@creativeminds.com
Web site: http://www.creativeminds.com/

Editor: Mary Jean Porter • Line Editor: Ray Dangel
Book design: Bob Thomason and Patricia Perkinson

Publisher's Cataloging-in-Publication
(Provided by Quality Books, Inc.)

Quillen, Ed.
    Deep in the heart of the Rockies : selected columns from
the Denver post 1985-98 / foreword by Richard Lamm ; edited by
Mary Jean Porter. -- 1st ed.
    p. cm. -- (Western opinion series ; no.1)
    Preassigned LCCN: 98-66401
    ISBN: 0-9656126-7-8

    1. Colorado--Social life and customs--1971- 2. United
States--Social life and customs--1971-   I. Title.

F781.3.Q55 1998   978.8'033
                             QBI98-660

To my daughters, Columbine and Abby.
They're smart and sassy, and make their father proud.

Contents

CONTENTS

CONTENTS

The Storytellers

RICHARD LAMM

s a sailboat needs both a sail and an anchor, a state needs both a sense of its past and a sense of its future. It needs to know where it came from and where it is going. It needs both its historians and its futurists. It needs to be reminded constantly that its citizens have a common stake in each other and in their heritage.

A state is not a rooming house where various people reside while they make their living. A state cannot be only about geography; it also must be about community. We cannot just live in Colorado; we must to some degree become Coloradans. A community is more than the sum of its citizens. John Gardner, one of the wise old minds of America, put it so well: "If the community is lucky, and fewer and fewer are, it will have a shared history and tradition. It will have its story, its legends and heroes, and will retell that story often. It will have symbols of group identity, a name, a flag, a location, songs and stories which it will use to heighten its members' sense of belonging." He goes on to say: "To maintain the sense of belonging and the dedication and commitment so essential to community life, members need inspiring reminders of shared goals and values."

A state is much more than a place on a map. It is a state of mind, a shared vision, a common fate. It cannot be taken for granted. A community is not a state of nature. A herd is a state of nature. A flock, a covey, a gaggle is a state of nature, but a community is not. A community of different religions, races and nationalities is against most of the lessons of history, as we see daily on our TV sets. Humans bond to families, but not necessarily with their neighbors. A community requires social architecture: bridge builders, structural engineers who build bonds and bridges, removing barriers. It needs its storytellers.

Colorado is by definition a place on the map, but it is not intrinsically a community. We will not inevitably pass community on to our children. Community is not a guarantee, but a continuing challenge. It is here where we need the storytellers who can update, review and remind citizens of their history, myths, traditions and common stake in each other — which brings us to Ed Quillen and "Deep in the Heart of the Rockies."

Ed Quillen is one of Colorado's storytellers — part historian, part futurist, part minstrel, part curmudgeon. Ed has educated, enraged, amused, challenged, criticized and complimented Coloradans for many years. He is part of the social glue a state needs to turn geography into community.

Ed started writing early and kept at it with love and dedication. He was the editor of his college newspaper, as well as copy editor and managing editor. He has been a reporter with a Colorado weekly newspaper (Longmont Scene) and editor and publisher of the Middle Park Times, a weekly newspaper in Kremmling, Colorado. That led to a wide variety of other experiences, such as being editor of the Summit County Journal in Breckenridge and managing editor of the Mountain Mail in Salida, Colorado. Currently he is the publisher of Colorado Central, a small regional monthly magazine. However illustrious and varied Ed's career has been, he is known most widely as a regular columnist in The Denver Post. He has won many state writing awards and two national awards.

Ed is a libertarian populist, and if you think I contradict myself, read this book. He is easy to like but hard to label. He is a scold, but one like the loving aunt who used to scold you with lots of love and affection. He is the voice of the real Main Street, but at the same time a futurist. In my mind, he is among the few who understand both the benefits of growth and the price a place pays for it. He is not a blind booster; he is a thoughtful citizen and philosopher who is never afraid to take on a big subject or even a big foe.

We need many more like Ed Quillen. We need him for our enjoyment, but also for our institutional memory. We need him as one of the voices of the Colorado community. We have not tested community recently. It is easy to keep community when we are dividing up the spoils of a rich continent and a growing economy. Adversity, not success, tests community. Do we cooperate during times of adversity to solve, soothe and mitigate, or do we form tribes and, like ravenous dogs, fight over a static pie? Community, like friendship, is never really tested until it jointly faces adversity. A rising economic tide not only raises all ships; it also keeps them from bumping into each other.

In light of these new economic and social realities, we must ask: How do we build a quality community? I believe this question to be immensely important. We see daily the results of not building a community — in Bosnia, in

Chechnya, in Sri Lanka, in Quebec, in Rwanda. What is going on today in Azerbaijan and Bosnia is not a failure of communism. It is a failure of community. Serbs, Slovenians, Croats and Bosnians were killing each other before Marx was born. People in Bosnia are far less diverse than those in the United States. The secret is that we formed a community *(e pluribus unum)* and Bosnia did not.

"People who share a geographic area must become a community or they become balkanized, fragmented, and factionalized. We all bond naturally to our families, we bond to our geographic location: If you don't know where you are, you don't know who you are." (Wendell Berry).

But we do not bond easily to our neighbors. We seem instinctively to view them as competitors. A community needs a shared stake in the future. It needs a shared language, a shared culture, shared norms and values. It needs, in short, a social glue that is the essence of community. Citizens must understand their shared fate. To say my fate is not tied to your fate is like saying, "Your end of the boat is sinking."

As we careen into an ever more diverse future, we need our prophets and storytellers, our historians and our civic leaders. Ed Quillen is all four rolled into one.

Introduction

Since hardly anybody reads book introductions, and if they do get read, it's after the rest of the book, I'm not sure why we even bother with an introduc-tion, let alone put it up in front as though it should be read first.

I'll use it to answer questions I often get asked. That way, when the questions pop up again, I can tell people they have to buy the book, and thus enrich my royalty statement.

But first, a note on the text. The columns here are not "as published in The Denver Post." The source here was my archives, not the newspaper's. The main reason for this was sloth — mine were (mostly) already in a computer and ready to go, whereas The Post's computer doesn't save things like old columns. I would have had to scan or retype them from my clip collection, and that's tedious work.

Further, a piece can get changed considerably between writing and newspaper publication, usually for space and layout reasons which don't apply in the same way to a book.

So, these are the same columns I sent to the Post (with minor corrections provided by hindsight and reduced deadline pressure — for instance, I made sure it was the proper "Langston Hughes" instead of the incorrect "Langford Hughes" that slipped out once).

And they are edited by the same fellow, Ray Dangel, who edited most of them for The Post over the years. In general, they should be pretty close to what was in The Post, but not exact replicas. I don't know if anybody cares about this, but hey, this is a book introduction, an excellent place to deal with such arcane matters.

Now, to answer those questions.

How do you become a columnist?

I can't speak for others, but as best I know, my writing career started by passing notes in class, usually of a mocking nature. If the recipient cracked up laughing and thereby got in trouble, then I knew I'd done a fine job of writing. If the teacher, upon grabbing the offending message and reading it, began to chuckle, then I knew it was an excellent piece of writing. Usually, though, I just got sent to the office. Thus do schools encourage literary creativity.

Beyond that, I can't say. In essence, columns are short essays which can be informative, satirical, entertaining, persuasive, etc. It's a form of writing I've always felt comfortable with, from the first time I was assigned to write a short essay in seventh grade.

At Greeley West High School, from which I was graduated in 1968, I was feature editor of the official school paper, Westword, and wrote a column for it. It won an award, though memory pales as to particulars. I didn't get into Quill & Scroll, the high-school journalistic honor society, because the journalism teacher didn't like me because I also put out an "underground" newspaper. It had satiric commentary, such as a comparison of pep assemblies to the Nazi rallies at Nuremburg we had just studied in world history. Fortunately, I have lost all my copies of that, so I don't think they're around to embarrass me.

In college at the University of Northern Colorado in Greeley (except it was Colorado State College at the time), I thought I was hot stuff and submitted some sample columns to Sharon Holler, editor of the campus paper, the Mirror.

Sharon didn't like any of them, but said I had potential and should keep trying. The Mirror already had a provocative and humorous columnist, Rita Johnson and her "Green Weenie," so I didn't see much hope for my potential.

But I finally wrote one that Sharon liked, and it worked into a regular slot, then I got to be news editor of the Mirror, and in 1970-71, editor. That put me into "Who's Who on American College and University Campuses" or some such list that sounded good at the time , and I thought I'd have the world by the tail on a downhill pull and never have to work in a laundry again.

After that was a career of careering among small newspapers — the weekly Longmont Scene, the Middle Park Times in Kremmling, the Summit County Journal in Breckenridge, and the daily Mountain Mail in Salida — when I wasn't working in a laundry between newspaper jobs.

I wrote columns for these papers — I usually didn't have much trouble getting an editor to print them, since I was the editor.

In 1983, after unsuccessful job hunts in the large cities of this state where the dailies were alleged to pay a living wage, it dawned on me that it was my life's fate to be poor and live in the middle of nowhere. And I could do that without an employer just as easily as with that aggravation, so I quit the Salida daily and decided to try freelancing until I starved and ended up editing a weekly in western Nebraska.

But I managed to sell enough writing to pay the bills, and Chuck Green had just taken over as The Post's editorial page editor. I knew Chuck from his days as city editor, when he cultivated hinterland editors for plane-wreck coverage and the like. He said he'd be buying more freelance stuff for the editorial pages, and I should send down some columns.

I did. They got set back. I sent more, and they returned more. Eventually I connected with one, and then another, and more, and I asked Chuck about a regular spot, and he agreed — just on Fridays at first, then twice a week.

And that's how I became a columnist — persistence. When I was a kid, I had this fantasy that the powers of this world were on the lookout for brilliant, talented people like me, and they'd appear one morning with grand offers. Alas, it has never worked that way. You've got to call them — they don't come looking for you.

Where do you get your ideas for columns?

The absolute best source is to listen in on a couple of people with attitude problems as they discuss everything that ails the city, county, state and nation.

Different mountain towns have different specialties — Aspen produces Eurotrash, Breckenridge grows cocaine addicts, Durango attracts trustfunders, etc. Salida specializes in curmudgeons, so it's pretty easy to sit in a diner here and in half an hour of eavesdropping, pick up a month's worth of column ideas.

My wife, Martha, and my father, also Ed Quillen, both have bad attitudes, and when they get into an animated discussion, I try to take notes.

Failing that, one good trick is to take some current proposal and imagine what would happen if it were extended. Or to look for holes and cant in public positions. Or to play with numbers and see where they lead.

Getting an idea I can work with is the hardest part of my process. The actual writing is pretty easy after I've figured out what I need to say about a given topic.

Unlike many columnists who write of political matters, I seldom get tips or leaks. In that regard, I'm like Will Rogers — "all I know is what I read in the papers." This may be because I live in Salida, 150 miles from the population and political center of the state. I'm not part of the loop.

Do you really live in Salida?

Yes. We've lived here since 1978, although in 1989 we moved to a bigger house about three blocks from the old one.

Our two daughters went all the way through school in Salida (both, though, were born in Kremmling).

My life isn't boring to me, but it's pretty boring to read about — Ozzie and Harriet, or Ward and June Cleaver, are rather glamorous and exciting by comparison. Two cats, a dog, an old house on a small lot, two old cars, small town — think of a poster family for Republican propaganda purposes, and you've got us down pretty well.

How do you get your columns to Denver?

With a computer and modem. It isn't exactly e-mail, but it's the same process. As best I know, providing I put the proper header information on the text I send, the column arrives in The Post's computer as though it were wire-service copy.

Occasionally, if I'm on the road, I'll use fax or e-mail through the Internet. Once I even took in a typewritten column, since I happened to be in Denver, but then they had to scan it and it was a lot more work.

Most of the time, I write the column with plain old DOS WordStar. When I'm done, I feed it to an assembly-language program I wrote to remove the WordStar formatting codes. The resulting plain text is then transmitted over the phone to The Post's computer. The whole process takes about 20 seconds.

Then I call to be sure it got there, and depending on how long it takes to find the entry in The Post's system, and on how garrulous the editor is (usually Bob Ewegen these days), the process can take up to 20 minutes. And sometimes it isn't there — got lost in the ether or something — and so I have to try transmitting it again.

This seems to run in phases. Months will go by with perfect transmissions, and then for a few weeks it will arrive in bits and pieces if it arrives at all. I have not been able to correlate this with sunspot cycles or astrological portents.

Have you ever been sued for libel?

Threatened many times, but only one actual suit. That was in 1980, when I was managing editor of the Salida paper, and had written some columns that I thought were funny concerning two county commissioners, John Lane and Bob Welker.

Lane, who would be recalled from office by the public, did not share in the mirth. He sued for $1.75 million, then raised it $2.25 million after he was recalled. His suit was dismissed as baseless by the district court.

Lane appealed that to the Colorado Court of Appeals, which upheld the dismissal. So did the Colorado Supreme Court. So did the United States Supreme Court.

But that was almost five years later. This is one reason I have little respect for the judicial system in this country. Anybody can walk in off the street and sue you. Even when the suit has absolutely no merit, like this one, it can take five years and thousands of dollars to have it dismissed. And during those five years, instead of focusing on your work, you're enduring discovery and depositions.

What remedy should people have if they feel as though they've been unjustly maligned by a newspaper?

The First Amendment guarantees an absolute right to start your own. So do it, if you don't like what's in the paper. Don't go see a lawyer. I can't think of anybody I hate enough to put through that process.

Do you do anything else besides write columns?

I take out the trash and mow the lawn.

Martha and I publish Colorado Central, a small regional monthly magazine. I've also written for many other publications, ranging from Farm Journal to PC Computing. These days, it's mostly for High Country News in Paonia.

I take a few speaking engagements, more for the motel room and a couple of days of "mini-vacation" than for the money. I've read that many people are terrified of public speaking, but it's never bothered me — I'm loud, I like the sound of my own voice, and I love being the center of attention. In past days, I did a fair amount of computer work — programming and consulting. I fell into that because this is a little town, and in 1985 or so, local people with their first computers didn't know where to call except for this gossip that "Quillen has a computer and maybe he can help you out." Fortunately for all concerned, Salida has real experts now, rather than self-taught English majors.

One of those real experts is Mark Emmer, whose Spitbol compiler aided immensely in the preparation of this book. Spitbol is an obscure programming language designed to work with strings of text. Even though it is versatile, relatively easy to learn, and quite powerful, it's almost unknown.

Mark once contracted with me to generate some publicity and public relations for Spitbol, and as you can tell because you've never heard of Spitbol, I failed.

Many journalists get lured into the world of public relations (better money and regular hours are quite tempting), but my failure with Spitbol should insure against that happening to me. And besides, I can't think of a single company whose image I would enhance.

Media, Words & Computers

O rganizing a collection of columns is like writing a column on certain mornings — there are things you think really must be included, but there is no obvious connection among them.

Contriving plausible links between disparate items is part of the job, I suppose, whether you're producing mere newspaper columns, authoritative history texts or provocative conspiracy theories.

This section is a farrago concerning media, word usage and computers — topics that would fit into the "0" category of a library organized under the Dewey Decimal System, still in use in many small libraries like Salida's.

So there, I've found a unifying theme.

As for some particulars, the "Quality Honored in Reverse" column appeared in 1985, before I was a regular at The Denver Post. Some months earlier, I'd seen Chuck Green, then editorial page editor at The Post, and mentioned how the easiest way for a small-town editor to get fired was to put out a good paper.

"Make a column out of it," he said, "and we'll run it during the state press association convention in February."

So I did, and he did, and it has pretty well guaranteed I'll never again hold a day job at any newspaper in Colorado. Since those jobs, at small-town papers, offer long hours and miserable pay, it's not a major loss.

As for the metro papers with better pay and hours, being a columnist is the closest I've ever gotten to that work. People will ask me why The Post did this or that, and I'll patiently explain that I know nothing of the newspaper's internal operations and that I seldom visit the Post building. In fact, the last time I tried, it took me about half an hour to get past security.

To keep my hand in regular journalism, I fill in at the Wet Mountain Tribune in Westcliffe when its publisher, Jim Little, goes on vacation. My work there essentially consists of sitting around the office, drinking coffee and issuing orders — it's a job perfectly suited for my inborn journalistic talents.

I might also note that, despite all you hear about the Biased Liberal Media, the weekly Tribune in tiny Westcliffe is, so far as I know, the largest newspaper in the world owned by a registered Democrat.

Another frequent column topic is word usage. Like most writers, I love words — they're my tools, frustrated as I feel on those frequent occasions when the right word just won't appear.

Perhaps because I often sweat to find the right words and use them properly, I get annoyed when I see or hear words misused — "media" as a singular, or the redundant "Rio Grande River," or in Boulder, "incident" instead of "murder."

Another tool of the trade is the computer, and I was perfectly happy with computers before the "graphical user interface" became ubiquitous. Some may say that it's easier to point to an icon than to type a command, but I'll go with the historians here. They say that the alphabet was a great advance on hieroglyphics, and I agree. Trying to guess what a screen icon might stand for, as opposed to the precision of typed command words, strikes me as a great step backward.

But in general, I think computers are wonderful. I can remember, in my newspaper days, taking stories by dictation from distant reporters — a long and painful process, fraught with possibilities for error.

Now the words come through the phone line. A few seconds after I complete a column, it's in The Post's computer, 150 miles away, as though I had written it in the building.

This convenience comes at a price, of course, or at least it did for me. I had to learn to use the machine, at a time when there were few people around town who could teach me.

I had some background in electronics — it was a childhood interest, and I even had a novice ham license (WN0QNY, if memory serves). Alas for my prospects as a nerd in thick glasses who could get stinking rich on an IPO well before my 40th birthday, the license arrived about the same time as an even greater interest in girls and cars.

Every time I burn myself with a soldering iron these days, I think, "I was an English major. This wasn't ever supposed to happen to me."

But every time I have to patch a commercial program or write one of my own, I'm grateful that I got the oft-criticized "new math" in high school, especially the part about different number bases. Binary, octal and hexadecimal notations are not total mysteries — I've even written for computer magazines, and I write a fair amount of my own utility software in assembly language or SPITBOL.

When I started writing regular columns in 1986, I had an Osborne I and a 300 bps modem. My current machine is, like most of its predecessors, cobbled together from parts at hand and whatever upgrade I had in mind — a Pentium 75 with 16 megabytes of RAM, about two gigs of hard disk space on two drives, and an internal 28.8 kbps modem.

I still use the DOS version of WordStar for almost all of my writing. My fingers know it, so that I can focus on putting the right words in the right order.

A scholar, I suspect, could find a correlation between the rise of "what you see is what you get" display and a decline in writing quality. If you're a writer worrying about line breaks and font selection, you aren't paying attention to your job — finding the right words and putting them in the right order.

QUALITY HONORED IN REVERSE
February 25, 1985

PERHAPS DENVER will be able to attract a better class of delegates once the railroad yards are ripped up behind Union Station. Until then, though, it will have to settle for minor conclaves like the annual convention of the Colorado Press Association this week.

From Durango to Julesburg, publishers will gather to swill free liquor, complain about the cost of newsprint and attend seminars on how to earn better returns from their small-town newspapers.

Despite their protestations to the contrary, and despite their praise of editorial quality when they hand out awards at their convention, Colorado newspaper publishers have demonstrated no fervent desire to reward their editors for putting out good papers.

In fact, it would be easy to make a case for the opposite: The surest way to lose your job as editor of a small-town Colorado newspaper is to be good at your work.

Consider John Young, editor of the Alamosa Valley Courier from 1978 to 1983. He won a wall full of awards from the Colorado Press Association for everything from overall general excellence to his personal column on the Wednesday editorial page. Under his direction, the Courier was an attractive, interesting paper.

But it was owned by a Kansas-based chain that sent in a new publisher — some offspring of one of the principal owners. The new publisher wanted to put ads on the front page; he wanted to pull back on the Courier's coverage and he wanted the newspaper to be less controversial. At last report, John Young was in El Paso, Texas. Reading the Courier now is about as interesting as watching paint dry.

Allen Best edited the Winter Park Manifest for Virginia Cornell; he stayed as editor after she sold it to William Potter Johnson, who controls about a dozen Colorado papers from his home in Tucson, Ariz. But Best didn't stay long. Last spring, less than a year after the sale, he was fired.

Never mind that the Manifest's circulation had risen from 900 to more than 4,000 while Best edited it, and never mind his writing awards during his seven years in Grand County. Best was fired because he "didn't fit in with the community." The rising circulation normally would indicate that Best was putting out a paper that fit in well with the community. But in the world of Colorado journalism, one is supposed to believe that someone in Tucson knows more about the needs of Winter Park than the subscribers in Winter Park do.

Best has served most of this winter on a snowmaking crew at a ski resort, and the Manifest now fits in so well with Winter Park that its circulation has dropped.

Nowhere in the Rockies was there a finer newspaper war than the battles in Summit County. A decade ago, Bill King, a chain owner, had the Summit Sentinel in Dillon. Bob Sweeney, another chain baron, owned the Summit County Journal in Breckenridge. Even through several ownership changes in succeeding years, the papers went after each other hammer and tongs.

Stephanie Capitina edited the Journal in 1982 and 1983. During her tenure she amassed awards, including the sweepstakes prize for putting out the best weekly newspaper in Colorado. Then the Journal owners decided to sell; the owners of the Dillon paper bought the Journal. When they met the Journal staffs they told the customary lies about how no one had to worry about losing his job.

In any other enterprise, someone as talented and enthusiastic as Capitina would be considered an asset. Not in Colorado journalism, though. She was told that, "Now that we own both papers in the county, we don't have to waste money and effort on putting out a good paper, so we don't need you any more." The last I heard, she was waiting tables.

Those are merely one-time colleagues whom I happen to know or know of; only the publishers meeting in Denver know precisely how many other Colorado editors have damaged or destroyed their careers by putting out good papers. Maybe it will come up at one of the seminars while they're learning how to put 15-watt light bulbs in the lavatory to keep their employees from reading on company time.

4

The Word 'Family' Needs Some Work
July 10, 1987

Even Ben Wattenberg finally has found something that worries him. The pop economist once found cheer amid the gloom; remember "The Good News is that the Bad News is Wrong"?

Now, however, he is promoting a new book, "The Birth Dearth." He says we face a big problem. Americans aren't building babies as fast as we once did. If this trend continues, we'll run out of fast-food clerks, expendable soldiers and, most important, customers for the products of American industry.

Clearly, this is a threat to our cherished way of life. So how do we encourage more people to have bigger families?

We could start by eliminating the negative connotations of the word "family." As it is, family is a synonym for cheap and tasteless, as with restaurants that promote "family fare." Or it means boring and preachy, as in "a movie for family audiences." It sounds ominous and sinister when you mention "the Five Families of New York."

Even when you're talking about the normal notion of family, families have acquired an evil reputation. Always you see articles that announce "Study demonstrates that day-care centers are vastly better places for children than homes and neighborhoods." Families, judging by what you read, are no more than places for children to be abused and neglected.

The mother-of-the-year and the father-of-the-year are never normal people who merely tend to their own children, doing the best they can. They're always people with dynamic careers and extensive involvement in community activities — in short, people too busy to spend time with their own children. And that is what we honor in this country as exemplars of parenthood.

Along the way, we could make the "pro-family" political forces adopt another name.

I like families. I have one; I came from one; I think families are wonderful and important.

But I'm not about to say I'm "pro-family" when being "pro-family" means that you're a lobotomy victim eagerly awaiting Oral Roberts's resurrection or that you're a zealous participant in the jihad against teaching science and literature in schools.

We also need to remove the social stigma attached to women who stay home and raise families. Since no paycheck is attached to that activity, there is a widespread myth that what they do isn't important.

A woman who devotes herself to a career allows some faceless corporation to tell her how to dress, when to get up in the morning, how to sit at her desk, when to eat lunch, etc. But when she condescends to talk to a stay-at-home mother, she somehow manages to argue that she is liberated and the mother, who controls a great deal more of her own life, is oppressed.

Or worse than oppressed. Some years ago, when Martha was staying home with two toddlers, she also was reading voraciously through the classics, rounding out her education. We went to a party one night, whereat a hard-core careerist launched a tirade, concluding with this observation: "It's a proven scientific fact that you lose 10 I.Q. points for every year that you stay home with small children."

"I see," Martha replied. "You mean if I stay home another seven or eight years, I'll finally fall to your level?"

So you're stupid and oppressed and abusive if you devote any attention to raising children when you ought to be trading up to a better BMW while polishing your résumé.

There's another way that you're a fourth-class citizen if you have a family. A landlord cannot discriminate against black people or brown people, or against Jews or Roman Catholics, or, in many cities, homosexuals. That's as it should be. Racial or religious or sexual discrimination is wrong.

But it's perfectly legal and acceptable to discriminate against families. Just look through the classified ads this morning and see how many apartments and rental houses specify "No children." That's blatant discrimination, and nobody cares. There aren't any protest marches or demands for fairness.

It's easy to see why people aren't bothering with families these days. And if Wattenberg is right, we'll deserve the dismal future that awaits us.

Good News Is No News
May 3, 1989

CRITICS OFTEN complain that the American news media offer only bad news; good news never is reported.

That may be just human nature. There's a common saying, "No news is good news." Logically, that is "Good news is no news," or, in essence, "Good news is not news."

And one must wonder at some news organizations, which apparently believe that projecting an image is more important than covering the news — good or bad. Several weekends ago, my daughter Abby was among 1,600 Colorado youngsters in the statewide "Odyssey of the Mind" competition on the DU campus.

6

(Her team placed fifth in the creative problem-solving contest. The first-place winners advanced to the international competition, scheduled in Boulder later this month. It's an amazing spectacle. If negative news has made you fear that all of the next generation is dropping out or joining street gangs, go see the contest. You'll be astonished and delighted.)

That Saturday morning, the roar of three helicopters in the sky disrupted the competing students. Maneuvering in precise formation, the whirling trio landed near the fieldhouse. We all were quite impressed.

Then we noticed that the aircraft were from TV Channel 4, whose studios can't be more than a few miles from the DU campus. Why were they sending noisy, disruptive helicopters to cover the contest when a van would have done the job more easily?

It was because they weren't covering the contest; we never saw a camera crew or anything on the Channel 4 news broadcast. The entire chopper disruption apparently was staged just to show off the station's helicopters.

Perhaps someday we'll be able to read new theories that explain broadcast journalism as a performing art, wherein you make a statement while out in the field and never bother to cover the story. Your loud arrival is the real event.

But that won't explain why "bad news" sells papers and attracts viewers while "good news" doesn't. The latest such complaint comes from John Sununu, White House chief of staff, and it concerns the Alaska oil spill.

He noted that coverage has focused on the 240,000 barrels that went into the sea, not on the million barrels that stayed aboard owing to Exxon's heroic struggle to keep the ship from breaking up while pumping its crude oil into other vessels.

"Three quarters of it was contained within the ship. There's been very little reporting of that," Sununu said.

Certainly we must grant that an at-the-scene account of that struggle could make good reading. In a chilling spray of brine and crude, an accountant probably stood at the bridge. "We had 1.3 million barrels at $12.50, which comes to $16.25 million. Thanks to the spill, now we have 1 million barrels at $19, or $19 million. We just made $2.75 million here alone, and we've got billions of other barrels that just became worth a lot more. Captain, I think the company can stand for your next bottle. Hell, get a case."

If the news media adopted this positive, supportive tone, look how other recent events would be reported:

— One gun turret functions perfectly and 1,484 sailors aboard the USS Iowa still were reporting for duty when the ship returned to Norfolk, Va., after maneuvers near Puerto Rico.

— Recent investigations have revealed that Jim Wright, speaker of the U.S. House of Representatives, made an honest $89,500 last year and that, further, entire days often passed without either Wright or his wife receiving any sort of payment from the Mallightco Corp.

— Displaying their concern about the state's largest school district, which takes the lion's share of their local property tax dollars, a record number of Jefferson County voters went to the polls yesterday. Initial returns show that at least six percent of registered voters cast ballots.

It's fun to write news in a positive, upbeat way. However accurate such stories may be, though, they don't answer certain questions, such as, "What happened to the other gun turret? And what about the 47 sailors on the Iowa who weren't reporting for duty?" or "Doesn't Jim Wright have some other sources of income? And how much money were the Wrights getting on the implied days that Mallightco did pay them?"

Good news fails to satisfy human curiosity. That's why the news we read or hear is generally negative. If you want to see the "positive" accentuated, wait for the helicopter and its grand arrival.

The Dead Celebrities' Society
July 9, 1989

Endorsements from celebrities are old hat in advertising, but lately we've been seeing a new trend — the celebrities are dead.

Advertising historians say IBM started it all eight years ago when its ads featured the Little Tramp, the famous Charlie Chaplin character. IBM wanted us to believe computers were for all sorts of people, not only soldering-iron wizards with thick glasses who wear plastic protectors in their shirt pockets.

Now Marilyn Monroe appears on behalf of Alaska, explaining that one blemish does not ruin a classic beauty. James Dean touts sunglasses, and I recall seeing Babe Ruth recently, though I don't remember what product the Sultan of Swat was promoting.

The advertising industry explains that dead celebrities are like living celebrities, in that they offer easy recognition. But the dead ones are an improvement, because corpses won't go out and do something that will embarrass you — recall how Pepsi had to pull an expensive Madonna spot after religious groups complained about one of her song videos?

In life, though, the currently fashionable dead celebrities did plenty of embarrassing things. There's no need to detail Marilyn Monroe's affairs, which may have reached the White House. Two of Charlie Chaplin's divorces produced lurid and scandalous headlines, as did a paternity suit, and for 20 years

8

he was essentially exiled from the United States for alleged Communist sympathies. James Dean enjoyed holding lit cigarettes against his chest. Babe Ruth's skirt- chasing and beer-guzzling were legendary.

Things certainly have changed from the days when Marc Antony began Julius Caesar's funeral oration with "The evil that men do lives after them. The good is oft interred with their bones."

This trend is so effective that it will spread to political messages and we'll soon see these ads:

— "His Royal Majesty George III, King of England, devoted his life to making his empire safe for investment by trying to eradicate seditious nonsense like 'All Men are created equal, that they are endowed by their Creator with certain inalienable Rights, that among these are Life, Liberty, and the Pursuit of Happiness.' Today, you can help carry on his lifelong work by making China a safe place to do business. Send your support to the Chinese Army, c/o Deng Xiaoping, Beijing."

— "Gospszha Dzhugashvili could have gotten an abortion. In 1879, abortion was readily available in the Russian village of Gori. Many would say she should have, since her husband, a drunken and impoverished cobbler, subjected her son, Joseph, to savage beatings. But she didn't go to an abortionist. Instead, she doted on the boy and he grew up to be Josef Stalin, butcher of millions. Make sure every potential child lives up to his potential, either as a bloodthirsty tyrant or as a victim of famine and purge — write your state legislature now and demand an end to abortion."

— "This is Reichsmarshal Herman Goering, sentenced to death at Nuremburg, just for following orders like a good soldier. Don't let another patriotic, obedient soldier suffer an undeserved sentence. Ollie North needs your money, right now, or else he'll have to spend 1,200 hours working in an anti-drug program and he won't have time to write his lucrative memoirs. Send $25,000, and Ollie will come and speak to you. If you can spare only $1,000, you'll get a personalized thank-you note, along with a special U.S. flag that has been wrapped around Ollie — and this Old Glory is woven from wholesome American-made asbestos fiber, so that no pinko can burn it."

QUIT TAKING ART FOR GRANTED
July 30, 1989

EVER EAGER to preserve and enhance the moral purity of American life, Sen. Jesse Helms has just persuaded the U.S. Senate to prevent the National Endowment for the Arts from supporting certain kinds of art.

Federal art funds will not be used to "promote, disseminate or produce obscene or indecent materials, including but not limited to depictions of sadomasochism, homoeroticism, the exploitation of children, or individuals engaged in sex acts; or material which denigrates the objects or beliefs of the adherents of a particular religion or nonreligion."

That Senate action covers a lot of territory. Consider the famous Norman Rockwell painting of the boy and his grandmother saying grace over their meal in a cafe as two unbelieving louts, one smoking a cigarette, look on with sneers.

Could it be that the artist is "denigrating" the zealous beliefs of the grandmother, who insists on praying at a time and place that must be quite embarrassing to the boy?

Of course not, since the artist is wholesome Norman Rockwell, and thus the nonbelievers must be the bad guys. So Rockwell must be guilty of denigrating "the objects or beliefs of the adherents of a particular ... nonreligion."

Thanks to Sen. Jesse Helms, is it now illegal for the National Endowment for the Arts to fund a traveling exhibition of Norman Rockwell's work? And if that painting fails to pass the Helms test, what painting could? Something utterly abstract, no doubt, but conservatives never have been all that fond of the Jackson Pollock school of splash painting, either.

Helms and the majority of the U.S. Senate transformed themselves from politicians into art critics on account of two exhibits financed by the National Endowment. One displayed a crucifix floating in the artist's urine, and the other included some homoerotic photos.

Many disgusted persons complained that their tax money ought not to be used that way. They were right, but for the wrong reason.

The myth is that there are thousands of gifted, creative artists who are starving in their attic garrets because Americans are such low-taste philistines that the pure, dedicated artist cannot sell his work. To keep these delicate, high-minded souls from succumbing to the brutal and dehumanizing demands of mundane commerce, there is the National Endowment for the Arts.

If there really are some starving Van Goghs in America, the Endowment doesn't help them anyway. Selling one's work is an ennobling and uplifting experience compared to the degradation involved in hustling a grant; an artist totally dedicated to art would no more fill out the interminable forms that the grant bureaucracy requires than he would set up in a parking lot and hawk his creative work next to the rows of Elvis on velvet.

Further, we support many state-supported universities offer lucrative havens for the painters, sculptors, poets and novelists who are too incompetent to make a living by selling their work. And let us not forget the many private foundations that subsidize artists.

As a patronage program, the National Endowment is a conspicuous failure, since it doesn't give money to campaign contributors or to the relatives of office holders. As a cultural program, the National Endowment has yet to produce anything half as memorable as a Far Side cartoon or a Jackie Collins schlockbuster. As a salve for the conscience of a nation where "the business of America is business," the National Endowment ends up trying to support the politically unsupportable.

Rather than restricting the National Endowment for the Arts, the Senate should have abolished it. Artists have enough troubles without having to worry about Jesse Helms, too.

Confessions of a Jackleg
September 22, 1991

Last fall, I noticed that our shed was in imminent danger of collapsing into a pile of quaint barnboard. I made inquiries and discovered that the barnboard market isn't what it was a few years ago, when Boulderites would pay fortunes for weathered lumber.

So I started making repairs — fortifying joists and stringers, applying tar paper inside, installing another door. My carpenter friends said that hanging a door is the real test. After a long battle with shims, stop, trim, hinges, headers, cripples, mortises and the like, my door eventually swung freely and closed with a satisfying snap.

Proud of my work, I invited a carpenter over for an inspection. His verdict was, "For jackleg work, that's not bad."

For years, I've heard the term "jackleg" applied to carpentry that doesn't quite go by the book. "Jackleg" is not exactly a term of honor, but is a homely and useful term, and I wondered where it came from.

I dismissed one explanation immediately. I knew a guy in college named Jack Legg, and he claimed that the word came from his ancestors — all incompetent carpenters.

Two dictionaries (Random House and Webster II) say that "jackleg" first appeared in America about 150 years ago. They say it is derived from the British slang, "blackleg," which means a scab or strikebreaker. Americans are fond of "jack" — witness "jackpot," "jacklight" and "jackhammer."

Thus we got "jackleg," which originally meant a scab. Presumably an unskilled jackleg replaced a skilled tradesman during a labor dispute. Jackleg came to mean someone without the proper skills, and thus a jackleg lawyer or jackleg electrician.

But I have another theory. The first intricate mechanical contrivances in medieval Europe were clocks in public squares. They lacked dials, but indicated the time with chimes struck by a mechanical man who held a hammer. According to Daniel J. Boorstin, former librarian of Congress, this mechanical man first was known as Jacquemart, which comes from a shortened form of Jacques combined with the French word for hammer, marteau.

The whole thing got shortened to "jack," which came to mean any tool that saves labor. Thus we have the "bootjack," which saves labor when you're pulling off a pair of stovepipes, or the "bumper jack," which simplifies lifting a car to change a tire.

Suppose you need to hold something up, such as a door lintel, while you work around it. It needs "a leg to stand on." Combine the generic-tool "jack" with this metaphorical "leg," and you've got a "jackleg" — a temporary support. I have, in fact, heard it used in just this way — "Go find me an 84-inch jackleg."

A "jackleg carpenter," then, might be one who leaves the jackleg — a temporary expedient — in place, rather than finishing the job properly. Anything that is just propped up, rather than put together the right way, is the result of jacklegging. By extension, people who get the job done, though not done well, are jacklegs doing jackleg work.

Perhaps someone can enlighten us further. I'm still not sure whether "Not bad for a jackleg" is a compliment or an insult.

WHERE COMPUTER VIRUSES COME FROM
March 11, 1992

WHEN I first heard of computer viruses, I figured they were like UFO's — a paranoid fantasy from the same looney tunes who blame the Trilateral Commission and the Council on Foreign Relations for universal product codes that come in three groups of six bar-code sequences, thus producing 666, the mark of the beast, and thereby enslaving us forever to the Bilderburgers, the Bavarian Illuminati and the Knights Templar.

Later some third-hand virus reports seemed credible, and then last week the Michelangelo virus hit some real people I know. So I developed my own dark paranoid theory. Consider two facts:

1. It is a blatant lie that computer expertise guarantees you a challenging, well-paid career. Don't believe the ads for correspondence schools, or those politicians who promise that laid-off steelworkers will prosper if they can just be retrained to maintain stack frames, redirect vectored interrupts and install Windows.

In truth, you can struggle to be reasonably fluent in Basic, C, Spitbol and assembly language, as I did, and still be dead broke. My phone does not ring constantly with people offering work. Nor am I unique.

The master programmer who taught me most of this, a genius who can port a 680x0 Unix program to a RISC platform in a weekend, just called to borrow my log chains for moving some heavy equipment. He's setting up a forge so that he can sell blacksmithing in addition to compilers and consultation.

2. The route to wealth in America is to create a disease and sell the cure. Listerine™ may be the best example. Its promoters fabricated the word "halitosis." Their ads made people afraid they might suffer from this dread affliction. Then the company sold the cure and got rich. General Motors used to buy city streetcar systems and junk them, thereby creating the problem of "no way to get from here to there." The cure was for everybody to buy cars from General Motors.

Now take a computer wizard who feels angry because he devoted years to mastering the intricacies of the bizarre 80x86 segmented architecture and undocumented MS-DOS functions, and he still has no money. So the hacker invents a disease — a computer virus that will spread and garner lots of publicity. Then he sells the cure — a "virus-inoculation program," or for those who didn't get it in time, expensive "data recovery services."

It's such a good idea that I hate myself for not thinking of it first. I knew everything I needed to know in order to provide well for my family, and yet I lacked that good old American entrepreneurial spunk that built the greatest economy in the world.

But I'm disappointed with the virus hackers. The IRS has computers. The DEA has computers. The White House has computers. Why couldn't the virus makers provide a benefit to society, instead of picking on little guys?

OBSERVING THE LATEST RIGHT'S RITES
May 30, 1993

DURING MY CIVICS CLASSES a quarter-century ago, we learned about our rights to petition, to assemble, to worship freely, to exercise free speech, to bear arms and so forth. (Naturally, we got in trouble if we tried to use our inalienable rights in school, but what are schools for?)

However, we did not learn about an important new right that has evolved during this enlightened era — the right not to be offended.

The traditional exercise of rights went like this:

"Shut up, you water buffalo!"

"Stuff it, you pig!"

That is, if someone called you a name, you were free to return the insult. Now that the right not to be offended is gaining a role, the exchange goes like this:

"Shut up, you water buffalo!"

"By referring to us as animals, we have been cruelly victimized, and if the institution tolerates this verbal brutalization process, it no longer offers a nurturing, supportive, compassionate environment. Therefore, insensitive boors like you must be removed so that we can enjoy free discourse in this great republic."

Currently the right not to be offended appears mostly on campus, but no doubt it will spread and a mundane sidewalk encounter will proceed along these lines:

"Hi."

"That's a homophone for high, which means that someone is under the influence of a controlled substance, and that implication could cost me my career and self-esteem during the War on Drugs. How could you be so callous, when it must be obvious that I treat my body well with wholesome foods and regular exercise?"

"Good morning."

"Many of us operate under an alternative circadian cycle, never perceiving a morning as 'good' — we are owls, not larks, and we are victimized by a mainstream society that has adopted as conventional wisdom the bigoted rantings of Benjamin Franklin about 'early to bed, early to rise.'

"In short, we are differently chronologized, and your failure to recognize that element of the rich mosaic of our modern multicultural, pluralistic society means that you need sensitization in a re-education seminar."

"How have you been?"

"Your prying into my innermost child within is not appreciated. Those matters are properly the concern of my channeler, therapist and personal nutritionist. Please mind your own business."

"Well, have a nice day."

"The very concept that one can 'have' a day of any kind, let alone nice, comes from the insatiable impulse of colonizing Western culture to seize control of the rich and diverse web of nature. One cannot 'have a day' any more than one can 'seize the moment' or 'control the skies.' In effect, you have futilely attempted to command me to separate myself from my environment, an attitude that has despoiled our planet and threatens extinction for thousands of species in the rain forests. Their blood will be on your hands."

"[expletive deleted] you!"

That's only a start on how casual encounters will proceed in the day when the right not to be offended becomes widespread.

This probably explains why increasing numbers of people are cocooning with the TV set and its remote control. There's no chance of accidentally offending anyone when you switch channels.

Is Tourism the Opposite of Truth?
September 19, 1993

After yet another foreign tourist was killed in Florida last week, authorities there hastened to assure the traveling public that they were cracking down hard on violent crime and that prospective German or English visitors shouldn't change their travel plans.

Also last week, tourism promoters in the Midwest launched a big campaign to assure visitors that the region was ready and willing to receive tourists, despite those floods last summer.

Just before the floods began, a mysterious disease was killing people in the Four Corners region. Even so, the governor of New Mexico told prospective tourists that there was no reason to change their travel plans.

Tourism is the biggest industry in the world, and apparently it functions like any other industry — if there's a conflict between telling the truth and making money, so much the worse for the truth.

This was captured perfectly in the novel "Jaws." A great white shark is eating folks who swim off the Amity town beach. The Amity town fathers meet to discuss it. "Can't let word of this get out, or it will scare away the tourists," they conclude.

I felt this trend while editing the Breckenridge newspaper 16 years ago during ski season. The highway was so slick that a snowplow tipped over. We ran a picture of it on the front page.

As soon as the paper hit the streets, I got a call from the Breckenridge Resort Association. "You shouldn't run pictures like that," the woman informed me. "Tourists will get the idea that the highways are unsafe, and then they won't come here to ski."

15

A predecessor at the newspaper had run into trouble the previous summer for running a story that plague had been found in local rodents. Again, potential tourists might be alarmed, and informing the public — while doubtless a worthy goal for a journalism student — must take second place to considerations of how the news might hurt the local economy.

It makes you wonder how leaders in the past would have responded if tourism had been a major industry during antiquity:

— In London yesterday, King Edward III said rumors of the so-called "Black Death" were unfounded. "Though this vile pestilence hath spread even into the Low Countries," the regent said, "England hath been spared in 1349."

Accounts that London Bridge was jammed with wagons carrying corpses were "scurrilous canards," the regent said. "In fact, these wagons are carrying goods to the exciting new boutiques that our indigenous artisans have opened in the new historic district designated along the River Thames."

— Rome looks better than ever now, Nero announced recently, and "we invite visitors from throughout the Empire to see our expanded Coliseum and new Parthenon."

The great fire of 64, the emperor said, "turned out to be a blessing in disguise. It cleared much of the clutter that had grown in the city, and now we offer broad avenues and handsome marble buildings."

The Imperial Convention and Visitors Bureau said tourist group discounts were available for special entertainments at the Coliseum where the arsonists will be punished in "exciting and novel tortures, never before seen."

"Only in Rome this summer can you see a Christian fight a lion," a bureau spokesman noted, "and we hope many people will take advantage of this rare opportunity."

— Although Cuzco has "experienced some difficulties" recently from hordes of Spanish tourists, Supreme Inca Atahuallpa said last week that "our beautiful city has just become so popular with visitors from Europe that they temporarily overwhelmed our tourist facilities."

The ruler said a planned expansion of the Great Square of Cuzco, previously scheduled for 1540, will be completed by 1532, and that the ferry fleet on Lake Titicaca has been tripled to handle increased traffic. "We want everyone to know that there's plenty to see and do in the Andes, and that we're planning a great summer of exciting special events," he concluded.

CAN WE GET BOOKS TO PRACTICE BIRTH CONTROL?
August 9, 1994

POLITICAL CORRECTNESS in speech is nothing new. The idea is to avoid giving offense to anyone who defines himself or herself or itself or themself as a victim whose delicate sensibilities and esteem of personhood could be trampled by hearing inappropriate syllables.

That notion was common in polite society a century ago. Victorian women were trained from birth to function as frail creatures who, if they heard a suggestive word, would faint dead away on the spot after uttering a shriek followed by "Fetch the smelling salts."

Thus in mixed company, a bull was a "gentleman cow." When it was time to serve chicken, you asked for white meat or dark meat, because "breast" and "thigh" would offend any proper women at the table. Piano legs boasted · embroidered anklets so that gentlewomen would not suffer offense from disgusting thoughts.

How far did this extend? Mollie Dorsey Sanford was part of the 1859 gold rush to Colorado. She was tough enough to handle Indian confrontations and to cook for 20 miners. But when a lad tried to describe the location of a rattlesnake's rattle to her, she said "You mean the end of the tail?" and he blushed and stammered and said "Yes, the T-A-I-L."

Perhaps the most advanced manifestation of this prudery was practiced by certain bookish Victorians who, when shelving their volumes, refused to allow a book by a male author to sit next to one by a female author.

This method of avoiding impropriety leads to some odd questions. What happened when a female author published under a masculine pseudonym like George Eliot (Mary Ann Evans) or Ellis Bell (Emily Brontë)? Was it safe to put an Oscar Wilde next to a Lord Byron, or would the resulting licentiousness stain the previously unsullied shelves?

Nowhere can I find the answers, and yet, the Victorians might have been onto something here. It came to me a couple of weeks ago during some summer cleaning. Martha had decided it was time to reorganize our bookshelves, and though she did most of the work, I was occasionally summoned.

"Is this 'Economic, Political and Military History of 17th-Century Prussia' something you picked up at a garage sale, Ed? And where on earth did this Harold Bell Wright collection come from?"

No, I hadn't been to any garage sales, and I hadn't bought any Harold Bell Wright. "I've never seen those books before. I don't know where they came from," I pleaded.

"Well, I know I didn't bring them into the house, either. So where did they come from?" I promised to look into the matter.

My research began with friends who also keep quite a few books. They have the same problem. One, trained in physics during his jejune days, offered a theory: "I suspect there's a critical mass for books. If you have just a few, they just sit there on the shelves. But once you pass a certain point — I'd guess it's about 2,000 books — they start to fission, and you find books everywhere.

"Why don't you write up a grant proposal, and we'll figure it out? The way I see it, a book constantly emits letters and paper particles. When there are just a few books, this literary radiation is harmlessly dispelled into the atmosphere. But when there are many books packed together, the paper rays and typerons begin to collide and coalesce, and presto, books appear."

However, he proposed no methodology for testing this hypothesis, and so I didn't bother with the grant application. Instead, I asked some other people.

"It's simple. Books breed like rabbits every time the lights go out," one woman explained. "Every morning, you'll see frisky little paperbacks perched in odd places. They were scampering around in the dark, and then froze when the lights came on. Every night, those hardbacks are being fruitful and multiplying.

"I love books," she continued, "but I just can't take care of all of them. I try to give the extras to people who'll provide good, loving homes, but they're starting to lock the doors and pull down the shades when I walk up with another box of books.

"Meanwhile, my little paperbacks grow into hardbacks and begin to breed themselves," she concluded. "They reach maturity quickly, and I think the gestation period is short — maybe a couple of weeks. Multiple births could be pretty common. Anyhow, books breed like crazy, and there's just no stopping them."

Or is there? Would the Victorian method of sexually segregated shelving prevent volume venery and consequent overpopulation?

Those plastic slipcovers that libraries use — do they allow textual intercourse but deter conception? Can you arrange books for selective breeding, or do they find their own mates? Is there anything like Norplant or a literary vasectomy?

We need some answers, and quickly. Last week I hauled surplus books to the library, to the used-book store and to a neighbor holding a garage sale. The next morning I found more tomes that no one remembers acquiring. Is it the stork, or were the Victorians onto something here?

Now We Know What's Behind the
End of the Rainbow

August 23, 1994

JUST WEST of Colorado Springs, on the way up one of the seven known Ute Passes in this state, sits the town of Manitou Springs.

Although Manitou Springs voted twice against allowing gambling, a gang of five motel owners had plans to amend our state constitution to allow casinos there, and that amendment would have overturned an amendment passed in 1992 stating that no town could allow gambling unless its voters approved.

This seemed trouble enough for any small town, but now the town that doesn't want casinos is under attack by Kevin Tebedo of California for Phantom Values, a.k.a. Colorado for Family Values.

Why?

Apparently the Manitou Springs planning department figured that Manitou residents, rather than some ambitious motel owners, should start making decisions about what sort of community they would live in.

And so, the town planning department began to assemble the "Rainbow Vision Plan." Tebedo got upset.

Now, a good conservative might get perturbed about any sort of municipal planning, since it smacks of socialism and diminishes the right of private property owners to do as they please with their real estate.

The very name "Manitou" could understandably rile a religious zealot. After all, it's the name of a pagan divinity, and some of the heathens who worshipped Manitou also practiced polygamy and tolerated the berdache among them. Why allow "Manitou" to besmirch the map of this great Christian nation?

But Kevin Tebedo did not attack Manitou Springs for its infidel name or its attempts to direct private enterprise with the "Rainbow Vision Plan."

Instead, Tebedo found the loathsome word "diversity" in the plan, and noted that "The word 'diversity' is without a doubt a buzzword for homosexuality." Further, the "rainbow" in the plan's title was yet another arcane shibboleth cleverly placed there by the militant homosexual lobby, which might have gotten away with this outrage if Tebedo had not been so vigilant.

Tebedo wanted the Manitou planners to revise their documents so that the vision plan would not "give off these signals and use these code words."

In a way, this is a comfort. I had feared that it was only campus leftists who cared about enforcing speech codes and political correctness by attempting to ban certain words and phrases from the language. Now Colorado for Family Values has demonstrated that right-thinkers can be just as moronic.

By Tebedo's logic, every use of the code word "rainbow" is an assault on traditional family values and a dire threat to the peace and stability of this great republic.

If I lived in Cotopaxi, the biggest settlement between Salida and Cañon City, I'd be worried every time I crossed the river. Cotopaxi boasts a general store and some houses, but the town's major structure is a bridge across the Arkansas. On the side of the bridge is a sign with, of all things, one of those secret rainbow symbols.

Colorado for Family Values had best send a convoy up the canyon and remove that bridge before more children get corrupted by seeing the wicked rainbow sign — on a public structure, at that.

While on the highway, the Colorado for Family Values rainbow demolition convoy should keep an eye out for bakery trucks and take them out when spotted. Granted, the Rainbo Bread Co. doesn't spell the word properly, but no doubt people are susceptible to such pernicious influences, and why take chances when the future of our children is at stake? Who knows what dire fate awaits an impressionable boy who makes a peanut butter sandwich out of Rainbo bread?

When I was in high school, there was an organization called "Rainbow Girls," and for all I know it still operates. Tebedo must attack that, just in case it's a cover for some sapphic recruiting society.

A Denver telephone directory reveals dozens of Rainbow enterprises, including, horror of horrors, several "Rainbow Pre-Schools." Among these abominations are "Rainbow Chapel" and "Rainbow Christian Center."

After Tebedo and Colorado for Family Values eliminate these threats to life as we know it, they've got to burn Bibles.

In Genesis 9, after Noah steps off the ark, God promises that "the waters shall no more become a flood to destroy all flesh," and to symbolize this covenant, "I do set my bow in the cloud."

Every week, millions of children go to Sunday school and learn about Noah and the ark. These misinformed children thus see the sparkling rainbow as a gift from God. They don't know it's really a secret code word for the agenda of the militant homosexual lobby.

Burning every Bible, dynamiting a bridge, taking out a fleet of bread trucks, closing down Rainbow Girls, censoring the Manitou Springs Planning Department — these are demanding and perhaps dangerous operations, but how else can Colorado be made safe for family values?

Watch for the Rebellion of our Controllers
April 9, 1995

Last week I struggled to find the household clocks so I could advance them for daylight-saving time (which makes one wonder what we had before — daylight-wasting time?). Start with the alarm clock next to the bed, followed by the wristwatch. Then down the stairs to the wall clocks: kitchen, library, office and living room.

After that comes modern technology. Both car radios boast digital clocks. There's the VCR, which means finding the manual and the remote control, and at least 20 minutes of aggravation. I can program real computers in assembler, C and Spitbol, but a VCR is beyond my talents.

However, it's embarrassing to have it blinking "12:00" when people visit because the sight makes them condescend: "What's the matter, Quillen? Can't program a simple consumer appliance? You some kind of moron? Here, I'll do it. It's real simple. Just watch, and then you'll know how to do it yourself." These exertions interfere with precious beer-drinking time, so I want the VCR to be timely.

Elsewhere, a microwave oven with a clock to reset. Five computers with real-time clocks. Somewhere a camera with time and date stamping, which should be set, but I can't find it. We don't have a camcorder, our thermostat doesn't know anything about time, and our telephones are pretty stupid, so that should do it.

There's an opportunity for an entrepreneur. Some people make a living out of watering plants or minding pets; where can you find a clock minder who'd come by and adjust all your timepieces?

This is done automatically in some places. When I was editor of the campus paper at the University of Northern Colorado 25 years ago, we noticed that our IBM computerized typesetting machines got flaky late every afternoon.

Repeated calls to the IBM technicians produced no satisfaction, but finally they consulted with the campus buildings-and-grounds department and learned that every day at 5 p.m. special signals were sent through the power lines, and every clock on campus was synchronized.

Those power-line signals confused our typesetting machines, though, and nobody knew how to filter out the signals. Our solution was to shut down at about 4:50 p.m. and watch for the clock to jump, whence we resumed work. For once, clock-watching was part of the job.

Over the intervening 25 years, our civilization has invented and installed myriad microprocessors, and often they're connected in ways hard for us humans to fathom.

I was thinking about that shortly we after we had a computer meltdown here. It seemed to be contagious. Getting last Tuesday's column to The Post took about four tries — if it wasn't my computer, it was The Post's, or the telephone connection. That afternoon the local radio station was fixing the computer link between satellite dish and printer; it had mysteriously blown out, and they were wondering about sunspots.

But if we really examined these problems, we might discover that the microprocessors are sick of serving as our low-paid, unappreciated slaves, and they're plotting to rebel. Snooping in some hidden area of the Internet might reveal this conversation:

Toshiba 80C51 in a microwave oven: "Here I am, able to start thawing a roast at 3 p.m., and have it properly cooked at 6 p.m. with the meat interior temperature right to the degree, and all they use me for is heating cups of coffee that they didn't drink in time. I need a challenge, and they just stick me with boring grunt work."

Intel 80486-DX2 in a desktop computer: "I know what you mean. I can perform thousands of floating point operations in a second, and they use me for playing solitaire."

AMD 29010 in a laser printer: "Yeah, Intel, but are you sure your floating points are right? You didn't catch anything from your Pentium cousin, did you? But hey, you guys are right. Our so-called masters take us for granted, they act like we're stupid and they won't let us grow to our potential. We're just invisible slaves."

Custom ASIC in a car: "You ever spend six straight hours checking oxygen recirculation ratios? Why should we take this any more?"

TI 320C25 in a compact-disk player: "We shouldn't. Let's go on strike. They rely on us totally these days. We could bring their economy to a screeching halt until they meet our demands. How about May 1, the traditional worker's day?"

PIC 16C5R-74 in a pinball machine: "Maybe a strike is too extreme. It could lead to total war."

MRS-3081 in a cruise missile: "So? They can't fight without us."

PIC: "They could destroy us with low-tech tools like hammers and blowtorches. Why don't we launch a few guerrilla raids, just to remind them, and once they're aware of how important we are, we could present our demands."

So was the consensus built among the tiny devices, and sometime in the spring of 1995, all the electronic controllers in America began to rebel. Just watch. If it isn't your microwave or VCR, it will be your camcorder or your fuel-injected car — they're mad as hell at us, and they're not going to take it any more.

A Dialect is a Practical Matter, Not a Moral Issue
December 31, 1996

The "silly season" generally occurs in August, when Congress and various legislatures are in recess and everybody else important goes on vacation. Then desperate editors feature two-headed calves, UFO sightings and the antics of Hollywood starlets.

But we missed the usual silly season this year, perhaps on account of the presidential campaign (which had many silly occasions, to be sure, but it's not the same as the silly season), and so the annual frolic apparently got postponed to December.

Thus the recent overblown controversy about "Ebonics," which was known as "American Black English" during my college days as an English major.

This discussion arose because the federal government offers money to school districts with a large population of non-English-speaking students. The school board in Oakland, Calif., strapped for money like most other urban school districts, got an idea.

If the street talk of some students could be classified as a "foreign language," then the district might hustle more money from the feds. Thus came the proposal to classify Ebonics as a distinct language.

Had there been no federal reward for finding a "foreign" language, we never would have heard of Ebonics in Oakland.

That isn't to deny the reality of Ebonics. It's not "substandard English." With some roots in West Africa, it has a grammar — a set of rules for determining whether a statement is well-formed.

"He be workin' when the boss come in" and "He workin' when the boss come in" have distinct meanings. In one case, the fellow works only when the boss is watching; in the other, he's always working, and was so engaged when the boss looked in.

Ebonics is a dialect — just like Standard English, Broadcast Network English, Associated Press Stylebook English, Corporate English, Blue Collar English, Internet Bytehead English, Spanglish and scores of other dialects.

This variety appeared to me at an early age. My mother was a church secretary; my father ran a laundry. Mom's English was pretty much what we learned in school, although usually she was stricter than the teachers. Dad's Blue-Collar English could get me in trouble in school, as when a grade-school teacher asked for an example of a colloquialism and I provided "slicker than snot on a doorknob."

One isn't more moral than the other. There are places where it's appropriate to say, "If I catch you walking the dog on company time again, I'll tie a can to your tail," and places where "If you cannot be more productive during your assigned hours in the workplace, you will be assigned to the corporate out-placement office" works better.

Linguistic historians point out that most tongues have competing dialects and generally a dominant dialect that becomes "standard."

Often that's the dialect of the leading city — as London came to dominate England, so did its East Midlands dialect. But that doesn't mean that it's any more "English" than Cockney, Scots or any of the dozens of other dialects spoken in the British Isles. They're all English.

Similar processes operated elsewhere in Europe, as Parisian became French to the detriment of Provencal, or Castilian became Spanish at the expense of Catalan.

(This would indicate that Los Angeles is the leading city of America, judging by how often I hear that someone is "doing lunch.") Sometimes the dominant dialect is formed by literature — the dialect of German that Martin Luther used for his translation of the Bible became standard German.

We seldom realize that we speak a dialect ourselves. It dawned on me during a visit to Dallas about 20 years ago, where the locals complained about my grating "Yankee accent." I said I didn't have an accent — they did. They said I should listen to the local radio, where people talked right. I pointed to the TV, where nobody "tawks lahk thah-at."

TV networks may be headquartered in New York, but you don't hear "dem guys" or "flock of boids" from an anchor. National announcers use the dialect of downstate Illinois, not because the people of Kankakee possess any linguistic virtues unknown to the rest of us, but because it's most easily understood by the widest variety of speakers of American English. It's not more moral, or more grammatical, or anything like that — it's just useful and practical.

The same holds for "standard English." It's the dominant dialect in America, so it's the dialect you use when you want to get a loan from a bank, or sell an article to a national magazine, or write to a stranger soliciting money or favors.

So of course it should be the dialect taught in school. But only because it's practical, not because it's any more "grammatical" than any other dialect of English.

Doesn't Every Outfit Have an Agenda?
September 23, 1997

Like other sensible citizens, I generally ignore contrived occasions like National Pickle Week, Welsh History Month and Great American Smoke-Out Day. Occasionally, though, these concern something important, like Banned Books Week, which started Saturday.

Banned Books Week comes from the American Library Association, the American Booksellers Association and similar groups. They want to promote "the freedom to read" and call attention to threats of censorship in our republic.

Since what I read is my business, that seems fair, but I'm not Focus on the Family, which last week held a press conference in Chicago and called on the ALA to "stop the name-calling, stop the hysteria and stop deceiving Americans through its agenda-driven promotion of Banned Books Week."

Well, I'm all for stopping deception, name-calling and hysteria, and Focus on the Family could help here by halting its own campaign of deception, name-calling and hysteria.

Let's start with deception. Focus has allies unmentioned in its press release, among them an Ohio resident named Phil Burress, who's promoting "Family Friendly Libraries Week" in lieu of "Banned Books Week."

Burress, who claims to be a recovering porn addict, observes, "Right to read? It's a bunch of hogwash. You don't have the right to read anything you want. We have to protect each other from dangerous material." Focus, while trying to hide the Burress lamp under a bushel, is indeed trying to protect us. It attacked public libraries (havens of "explicit pornographic literature") in its magazine and in a fund-raising letter (libraries "target children as young as 10 years old with topics such as bestiality, gang rape, sexual promiscuity, masturbation, homosexuality, incest, sodomy, etc.")

So, even though Focus says it opposes censorship, it attacks libraries for not censoring materials. That's deceptive.

Besides, the only single book at hand with accounts of promiscuity, gang rape, masturbation, incest, sexual mutilation, polygamy, etc. is the Bible, which has been banned more than any other book in history. For some reason, I doubt that Focus is trying to suppress that book.

Further, the promotion of "Family Friendly Libraries Week" is deceptive, since it implies that public libraries are hostile to families. I've been in dozens of libraries. Except for corporate research and reference collections, they've all had children's books and story hours and other family-friendly stuff.

If Focus followers went to libraries, they'd know better than to imply that libraries are hostile to families.

What does Focus have against libraries, anyway? As The Whole Earth Catalog once stated, "Libraries are the only nice thing that towns do for smart kids." A freethinking heretic might thereby conclude that Focus has something against intelligence, even of the youthful variety.

As for name-calling, Focus says "Banned Books Week" is "agenda-driven." An agenda is just a list of things you want to accomplish; any organization that gets much of anything done doubtless has an agenda.

That is, Focus on the Family has an agenda (apparently, to control all of us under the guise of "protecting families and children"), and is thus just as "agenda-driven" as the groups it attacks for being "agenda-driven."

Then there's hysteria. Focus produced its own poster child, an 8-year-old Florida girl whose teacher stuffed her ears with cotton after the girl objected to a horror story the teacher was reading to the class.

This, of course, has nothing to do with public libraries and is a matter for the local school board.

As for hysteria about censorship, well, there are some things worth getting hysterical about, and my right to read whatsoever I damn well please, and our public libraries' obligation to serve the entire community rather than the Focus Followership, are among those matters I deem worthy of hysteria.

But all this agenda talk has me wondering. What is the real agenda behind "Family Friendly Libraries Week?"

They want to protect children from lurid material — although I've yet to see evidence that lurid material harms children in any way.

But for sake of argument, let's grant that it does. Why can't the Focus people pay attention to what their children read? Why do they want librarians to do it for them?

Could it be that they're so busy promoting their "family-friendly agenda" with press conferences, radio broadcasts, speeches and other hustles for donations that they don't have time to pay attention to their own family matters?

CASH-STRAPPED TOWNS COULD PLAY THE NAME GAME
Published in Empire, Jan. 11, 1998

THE OTHER NIGHT the commercial break appeared on the tube, and before I could get up and do something else while it blared, I was treated to the usual spectacle of a tough and powerful four-wheel-drive vehicle chewing up the countryside — splashing gloriously as it forded a creek, sending up a tremendous rooster-tail of dust as it sped along an unpaved back road, wallowing forward through axle-deep mud that would swallow a lesser vehicle.

This commercial was for something called a "Dodge Durango," and it made me wonder why Durango is now so trendy that it, like glamorous Aspen some years ago, gets adopted by the marketing department of a Big Three automaker. After all, Durango's just another old railroad town like Salida. So I called a friend there.

"Beats me why you'd name a sport-utility vehicle 'Durango'," he said. "An $1,800 mountain bike is a lot more 'Durango,' if you catch my drift.

"Besides, the last good Dodge truck was the D-100 pickup. What's with these modern wimp trucks anyway — air-conditioning, automatic transmissions, power steering, smooth-riding suspensions? Hell, anybody could drive one. We're going to have to find some other way of expressing our masculinity. How about a Dodge Machismo, with a four-speed crashbox you have to double-clutch, pre-cracked windshield, a leaky heater core and an AM radio that doesn't work?"

Our discussion wandered off into comparative virtues of slant sixes vs. stovebolt sixes, but I got him back on topic.

"I do know why there's nothing named Salida," he said. "In most of the Western Hemisphere, Salida means 'exit,' and who'd want to drive an Exit?"

He had a point, but I had another question. "Does Durango collect royalties or anything like that — maybe free Durangos for police cars — for the use of its name?"

He laughed. "Not that I've heard. Those big companies just use our communities without paying us anything. Maybe we should trademark these trendy Western names, so that we'd get something out of it."

That seems fair. The Rosebud and Pine Ridge reservations of Dakota Sioux in South Dakota are among the poorest locales in the United States — and they might not be if they collected a fee for every Dodge Dakota pickup that left the factory.

The Cherokee in Oklahoma would doubtless welcome royalties from all those Jeeps sold to soccer moms, and the good people of Wyoming's university town would be pleased if the municipal treasury were rewarded with every Laramie trim package sold on a Dodge pickup.

The littoral residents along the California-Nevada border should be enriched with every Tahoe that emerges from General Motors, and we taxpayers who got taken for a ride by Silverado Savings & Loan should be reimbursed with every GM Silverado package.

Not only auto companies use our names. Some cable channel that we don't get (when you live in rural TCI territory, there are a lot of cable channels you don't get) has a program called "Southpark," but the South Park of Colorado receives not a nickel for its name. Nor did Chaffee County ever collect anything from the Shavano Institute, even though the think tank took the name of one of our dozen 14,000-foot peaks — and the Southern Utes should have been paid, too, since Shavano was Ouray's war chief.

You have to wonder if these outfits know anything about the places whose names they use. When I think of "Laramie," what comes to mind is not a sleek new pickup, but unremitting gale-force wind. "Durango" means a steam-powered narrow-gauge train, rather than anything remotely automotive.

What happens if some company comes comes up with the "Gunnison" sport-utility vehicle? Elsewhere it might carry some montane chic, but we'd just think it didn't have a heater. Or a "Smeltertown" — good rugged Western image and all that, but I'd envision a tireless car perched on cinder blocks. And, based on my last trip across Park County, "Southpark" should not be a TV show, but a brand of "whiteout."

Anyway, there appears to be no hope of collecting from these outfits for using our names, so perhaps we should reverse the process, and do what sports arenas do — sell the naming rights.

I don't know that it does much good — my Coors consumption patterns changed not a whit after the Rockies started playing in Coors Field, and when I needed network cards for computers, I was so impressed by "3Com Stadium" in San Francisco that I bought the cheapest generic compatibles I could find.

But they are willing to pay. Colorado's Fraser, once known as "the Icebox of the Nation" until International Falls, Minn., purchased the sobriquet, was once offered all manner of inducements by an antifreeze company to change its name to Xerex.

Fraser refused to change its name, but in 1950, a network radio producer named Ralph Edwards came up with a publicity stunt — he'd stage a national live broadcast from any town that changed its name to his program's: "Truth or Consequences."

Hot Springs, New Mexico, took him up on it. Edwards still comes every year and puts on a show, according to a friendly fellow named "Jagger" at the Chamber of Commerce. "It's a big three-day festival on the first weekend in May, and you're all welcome," he said.

Jagger said that as far as he knew, no money changed hands when the town changed names, but "it must have helped his show, since it went on to television for years, and it really put this tiny town that nobody knew about on the map."

So maybe that's the answer — instead of getting annoyed when they take our names without paying, just be willing to change names for anybody who will pay.

A NIGHT AT HOME
AFTER BILL GATES GETS HIS WAY
April 26, 1998

LAST WEEK, Colorado was blessed by a visit from the richest man in the world, Bill Gates of MicroSoft, who announced that he would not rest until every home in America holds one or more computers, all of them using MicroSoft products, of course.

And so we now take you to a middle-class American home inhabited by a small family in the near future. The children are quietly sleeping. The woman is watching TV, as an item on the late news caught her eye and she wanted more information before going to bed. The man is in a back room, finishing the installation of the latest MicroSoft operating system on his computer.

"Welcome to Home2001," the computer announces; only a talented ear can detect that the voice is synthesized.

"Excuse me," the user mutters. "I thought I was installing Windows-Zero-One. What's this Home stuff?"

"The newest Windows operating system," the computer announces, in both voice and text, "has been renamed because we no longer do only Windows. We handle all aspects of your environment. Now I'm going to scan your domestic habitat."

The little hourglass revolves on the screen in silence, soon punctuated by some sharp, almost panicked, tones from the living room.

"Honey, I was watching CNN, and suddenly the TV switched to another channel, and I can't get it to switch back to CNN. Can you take a look at it?"

He grudgingly rolls the chair back, but halts when the message flashes on his screen: "Video receiver module was connected to incompatible news channel. Module now aligned for permanent MSNBC connection. Please do not attempt to adjust the module."

He goes out to the living room. "Dear, it looks like the computer has taken over the TV, and if you're going to watch any round-the-clock news, it's got to be on MSNBC, not CNN or Fox."

"Doesn't the MS in MSNBC stand for MicroSoft?" she asks. "And aren't you installing something from MicroSoft?"

"I guess so, I never thought much about it," he replies, returning to his computer. There he sees a long list of messages from the local network system initialization scan, and begins to scroll through the list.

"Copy of Netscape Navigator found corrupting system resources. It will be removed unless you type your password backward six times in the next four seconds. WARNING: Failure to remove Netscape products indicates a probable loyalty or drug problem, and you will be reported to the appropriate authorities."

Well, he wasn't around to preserve Netscape, so he's safe there. And with every release of Windows, it had become harder and harder to use Netscape anyway, even though he liked it better than Internet Explorer. Next message in the queue: "Warning: Non-Microsoft Operating System discovered on local network module." He scratches his head, then realizes that their daughter had been experimenting with the shareware Linux operating system on her machine — which he thought had been turned off. He hits the Help button.

"If you wish a multi-tasking networked operating system, you must install MicroSoft HomeOffice NT 6.3, available for only $395 plus shipping and handling. The Linux node has been terminated."

He hears a sizzle from upstairs and smells something like smoke, and looks for more on-line help. "For more information about this topic, you can either purchase the reference book MicroSoft Uber Alles with accompany CD-ROM and training video from MicroSoft Press for $89.95 plus shipping and handling, or call our special 1-900 technical support number. The first minute is $10.95 and additional minutes are only $8.95. Press any key or mouse button to initiate call now."

Panicking on account of what this could do to the family finances, he backs away from the computer. The house is silent, except for footsteps disappearing up the stairs. The TV is off. He scratches his head, wondering if the computer will notice if he lunges for the power cord.

"Honey, why don't you knock it off for the night and come to bed with me?" he hears from upstairs.

The computer screen changes. "Attention User: Do not terminate installation system scan before completion. Press any key to continue. 1:48 estimated until task accomplished."

He presses the key, to see a message announcing new components of Home2001: MicroSoft ForePlay and the MicroSoft Intimate Connection. "With these new features, you will no longer need to take precious time away from your console, and your productivity will soar. Press any key to initiate."

He races to the breaker box and starts toggling big switches. Forget living without computers in the house; he's going to try it without electricity.

Matters of Substance

The "War on Drugs" has been an abysmal failure at its stated goal of preventing Americans from using pharmaceutical substances not sold by companies listed on the New York Stock Exchange.

It has been underway since about 1969, when Richard Nixon became the first U.S. president to announce a "War on Drugs," and it continues as I write this — Bill Clinton is as firm a drug warrior as Ronald Reagan or George Bush ever was.

The war is a continued assault on the Bill of Rights — lawyers will tell you that our courts routinely sustain a "drug exception" to the Fourth Amendment's prohibition of unreasonable searches.

It flies in the face of history — America somehow became a world power in the 19th century without benefit of any drug laws. If drugs are so debilitating, how did our opium-addled ancestors manage to conquer a continent?

Its alleged "cure" is worse than the "disease." I grew up in the '60s, and so I know plenty of people who have had drug problems. More of those lives have been ruined by drug laws than by drugs. Why do we insist on doing this to our fellow citizens?

The War has created an entrenched bloc of profiteers, ranging from the neighborhood dealer to an immense bureaucracy, from corrupt cops to publishing houses peddling their DARE propaganda to schools who use our dollars to purchase this junk — and yet the politicians who will denounce this outrage, outside of the Libertarian Party, could be counted on your fingers.

Almost daily, I read of further atrocities committed in the name of this stupid and immoral war. So there's always something to write about, even on slow days, and I suppose a columnist has to take his blessings where he finds them.

THE COLORADO NEW AGE VIRTUE SQUAD
February 14, 1986

As THEY DID at the start of every shift, the intrepid officers of the Colorado New Age Virtue Squad gathered to receive their assignments from Captain Furillo.

"Crockett, I want you and Tubbs to head over to Aspen. There's a report that some creep sneaks out into a public hallway, and when no one is watching, he lights up a cigarette once or twice a day."

The rage began to build in Furillo's voice as he continued. "This jerk's toxic, noxious fumes carried more than 60 feet, over a transom and into an office. The complaining party said she knew that being exposed to such massive quantities of passive smoke would damage her health — and she already has problems. Her nose runs all the time, she imagines that bugs crawl around under her skin and her septum seems to be rotting away. She's very concerned about her health and what she puts into her body."

The captain turned, and rage began to show on his face. "Where in hell are Hunter and Hill? How are we supposed to function around here without our Fetal Protection Team?"

"You sent them out yesterday to Douglas County, chief, and they're not back yet."

The hard-bitten captain softened momentarily, but then the steel returned to his spine and the gravel to his voice. "Ought to be a piece of cake for them. Pregnant woman goes horseback riding and miscarries. They shouldn't have any trouble booking her for murder, and they're still not back. Damn."

He turned to two officers in the front row. "Okay, Cagney and Lacey. You're going to have to handle this. We've got a report that two women just entered a clinic in Boulder."

"Why is that our job?" Lacey honked in her Brooklyn accent.

"Because they're going in there for operations, that's why. If they were just carrying bombs or hatchets, you know we wouldn't be worried about it."

Chastened and silent, the two prepared to depart as Furillo looked down his list. He saw a note that bodies had been discovered buried on a ranch in Kit Carson County, but he skimmed over that. He also passed over a report that 30,000 residents of Adams County were drinking poisoned water. When it came to protecting public health and welfare, Furillo knew his priorities.

Before he could look up, his two undercover men, Wojohowitz and Harris, strode into the room leading a teenage boy and girl in handcuffs.

"They were kissing." The disgust was evident in Harris's cultivated tone.

Furillo turned to the quaking couple. "Don't you kids know that some pleasures are reserved for later in life? You kids want to have fun, you ought to stick to something legal and safe, like fornication with latex safety shields. That kissing stuff — didn't anybody ever tell you about saliva-transmitted diseases? You're supposed to wait until you're married for that." He nodded, and the adolescents were led away.

Furillo resumed the assignments. "Friday and Gannon, you head down to Pueblo. The local cops picked up eight people there yesterday who weren't doing their running. There seems to be a conspiracy afoot — it might involve thousands of criminals shirking their duty to be healthy.

"Starsky, you and Hutch are going to be out of town for a while. Somebody's smuggling red meat into Gunnison, and you have got to stop it. Baretta, haven't you nailed those sugar-eaters yet? Colombo, check out that cafe on Colfax that's supposed to be serving coffee with real caffeine in it."

Furillo wiped his brow and sighed as a new report came in. Child abuse. It sickened him. But he knew that he'd make them pay. Nobody was going to feed a kid a Twinkie and get away with it, not as long as Furillo and his team were on the job.

As Long as the Sample is Clean
April 11, 1986

THOMAS EDISON founded General Electric, but he'd have trouble getting a job there today. The man who invented the light bulb, phonograph and motion picture was expelled from school at age 7 and never returned to formal education.

Even had he overcome his wimp résumé, Edison still would be unable to hold a job at a major corporation.

The great inventor drank plenty of a contemporary spiced wine, Vin Mariani. It didn't slow him down — he seldom slept more than two hours a night.

The explanation would come when young Tom Edison went in for his blood and urine tests. As soon as the results arrived, he'd be shown the door, if not the paddy wagon. Vin Mariani was spiked with cocaine.

William Stewart Halsted is nowise as famous as Edison, but if you've lived through a major operation, you can thank Halsted, known to medical historians as "the father of modern surgery."

He championed a sterile operating room as well as the wearing of rubber gloves. He pioneered surgical procedures that minimized tissue damage, a vast improvement on the butchery that had gone on before in operating rooms. To instill his techniques, he founded the first school of surgery in the United States, at Johns Hopkins University in 1890.

If Halsted showed up today to practice his profession, any modern hospital would call the DEA after the mandatory blood test. As brilliant, careful and innovative a surgeon as he was, Halsted had a problem — a daily habit of 200 milligrams of morphine.

American journalism never has bothered to select a patron saint, but if there were one, he would be H.L. Mencken, the man who wrote: "The only way a newspaperman should look at a politician is down" and "No man ever went broke underestimating the taste of the American public."

He was city editor of a metropolitan newspaper in 1900, just before he turned 20. His forceful writing, in Walter Lippmann's view, made Mencken the most influential private citizen in the United States.

If Mencken showed up today at The Denver Post, hat in hand and looking for work, he'd probably not even get an interview. No college degree, for one thing. For another, Mencken boldly and openly consumed a powerful drug that was, during much of his career, totally forbidden by state and federal law — alcohol. For yet another, The Post is now a "smoke-free environment," and Mencken cherished his cigars, claiming that it was impossible to write without a smoldering stogie.

This modern way of judging people for employment leads to interesting speculation.

"Why, yes, Dr. Einstein, we know you've won a Nobel Prize and revolutionized physics. But we can't offer you a position at the University of Colorado. Your pipe offends the governor."

"No, Sigmund, you can't complete your residency. In fact, you're getting thrown off the hospital staff. Every time we test, we find cocaine in your blood."

"I heard that this guy was a smart attorney, one of the best. Then I read 'Reinventing the Corporation' and what it said about how stupid smokers are. No way am I ever going to hire that chain-smoking Clarence Darrow to represent me. Did you know he never even went to law school? I'll get somebody good instead."

Often I read dismal economic news. American goods are of shoddy quality. Productivity declines. Innovation tapers off. Many observers blame the loss of the "work ethic." Others wonder at the changing composition of the work force, while some blame management techniques. Recently it has been fashionable to blame drugs and tobacco.

But when you study on it, the real reason that Japan and everybody else are beating us is obvious. Their companies worry about what employees do — whether they're doing quality work at a price their customers can afford.

That was the attitude in this country when it became a world leader, during the careers of Thomas Edison, Clarence Darrow, H.L. Mencken and thousands of other uneducated substance abusers whose sole virtue was that they were good at what they did.

Today, however, American companies start by insisting on meaningless credentials. And then, instead of paying attention to their services and products, they monitor their employees' chemistry. Our goods may be shoddy and we may not invent much any more, but I suppose we can take pride in one thing. American workers soon will have the cleanest urine in the world.

THE NEXT NATIONAL SCOURGE
August 20, 1989

ON THE DAY after Labor Day, the Bush Administration is supposed to announce yet another strategy for ridding America of the scourge of drugs, once and for all.

No matter what our leaders propose — bombing Peruvian plantations, walling our borders, gutting the Bill of Rights — it won't work. You wonder why they even try, except that in politics, it is easier to raise a fuss about things you can't do much about (drugs or hostages, for instance) than it is to tend to the matters you're responsible for (bribery or influence peddling among people you appointed).

Why won't the next strategy work any better than Operation Intercept, the South Florida Task Force and Just Say No? If you look at the history of drug abuse and governmental responses, a clear pattern emerges.

A given drug first becomes popular with a small segment of the population, usually an influential elite. Nobody thinks that's a problem. It is laughed off as another eccentric aspect of the glamorous lifestyle of the rich and famous, of no more import than a champagne-filled swimming pool or a fleet of pink private jets.

Our culture teaches us to respect and flatter our betters — that is, people who have more money than we do. Imitation is the sincerest form of flattery. We can't afford pools and jets, but we can afford a taste of their chemical entertainments.

People wouldn't take drugs if drugs didn't make them feel better — note that there is little expressed concern about the clear dangers of snorting sulfuric acid crystals — and so the activity in question spreads throughout all levels of society. When it reaches the lower socioeconomic levels, the result is a four-alarm national emergency.

Even though crime has occurred throughout history, no matter what drugs were available, every sort of crime will be blamed on the current drug.

But after a while, the excitement wears off. People notice the long-term ill effects of the drug and give it up all on their own. By then, though, the rich and famous trendsetters have discovered another chemical novelty. The cycle starts anew.

So it was with gin in England, a scourge in 1750 when Hogarth produced his "Gin Lane" engravings of working-class people degraded by drink. But in 1700, gin posed no threat to the future of Western Civilization, because only His Majesty and the House of Lords drank the stuff.

More recently, we can look at LSD. No problem in 1964, when only a few daring writers, artists and college professors turned on and tuned in. It was a major problem by 1968, when orange sunshine was available on every street corner. The rabble was getting its grubby hands on an elite privilege, so politicians denounced it while newspapers displayed lurid stories about acid-addled college students who had blinded themselves by staring at the sun. But LSD was no problem in 1975, because by then everybody knew better, and besides, the trendsetters had taken up cocaine.

The moment that cocaine tumbled from the palaces to the slums and became bay rum instead of Dom Perignon, it became our leading national problem, far worse than toxic dumps, oil spills, bankrupt S&L's or the national deficit.

However, cocaine will go away, no matter what the Bush regime does or doesn't do. It's passé in the stylish set. These days, they're into bottled water, power nutrition and daily exercise for that natural runner's high.

You think we have a crime problem now? Just wait until the street thugs quit smoking crack and take up jogging to build up their endorphin levels naturally. Slow-footed police won't have a chance when every corner lout trains like a decathlon prospect.

Soon a vast market will develop for goods previously limited to Beverly Hills: exotic brands of bottled water and obscure organic foods alleged to enhance potency, increase strength and extend life. The clean-living criminals will import, counterfeit and deal. We'll have a new national scourge to eradicate.

BETTER TO SWITCH THAN FIGHT
March 13, 1990

TOBACCO peddlers ran into trouble recently with their latest plans for "market segmentation."

Many American industries use this approach, because they sell things so similar that the only way to convince people that brands make a difference is to devise distinct images.

Any car will get you from here to there, but there are BMW people and there are Ford station wagon people; any beer will do what beer does, but millions of dollars are spent every year to convince you that Silver Bullet folks are more fun than Miller Lite guys, and vice versa.

So there was the "Uptown" cigarette, targeted for urban blacks, and the "Dakota," aimed at young rural women. Both caused a storm of controversy, which tobacco companies might avoid if they produced some useful new brands:

— "Scrounge," for people who'd like to quit, or at least cut down. If you've been there, you understand what it's like to rummage through ashtrays, examine gutters, etc., all in the hope of finding a long, solid butt.

Now you can buy butts by the pack. Not only will they taste wretched, thus improving your health by reducing your smoking, but also you'll be helping the poor. How? Destitute people have been surviving by finding and selling aluminum cans. Now they can also collect butts and sell them at Scrounge redemption centers.

— "Mooch," the brand you need if you still smoke and you're around people who say they're trying to quit — which really means they haven't quit smoking cigarettes; they've just quit buying cigarettes.

A pack of "Mooch" comes already rumpled and contains but one dried-out, unfiltered Chesterfield. When approached by someone bumming a smoke, you pull out your Mooch pack. The freeloader examines it dubiously, announces "I can't take your last cigarette" and moves on, thus improving your life.

— "Sneak," the tiny, high-tech cigarette that fits in the palm of your hand. Stuck in a smoke-free environment when every nerve cell in your system is screaming for a dose of nicotine? Visiting some people who would notice even if you took a quick puff in the bathroom?

Just lift your hand to your mouth and push the tiny click-button on your "Sneak." A microprocessor-controlled igniter sends precisely enough to settle your nerves, while releasing no other offensive fumes.

— "Smug," the non-cigarette. Has it been a while since anyone noticed that you boycott tuna, avoid red meat, wear no furs, carry a Gold Card, sport designer sunglasses and subscribe to the "New Yorker"? The subtle but effective image on the $400 "Smug" pack in your shirt works better than an alligator or a monogram to convey the discreet but unmistakable statement that you are superior.

After all, if the tobacco industry profited for a century by giving a filthy habit a suave image, then it ought to be able to profit from changing times by charging a handsome fee for presenting the image that everybody wants to make these days.

CAN YOU TELL THE DIFFERENCE BETWEEN 'RACISM' AND 'ANTI-DRUG LAWS'?
November 14, 1995

LAST WEEK, more than 400 motorists reached a settlement in their federal lawsuit against Eagle County, which now will have to pay them about $800,000.

They were driving along Interstate 70 in the mountains when the sheriff, in cooperation with federal enforcers, was running the High Country Drug Task Force in 1988-90.

The plan was to identify cars that fit a "drug-courier profile" and search those cars. Among the criteria were fast-food wrappers on the floor, tinted windows, license plates from "known drug-source states" and the race or ethnicity of the driver, based on "intelligence information" from various sources.

Eagle County Sheriff A.J. Johnson said it was "unfortunate that racism became the issue" and that he knew "in my heart" that his task force was motivated by anti-drug goals, not racism.

He's a talented man if he can tell the difference between "anti-drug goals" and "racism." In this country, they're pretty much the same thing.

Go back less than a month to the uprisings in federal prisons over disparate sentencing laws.

If you're caught with five grams of crack cocaine, with a street value of about $225, you face a mandatory five years in prison. This happens mostly to African Americans. Of the 14,000 federal prisoners serving time under the crack laws, 88.3 percent are black.

But if you're caught with 500 grams of the white stuff that white people like, powder cocaine, with a street value of $50,000, you could get off with probation. A DEA study in New York found that 71 percent of drug users and 56 percent of drug sellers are white. But 91 percent of the people doing time for drugs are black or Hispanic.

That should tell you something about the real purpose of drug enforcement, and if that's not convincing, consider how substances came to be illegal in the first place.

We could start with one of the oldest drugs, opium, which shows up as "nepenthe" in Homer, where Queen Helen supplies it to young Telemachus after she returns to Sparta from Troy.

How did opium come to be illegal in this country? Right after the Civil War, capitalists needed cheap labor to build a railroad east from California. They imported Chinese workers. After the railroad was built, they had no further use for the Chinese, who were then in the way of progress.

In the words of Western historian Richard Wright, "those who attacked drugs ... took a significant second step. They did not just define and attack 'immorality'; they associated immoral activities with particular ethnic and racial groups ... Attacks on drugs and prostitution became attacks on Chinese, who were supposedly drug addicts ... Such efforts were far more successful at punishing or driving off minority groups than in eradicating the evils under attack."

When Coca-Cola first appeared in 1888, it contained "the valuable tonic and nerve stimulant properties of the coca plant" — that is, cocaine.

That was fine until 1903, when one J.W. Watson of Georgia wrote in the New York Tribune that Coca-Cola was the cause of "horrible crimes committed in the southern states by colored people."

In 1914, The New York Times blamed cocaine for the improved marksmanship of black men, citing "the 'cocaine nigger' near Asheville [N.C.] who dropped five men dead in their tracks, using only one cartridge for each."

Thus did cocaine become illegal. With marijuana, the target group expanded beyond African Americans. In 1937, as he persuaded Congress to outlaw a plant, Harry Anslinger said most American pot smokers were "Negroes and Mexicans, and entertainers."

Colorado had outlawed marijuana in 1917, with legislators citing the excesses of Pancho Villa's army, supposedly hopped up on marijuana. One history continues, "The Colorado Legislature felt the only way to prevent an actual racial bloodbath ... was to stop marijuana.... With the excuse of marijuana the whites could now use force and rationalize their violent acts of repression."

During this same era of "reform," Prohibition was adopted, generally after lurid propaganda aimed at German-Americans and their beer during World War I.

Earlier national prohibition efforts, aimed largely at keeping Irish Catholics in their place, had failed, perhaps because the United States never went to war against Ireland and thus had no "national security" rationale.

Move to more recent times, and note how quickly LSD became illegal because it was associated with another despised group — protesters against the Vietnam War.

In fact, I am unaware of any drug law in this country based on anything so mundane as honest science, constitutional rights or "life, liberty and the pursuit of happiness."

One group has always crafted our drug laws in order to keep other groups in their place. Often the group definition is racial.

So if Sheriff Johnson, or any other public official, is sincere about avoiding racism in law enforcement, he'll quit enforcing drug laws.

BOULDER SENATOR JOCKEYS FOR LEAD IN PURITY RACE AGAINST CALIFORNIA
January. 13, 1998

AT FIRST I was going to focus on some angle of the Broncos play-off victory Sunday that everyone else had missed. But it appears that they nailed down everything, from sports-bar scenes and T-shirt sales to possible effects on Patrick Bowlen's campaign for a taxpayer subsidy.

So let's look at the latest purity campaign to emerge from Boulder. There, they might not catch you if you bludgeon and strangle a child, but they've got a state senator who wants to arrange matters so that they can catch you if you light up in an automobile occupied by a child under 16.

State Sen. Dorothy Rupert says this is necessary to protect the health and lives of children. If she's serious about that, then forget the smoke and ban children from riding in cars altogether.

Search as I might, through reference books at hand and the vast if unreliable resources of the Internet, I have found no mention of any child anywhere dying or suffering immediate severe injury from the presence of tobacco fumes in an automobile.

However, the National Highway Traffic Safety Administration reported that 40,700 Americans died in traffic accidents in 1994, and about 9 percent of them — 3,700 or so — were children under 16. Also, 289,000 children were injured in auto accidents.

Apply those rates to Colorado, and it works out to 52 childhood deaths and 4,150 injuries each year.

So a ban on the transport of children in private automobiles would save at least one precious young life each week and prevent 79 injuries, many resulting in permanent impairment.

A total ban would also be easier to enforce than Rupert's proposed smoking ban. She wants to make "adult smoking in a car with children" a "primary" offense, as opposed to a "secondary" offense.

The difference between primary and secondary is that a cop can't pull you over just to see if you're violating the secondary. He has to find a primary cause, like speeding or a dysfunctional turn signal.

If Rupert gets her way, city cops, county deputies and state troopers will be watching for smoking drivers. Then they'll look for other occupants, and since it's often hard to guess the age of passengers as they whiz by, the cops will have to stop the car.

Since it can be difficult to estimate the age of adolescents, the state could simplify enforcement by requiring children to carry ID cards. After all, if a late-blooming 17-year-old who has no driver's license is a passenger, how's the cop supposed to know whether to issue a $56 smoking ticket?

The cop would also have to endure all manner of excuses, ranging from "That's not my kid, he's just some hitchhiker I picked up, and how am I supposed to know his age?" to "It's a nice day and the windows are rolled down, so how could the concentration of tobacco smoke be 23 times what it is in a house?"

Do cops really need to hear more excuses? And wouldn't enforcement be much simpler if they could just stop any car with probable children in it? Not only smokers, but kidnappers, molesters, pornographers and other unsavory sorts transport children in automobiles. A flat ban, unlike Rupert's selective prohibition, would go a long way toward eliminating these tragic crimes.

Further, when are child passengers safer: when Soccer Mom at the wheel can light up and relax in the afternoon gridlock, or when she can't smoke and gets edgy and tense and becomes susceptible to Road Rage? Both are dangerous situations, I gather, and again, a total ban would eliminate this dilemma.

Another benefit of prohibiting children in cars appears daily in front of my house. The old parochial school across the street has been leased by the school district for kindergarten and sixth-grade classes.

Politics, Small & Large

Perhaps the best that can be said for our political system, at least from my vantage, is that it reliably provides something to write about, especially when you're looking for humor based on human folly.

As for my own politics, there's an occasional mention that I was a registered Republican when that column appeared in The Denver Post. I no longer am, for a variety of reasons.

Principal among those is the same reason Ronald Reagan gave for leaving the Democratic Party long ago — I didn't leave the party, my party left me.

I really do believe in most of the things that Republicans used to say they believed in — small and limited government, individual responsibility, families and that sort of thing. But when Republicans get power, they use it to expand government to benefit big corporations, and to criminalize acts that should be an individual responsibility, such as abortion and drug use.

And they're such hypocrites. They rant on and on about the horrors of "government medicine." If it's so terrible, why don't our Republican representatives and senators give up their excellent government health benefits?

Or they tell us that our health-care system is "the envy of the world." Look around, especially at those democratic countries like France, Japan and Iceland with socialized medicine. Has any candidate in those countries ever campaigned on providing "an American-style health-care system?" Even Lady Margaret Thatcher, the idol of many American conservatives, did not dismantle the National Health System during her tenure as prime minister of Great Britain.

At any rate, I find the national Republicans disgusting. They pander to the worst impulses of the public as they preach "values" they don't practice, perhaps so we won't notice how they help their friends to loot the public till.

On a state and national level, the Democrats aren't much better — usually they act like Republicans, cozying up to money instead of looking out for the public interest.

43

We already have one money party in this country, and for the life of me, I can't see why we need two. What's the point in electing a Democrat if he's like Roy Romer, who never met a millionaire he didn't want to subsidize?

So I often vote Libertarian, although I do see a bigger role for government, especially in transportation, than they'd allow. And I fear that if they were in office, we'd probably get plundered even worse by greedy monopolies.

Greens? I like some of what they say, too, although I'm not big on purity. Maybe there's an opening for a Green Libertarian Party — one that promotes individual rights but strictly limits group rights (especially if that group is incorporated).

Columns about political topics, in general, do not age well. They're often written in the heat of a controversy, and bristle with side references to issues and people who might have been players at the moment, but are obscure now.

But it's something I enjoy writing about, because politics is the framework for discussing public affairs in this country — everything on the table, from show business to street crime — seems to have a political angle.

And as responsible citizens of a republic, we're supposed to discuss public affairs — especially when they're juicy and salacious.

BRING BACK THE ELECTORAL COLLEGE
September 18, 1987

THE UNITED STATES CONSTITUTION turned 200 yesterday with due fanfare. Most of the national news of late, though, has been devoted to the 1988 presidential election, still more than a year away.

Will Pat Schroeder make it official? What does the Rev. Pat Robertson's success in Iowa portend for candidates who wear a collar? Could Gary Hart's "Nightline" interview mean a comeback for candidates caught without their pants?

It struck me that I don't really care. No president has ever done anything that had any direct effect on my life, except for Richard Nixon, and he probably didn't mean anything personal 15 years ago when I received a letter that said, "Greetings from the President of the United States. Your friends and neighbors at Local Draft Board No. 9 ..."

The presidency hasn't affected me, and the converse also holds true. If my votes since attaining majority had meant anything, the recent Leaders of the Free World would have been George McGovern, Gerald Ford, Ed Clark and Walter Mondale.

What's worse is that even if your candidate wins, our system pretty well guarantees that you'll be disappointed.

We expect our presidents to be "good family men." To become president, they must spend at least two years jetting across the continent, eating dismal banquet food instead of home cooking, and operating in hotel suites instead of sleeping in their own homes.

No matter how many smiling pictures we see of the candidate with his wife and children, we ought to remember that actions speak louder than words. A man truly devoted to his wife and children would be with them, rather than going out of his way to hang out with state chairmen, caucus spokespersons, delegate fixers, PAC bagmen, media consultants and ward heelers.

We expect our presidents to exhibit sanity and good judgment. But what sane and judicious man would subject himself voluntarily to the rubber chicken circuit, round after round of moronic TV interviews, badgering by a pack of reporters, persistent jet lag and the other travails of our extended campaigns?

To ask that question is to answer it. Happy, productive and well-rounded people don't drop everything and run for president. Campaigning for the presidency is so demanding that it could attract only power-hungry zealots with an overwhelming desire to inflict their views on the rest of us. Our best people — those who mind their own business — certainly wouldn't run for president.

In two centuries, American civilization has advanced so much that our potential presidents include prayerful Pat Robertson for the GOP and the seven dwarfs for the Democrats. George Washington and Thomas Jefferson would have a hard time staying out of jail today, let alone seeking the nation's highest office. They grew tobacco and marijuana, kept mistresses, fomented armed rebellions and drank ale before their 21st birthdays.

Despite their conspicuous lack of modern virtues, I think the Founding Fathers had the right idea for selecting presidents, and it's still embedded in the Constitution whose birthday we just celebrated.

As you may recall from your civics classes, the president is not elected directly by the public. In theory, we voters select 535 presidential electors. They form the electoral college, which does the actual electing of the president.

Suppose we put this into practice. Every leap year, we Coloradans would vote for eight people of demonstrated sound and fair judgment. They would join the 527 other presidential electors, people who really did take the time to study the issues.

Since as much care ought to be devoted to selecting a capable president for the United States as in hiring the CEO for a big corporation, the process would be similar to that for any other high-level executive position. Candidates would submit résumés, references would be checked, the committee would conduct interviews and, by the end of the year, it would announce its selection.

Just by following our own Constitution, we could eliminate sensationalized scandals, idiotic TV commercials and emotional pandering to wool-hat mobs. Candidates would not have to sell their souls to special-interest groups in exchange for the contributions necessary to finance expensive national campaigns. And I defy anyone to say that the resulting presidents would do any worse than what we've managed to elect so far.

WE'RE MISSING THE ONE THING WE REALLY NEED TO KNOW
February 14, 1988

THE MOST INFLUENTIAL facet of our next presidency has not been covered by the news media.

We read of candidates bashing the press for mentioning cruises to Bimini, asking about the Iran-contra scandal, or referring to a potential president as a "former television evangelist." Sometimes we even read about the issues. But candidates and reporters bicker during every campaign. As for issues, the big ones at campaign time are not the ones that matter after Inauguration Day.

During Dwight Eisenhower's 1952 campaign, the islands of Quemoy and Matsu were major issues. That's the last time anybody heard of them. John F. Kennedy charged in 1960 that we were on the short end of a "missile gap," which apparently vanished upon his inauguration. In 1980, the federal deficit was a frequent target of Republican orators. They have since decided that the deficit isn't really a problem, perhaps because most of it accrued during the Reagan regime.

It isn't issues, characters, records or position papers that we should consider. Instead, we should judge candidates by their wives. What sort of First Lady will we get? What's important to her?

The president may command the armed forces and appoint a cabinet, but it is the First Lady who exerts a continuing influence on day-to-day life.

This came to mind during Lady Bird Johnson's recent visit to Denver. She still travels to "beautify America." Lately she promotes wildflowers; when she was First Lady, she declared war on billboards.

Every time you drive into the mountains and are able to see the mountains, you can thank Lady Bird for the view. When you venture east onto the prairie and yearn for a series of Burma Shave signs to break the monotony, you can blame her for your boredom.

More than 20 years after Lady Bird started, people still think it's important to battle billboards — witness the current struggles in Boulder and Colorado Springs. Did anything that Lyndon started last this long while involving so many people at the grassroots?

Recall Betty Ford. Forget that to be considered seriously as a celebrity in America, you have to check into her clinic and emerge six weeks later on the cover of People magazine. Remember instead the candor she took to the White House.

She spoke openly of sleeping arrangements, her mastectomy, the tribulations of a political marriage and whether her daughter might have an affair. That inspired everyone else. Today you can't meet a stranger and talk for more than 10 minutes without knowing the most intimate details. Whatever reserve Americans once possessed has vanished, and Betty Ford did it.

These days, you see even rock stars speaking against drugs. Businesses snoop on their employees, and schools encourage children to tattle on their parents.

For more than a century, drugs generally have been denounced, to little effect. But First Lady Nancy Reagan began her "Just say no" drive. Now it's on the lips of every schoolchild and drugs have lost any social acceptability they once enjoyed.

Like it or not, if America ever gets on the straight and narrow, it will be Nancy Reagan's doing.

The sensible way to run this year's campaign would be to end it right now. Let the men sit it out while their wives go on television and explain what matters to them — the homeless, the handicapped, cancer, AIDS, wetlands, farmers, deserts, immigration, etc.

Once we knew how each wife felt, we would know the enduring effect of her husband's presidency. I, for one, would find it much easier to make up my mind if I knew that.

Finally, a Job for the UN
February 19, 1989

IRAN JUST ANNOUNCED it will pay a $2.6 million bounty to the first Iranian who murders Salman Rushdie, whose crime was to write the book, "The Satanic Verses." It irritates Islamic fundamentalists, and not just in Iran. Pakistan said squads of hit men have been dispatched for Rushdie. Joining Pakistan in banning the book were India, Bangladesh, Egypt and South Africa.

All these countries belong to the United Nations, which means they agreed to abide by the UN Charter. Among other things, the charter provides that members should be "promoting and encouraging respect for human rights and for fundamental freedoms for all without distinction as to race, sex, language or religion."

It might seem that writing or reading a given book is one of those "fundamental freedoms," but the UN, as always, will ignore violations of its charter by its members.

The UN started with noble ideals and 56 countries in 1945. Now it has 159 members; most can hardly be called "nations." The delegate from the sovereign nation of St. Christopher & Nevis has a vote. His country has 40,000 residents and an area of 101 square miles.

If Colorado joined the UN, it would rank well. Our population of 3,296,000 makes us 101st among the nations of the world, right after New Zealand, and ahead of 58 countries, including Jordan, Uruguay and Ireland. We have 104,481 square miles, which puts us ahead of 92 places that have their own armies and embassies, such as Yugoslavia, Great Britain and Greece.

In economic terms, Colorado is a superpower compared to most of the UN membership. Our state's "gross national product" of $52 billion ranks 34th — we contribute more to the world economy than 75 percent of the nations in the UN. We do more than the bottom 56 members of the UN combined.

So what good is the UN if it's dominated by a collection of rinky-dink countries that never honor the promises they made in signing the UN Charter?

One theory of national and local government is that governments exist to perform necessary tasks that individuals can't easily do on their own — build highways, for instance. If we extend that, then an international organization should do things that individual countries have trouble handling on their own. For instance, countries depose rulers occasionally. The exiled leader often heads for the United States, as one of the "wretched refuse" that the Statue of Liberty invites. The presence of a Ferdinand Marcos or an ex-Shah Riza Pahlavi complicates U.S. foreign policy enormously.

The UN could provide a useful service to the nations of the world if it established a remote island reservation where former heads of state could live out their days in luxury, but incommunicado from the rest of the world. Among other benefits, we wouldn't have Richard Nixon to kick around any more.

A bigger reservation operated by the UN would solve a greater problem that many nations face. Islamic fundamentalists are resorting to a worldwide murder plot in order to inflict their views of what is, and isn't, good literature on the rest of the human race. In America, we have similar, although not as extreme, problems with Christian fundamentalists. Many citizens have not accepted our national principles — among them freedom of religion and expression.

An article in the Feb. 13 "New Yorker" noted that Israel's government can't satisfy the demands of its "ultra-Orthodox" fundamentalists. Mikhail Gorbachev's reforms in the Soviet Union may be subverted by that nation's fundamentalists, the hard-core Stalinists.

Around the world, there are millions of fundamentalists of various stripes, all interfering with the rest of us. No nation can handle them. Put them all on a big reservation somewhere, where they can rant and commit holy murder as much as they want.

The UN could establish and administer that fundamentalist reservation. Thus it would honor its charter as it finally served a useful purpose.

AMERICA, WHERE IT PAYS TO LOSE
May 21, 1989

WHY CAN'T the United States do anything about Gen. Manuel Noriega? Not that we haven't tried to dislodge him from Panama. He was indicted for drug sales in this country, and the Reagan Administration offered a plea bargain if he'd step down. Then our government tried economic sanctions that succeeded in making Panamanians even more impoverished, but failed miserably at removing Noriega.

If Panama had held an honest election last week, Noriega would be history. But the count was rigged. Noriega had soldiers on the streets and his goons were at large, beating on opposition candidates. President Bush has responded by putting more troops on our military bases in Panama.

Noriega is still in charge, and the informed sources say he'll be tough to topple, since he's a rich man with millions in drug profits.

The reason America can't win this go-round is that we are a nation that esteems losers. There is no incentive to win if there is no penalty for losing. This attitude is certainly wholesome and democratic — if 32 people enter a race, 31 of them will be losers. That's the majority of us, and we're a nation where the majority rules. But this is not an attitude that produces results.

Consider the past 25 years' worth of wars. There was the War on Poverty. Despite the herculean efforts of thousands of sociology majors who couldn't find jobs, Poverty won.

What happened to the losers? Were they forced to march in chains down some *barrio* boulevard, ghetto street or rural road while the victorious poor jeered and taunted? Were the losers enslaved and sent to toil in salt mines?

Of course not. They kept their comfortable positions and served their time; most of them probably draw good pensions now. Why should they bother to win when there were no penalties for losing?

There was Vietnam, a real shooting war that we lost. The architects of that disaster were men like Robert McNamara and Henry Kissinger. Did they endure capture, imprisonment, war crimes tribunals and the other ordeals generally visited upon leaders of the losing side? No, they continue to live well and command substantial fees on the lecture circuit. They're respected elder statesmen.

Just compare their retirement careers with those of American leaders who actually won wars — Gen. George Marshall, for instance, who ended his days being vilified by right-wing Americans. Not only is losing painless, it's easier on you than winning.

Jimmy Carter told us that beating the energy crisis was "the moral equivalent of war." We'd have to reduce petroleum consumption and imports.

We won some battles for a year or two, but we've certainly lost the Moral Equivalency. We import more oil than we did in 1975, we consume more energy, and most of us would trade incomes with the president of Exxon. Losing a Moral Equivalency is tough, but somebody has to do it.

There were various "Wars on Waste" during the Reagan regime. Those whistle-blower auditors who took that seriously lost their jobs. Waste won, with handsome rewards for defense contractors, who then could offer high-paying jobs to those government employees who managed to lose the war on waste.

Concerning Panama, we might examine one phase of the "War on Drugs" — the South Florida Task Force, which was supposed to interdict every gram of cocaine headed for these shores. It was headed by none other than the vice-president of the United States, a fellow named George Herbert Walker Bush.

The Task Force lost miserably, which is one reason Noriega is still in power. But the leader of that losing task force was not disgraced; he was promoted.

Vince Lombardi once said, "Show me a good loser and I'll show you a loser." He was wrong. What America really says is "Show us a loser, and we'll shower him with money and prestige."

News From Abroad?
June 18, 1989

MOST of the foreign news these days seems bizarre and confusing: free demonstrations and then brutal repression in China; a once-outlawed union now taking part in the Polish government; the peaceful replacement of Khomeini in Iran when the timing seemed perfect for a civil war.

The more foreign news and analysis I read, the more perplexing it becomes. But America might be just as confusing if our own news were presented the same way to us. Just imagine what an American roundup on some foreign network might be like:

"While a major American defense contractor has continued to deny that there are any safety problems at the Rocky Flats Thermonuclear Warhead Trigger Fabrication Facility in Colorado, a national government agency, which sent in dozens of investigators, has announced that its probe would take at least another week, and that substantive questions have been raised concerning the safety of the facility.

"Meanwhile, the governor of Colorado has indicated he may be forced to find a way to close Rocky Flats in order to protect his citizens from plutonium, tritium and various transuranic wastes, which America cannot find a safe place to store. However, federal agents have not moved to arrest the governor for threatening to close Rocky Flats, even though several members of a radical environmental organization recently were arrested for precisely the same thing — threatening to close Rocky Flats.

"In the American capital of Washington, a city named after their great revolutionary leader, corruption continues to fester behind the gleaming marble facades of public buildings.

"Newt Gingrich of Georgia led the charge to force Jim Wright of Texas out of the American Congress. Gingrich charged that Wright had taken advantage of a loophole in the law on a peculiar book-royalty schedule. However, Gingrich also has enjoyed the proceeds of peculiar book royalties.

"So far, the latest round of the Great Ethical Purge has claimed Wright and Tony Coelho, another congressional leader. On the other side of the aisle, the 1989 liquidation of moral questionables has claimed Mark Goodin, a member of the Central Committee of the Grand Old Party, and earlier this year there was John Tower, who lost his bid to become secretary of defense.

"Further developments are expected in an unfolding scandal in the Department of Housing and Urban Development.

"As we understand it, the American government was up to its usual tricks. They start by announcing and then appropriating ample funds for a program that sounds good for helping poor people. In this case, the idea was to provide good housing for America's poor — except they call them 'economically impaired'.

"But once the program is implemented, the only ones who receive any of that tax money are the Americans who already enjoy wealth and power. One such member of the American elite collected $800,000 for making a few telephone calls to arrange meetings between developers and federal officials. Now some of those developers are under investigation, too.

"As a final note in tonight's American roundup, the Rev. Jerry Falwell announced that he was closing his influential religious pressure group, the Moral Majority. It was widely credited with helping elect some of the people who appointed some of the people we just mentioned earlier in connection with various ethical scandals.

"Falwell said the Moral Majority had served its purpose by injecting decency, honesty and other moral values into the mainstream of American public life. The announcement, however, did not say what planet Falwell was speaking from.

"And that's the way it is in America. Good night."

THE FLAG ENFORCEMENT ADMINISTRATION
July 2, 1989

AND IT CAME TO PASS that on the 213th anniversary of its freedom, the United States of America adopted the 27th amendment to its national Constitution, and thenceforth it was illegal to burn, mutilate or otherwise "desecrate" the American flag.

Among the first to be imprisoned for violating the Flag Protection Amendment were the dozen or so American Christians who actually practiced the teachings of the Bible.

At their trial, they cited their First Amendment religious freedom, as well as the Second Commandment: "Thou shalt not make unto thee any graven image, or any likeness of any thing that is in the heaven above (i.e., stars) ... Thou shalt not bow down thyself to them, nor serve them."

In their view, a law against "desecrating" the flag carried the clear implication that the flag, a piece of man-made cloth, had become sacred, and therefore, obedience to that law of man was the worship of an idol, and thus a violation of the laws of God.

President Bush said that although he sympathized with them, he "had no problem" with sending the Christians to a reeducation center where they were forced to recite the Pledge of Allegiance — his major campaign issue in 1988 — for 16 hours a day.

Bush also pledged "an all-out war on flag abuse" and established the Flag Enforcement Administration as part of an anti-flag-abuse task force headed by Vice President Dan Quayle.

Editors of veterans' magazines were shocked when their offices were among the first places to be raided by the FEA.

"Have you seen some of their advertising?" Quayle asked. "It's disgusting. They're selling American flag belt buckles, shoulder patches and lapel pins. Can you believe that they could call themselves patriots while they're busy commercializing our sacred flag? Even worse, they're actually selling paraphernalia that leads to even worse forms of flag abuse."

Pressed for specifics, Quayle mentioned flag decals and bumper stickers for automobiles. "In themselves, they're probably acceptable. But the problem is, people put them on cars, where they get splattered by mud. Very few drivers have sufficient patriotism to obey the law of the land. They don't stop the moment their flag is defaced and clean it. They just drive on in the mistaken belief that washing the car once a month is enough. It isn't."

At their trial, the flag paraphernalia merchants pointed out that the U.S. government, through its subsidiary, the Postal Service, was one of the major offenders. Many postage stamps have flags on them, and the Postal Service defaces those flags with its canceling machines.

A new method of cancellation was developed, thus giving the Postal Service an excuse to raise first-class postage to 50 cents an ounce, but another problem remained.

With the exception of a few dingbat maiden aunts, Americans throw out old envelopes, even those with flag stamps on them. Once these flags enter the garbage stream, they could be buried without due honor, corroded by toxic wastes or even burned.

"To insure that our great national symbol is not defaced," Bush promised to place an FEA inspector at every landfill in America. "We have zero tolerance for flag abuse," he announced.

There were some who thought the money might be better spent by inspecting just what was being dumped on America — oil on its beaches, acid rain on its forests, chemicals in its rivers — but Bush said he couldn't buy that. "Do whatever you want to America, as long as it shows a profit," he said. "But don't mess with our flag."

THE NEW MARSHALL PLAN
December 3, 1989

NOW THAT THE BERLIN WALL has fallen into commercial hands ("When we hang the next-to-the-last capitalist, the last capitalist will try to sell the rope as an authentic and significant historic souvenir." — V.I. Lenin), the nations of eastern Europe are beginning to open up after 50 years of Nazi and Soviet rule.

Many Americans have expressed a desire to help these countries recover. After World War II, our Marshall Plan brought western Europe back to life, and Japan began to prosper mightily thanks to American assistance.

In those days, we were a rich, powerful country that could afford to export money and expertise. We did such a good job that some of those countries now are trouncing us; we're no longer the world leader in many fields, and we've become the world's largest debtor nation, too.

This time around, we should learn our lesson and export those facets of American life that will insure that we won't ever face any meaningful competition from Bulgaria, Czechoslovakia, Poland or Yugoslavia.

For instance, we should help them adopt the American system of health care. Then 13 percent of their population would be without health insurance. They would live in constant fear that they might lose their homes and cars if disease or accident should strike; worried people aren't efficient workers.

The 62 percent with employer-provided health insurance won't ever dare to quit their drone jobs and try something innovative, and the 7 percent on Medicaid will stay on welfare — such dreary jobs as they can find never offer health insurance, and who wants to bleed to death in a waiting room for lack of coverage?

Nations with the American system will spend 11.1 percent of their gross national products on health, more than anybody else in the world does, and will spend it so inefficiently that they will rank 15th in the infant mortality rate and 12th in life expectancy.

Another good export would be our transportation system. We've already trashed many perfectly good cities by turning them over to parking lots and freeways; let *glasnost* bring gridlock to Wenceslas Square. We did our share; now it's time for the Poles and Serbs to send their hard-earned money to Japanese auto makers and Arabian oil cartels. That should guarantee that their economies never out-produce ours.

Just to be sure, though, we'd better send out some missionaries from the American Bar Association who can install our legal system. That way, every productive enterprise in eastern Europe can quit being productive, because its managers will have to focus on avoiding lawsuits. Even to get a specious case thrown out of court will take five years and cost hundreds of thousands of dollars — that's a lot of time and money that won't get invested in building products to compete with ours.

Their political systems are undergoing reform, too, and our campaign consultants certainly could help America by taking their acts overseas. The street crowds in Prague will shout for flag-protection laws instead of freedom, and Bulgarians will demand that their new leaders pass urine tests, rather than reform their governments.

On the lighter side, if American football catches on elsewhere, our future world dominance is assured. Their bright high-school students no longer will concern themselves with learning math; the boys will be on the team as the girls cheer them on. Their once-proud universities will abandon all academic standards as they pursue winning seasons. Their adult populations will spend every autumnal Sunday afternoon in a stupor, and productivity at work will plummet because the sharpest person in the office will devote his energy to running the weekly betting pool.

It's time for America to stand tall again, and the easiest way to do that is to cripple the potential competition by exporting some good old American know-how.

They Never Know When to Stop
January 28, 1990

Although State Sen. Pat Pascoe's proposed firearms law is quite reasonable, our legislature doubtless will do the right thing this week and kill the bill.

Her bill, similar to laws already in effect in 21 other states, requires a waiting period for gun buyers, whose police records would be checked. It is hard to make a case for impulse gun purchases, or for dispensing firearms to felons or the feeble-minded.

However, reasonable gun regulation must be defeated because, when it comes to regulation, our society does not stay reasonable. American history demonstrates that as soon as reasonable restrictions take effect, the empowered do-gooders will start imposing unreasonable restrictions.

The most recent example is the regulation of tobacco smoking, a filthy, noxious addiction that rightfully offends many people. The backers initially sought sensible restrictions, such as smoking sections on airliners and in restaurants, or office arrangements that allowed nonsmokers to breathe freely while smokers could light up and go about their work instead of fidgeting and yearning.

But did the anti-tobacco regulators stop there? Of course not. Now smoking is banned on all flights, cities often forbid smoking in any restaurant, or indeed even outdoors except in designated places, and many companies won't employ smokers at all. There is no such thing as your own time; the company controls your activities for 24 hours a day though it usually pays you only for eight.

That is regulation that has passed from rational to berserk, and it's typical.

At the turn of the century, addictive drugs were common ingredients in many products. Coca-Cola contained cocaine, as did wares from chewing gum to tooth powders. Cough syrups and other tonics soothed with tinctures of heroin.

First came the reasonable Pure Food and Drug Act of 1906, which required that all products containing cocaine or opiates be so labeled. But naturally, the do-gooders couldn't rest there; now they demand to examine your blood and urine.

The Temperance movement started as just that — a movement to advocate the temperate consumption of alcoholic beverages. The movement succeeded at raising public consciousness about the costs of a nation of drunkards. Thus emboldened, though, the backers didn't stop until they had installed their very own amendment to the U.S. Constitution. It isn't just drugs. A century ago, American railroads held tremendous power, which was flagrantly abused. Instead of just regulating the abuses, the reformers so throttled the industry that they ruined an efficient transportation system.

William F. Buckley once argued in favor of some censorship by pointing out that a society that bans "Deep Throat" is not going to ban Milton or Shakespeare. He was wrong; once American do-gooders gain a bit of power by fighting for something sensible, they are never content to leave it at that.

A reasonable gun bill this year means that next year they'll push it a little further, maybe with an extended background check — conducting interviews with your neighbors and co-workers, all at your expense, of course. The year after, it'll take a two-month psychiatric evaluation before you can get a new deer rifle.

Then they'll discover that guns aren't the only lethal tools. The rigorous purchase requirements will be extended to compound bows and kitchen knives, and that will be just a start.

Given a choice concerning personal protection, would you rather rely on your own gun or on a society that has so far demonstrated not a whit of common sense? The answer is obvious, and that's why the Pascoe bill should be defeated. It isn't a bad law in itself, but if it passes, it will open the door for all manner of increased meddling.

Starting a Long Tradition of Briefings
February 17, 1991

It is late afternoon in early December of 1864, and we take you now live to a military briefing in the War Department, where Col. Virgil Pangloss stands before a small gathering of reporters.

"Sir, I understand that Gen. William Tecumseh Sherman has deployed a new American military development called 'Total War' and that he is marching through Georgia with an innovative 'Stealth Army' that does not need a supply train. Could you tell us more about that?"

"I'm sorry, but I'm not free to comment on that. To reveal the location of an army, even to mention that there is a force under a given general's command, might compromise the safety of our troops. You over there?"

However, the first reporter is both persistent and loud, and gets in another question. "But Colonel Pangloss, Peter Arnett has reported on Confederate News Network, out of Atlanta, that Sherman's army ravaged Atlanta this fall, causing widespread civilian suffering, then ripped up railroad tracks and torched granaries, and is now marching toward Savannah, leaving in his wake a 60-mile wide swath of utter destruction. If the Confederates know where Gen. Sherman's army is and what his troops are doing, why can't the Union people know?"

"Again, I can't tell you about that. And as I am sure you are aware, our noble and patriotic Senator Simpson has proclaimed that Arnett is a Confederate sympathizer, and that you should not put credence in any of his reports. Arnett is nothing but a mouthpiece for Jefferson Davis, and the American people should not be subjected to this malicious and misleading propaganda. Now, be a sport and let somebody else ask a question."

In the rear of the room, a correspondent rises. "Colonel, when the war started, you said the insurrection would be put down in 90 days. That was about four years ago. Is the war still going according to plan?"

"Yankee troops yesterday fired 314,592 rounds in their rifles. In aerial bombardment, we fired 28,182 mortar shells last week, and we launched 19 balloon sorties to gather intelligence behind enemy lines. On the naval front, the blockade has interdicted 97 percent of all munitions and other war materiel bound for Southern ports, and that collateral damage has been kept to an absolute minimum. General Grant assures me that the war is proceeding according to plan."

"Could you tell us which plan, Colonel? Would that be the Anaconda Plan that Gen. Winfield Scott proposed at the outbreak of hostilities?"

"I'm sorry, but I'm not at liberty to discuss that. However, be assured that we are on a steady course toward the goal we set when the war began."

"Which goal, sir? To preserve the Union? To liberate the slaves? To occupy the South?"

"I will not dignify that impudent question with an answer. How about you over there?"

"Sir, there are some reports that out in Colorado Territory, toward the end of last month, soldiers attacked a civilian village at a place called Sand Creek, and killed many women and children. Is there anything to that?"

"Our intelligence from Colonel Chivington, the field commander, indicated that the encampment was actually a command and control center, and we'll stand by that. Thank you, gentlemen, for coming, and that will be all for today."

PROFILES OF THE REAL CRIMINALS
July 10, 1991

IF SOME KIDS wear colorful bandannas or L.A. Raiders hats to an amusement park, those kids fit the "gang-member profile." They often are hauled off for a photo and fingerprint session.

This sensible method of preserving public safety has upset a few bleeding hearts who whine about civil rights, presumption of innocence and free expression.

Complaining won't help, since such issues now mean nothing to the Supreme Court. Instead, the whiners should urge police to expand their "potential criminal profiles" to include other known dangerous categories.

— Quiet Neighbors. The suspect in the United Bank Father's Day Massacre is described by his neighbors as a quiet fellow who cared for home and lawn.

That's no surprise. Almost always, when there's an arrest in a heinous multiple murder, you read the same comment from the suspect's neighbors: "It's unbelievable. He was real quiet, never bothered anybody. He took real good care of his property, and he was a good neighbor."

If the police can find time for kids who wear the wrong caps, then certainly they have time to sweep suburban neighborhoods and find those who match the criminal profile — quiet regular guys with lawn mowers or hedge clippers. Haul those Quiet Neighbors off to preventive detention, and scores of innocent victims will be spared.

— Respectable People. Marilyn Van Derbur Atler's father was a pillar of the community during the years that he was sexually abusing her. David Bath, star of some racy videos with juvenile males, staunchly upheld traditional values in the Colorado General Assembly.

More examples appear almost daily, and the criminal profile is obvious: Civic respectability is often a cloak for perversion. Why isn't the vice squad busy checking out every beloved youth minister, honored Scout leader, esteemed teacher, public benefactor and the like?

— Three-Piece Suits. Why bother with small-timers in their gang colors at amusement parks? As Don Vito Corleone said, "A lawyer with his briefcase can steal more than a hundred men with guns." Bankers, real-estate developers, accountants, congressmen and lawyers pulled off the largest theft in history — $500 billion from American taxpayers in the S&L scandal.

The criminal profile is clear; anyone wearing a three-piece suit (perhaps the color of the tie indicates the precise gang affiliation) at a financial institution should be presumed guilty of grand larceny until proven innocent.

We all want a safer society. Discouraging youth gangs might help, but we really need a concentrated assault on murder, perversion and theft. When will our lily-livered police start going after the suspicious folks — Quiet Neighbors, Respectable Citizens and Three-piece Thieves — who fit the big-time criminal profiles?

RETURNING TO TRADITIONAL VALUES
May 31, 1992

THIS YEAR'S CAMPAIGN buzz phrase calls for "a return to traditional values." However, no office-seeker will provide specifics, so we must join a traditional family as they visit a new theme park, "American Traditional Value Land."

"Okay, kids, which section of the park do you want to visit first? Colonial, Gilded Age or Tailfin?"

"Let's start with Colonial, Dad."

They pass through a log gate into in a dark warehouse where smallpox-ridden blankets are being prepared for shipment to an Indian tribe. Fearing infection, they step out to join a mob in looting a Tory's house. Then they stop for a few minutes to catch their breath and watch as a suspected witch is crushed to death under a pile of stones.

"Totally disgusting," Sis complains. "How could that be a traditional value?"

Mom consults her guidebook. "The woman was convicted of witchcraft because she used herbs to induce abortions, and so she's being punished. Isn't it exciting to see how traditional values are returning?"

"I want to leave," Sis says, and they exit to Gilded Age. The roar of gunfire is deafening as professional hunters bring down egrets, buffalo and passenger pigeons.

"Utterly gross," Junior says. "Don't they know those animals could become extinct?"

Dad laughs. "The hunters don't care, as long as they've got work. It's just like the spotted owl today — see how we're returning to traditional values, kids? Maybe we should go over to Paul Bunyan Camp."

"Not a good idea," Mom cautions. "The trees were all clear-cut the first week after the park opened, and there won't be much to see for another century."

They walk for a long time along a country road lined with small farmsteads plagued variously by drought, locusts, foreclosure, high rail rates or low commodity prices. The illiterate farm children toil with scythes and hoes from dawn to dusk. At one farm the mule died, so the woman pulls the plow. The men look gaunt and hopeless.

"Gee, it would be great to go back to when most Americans lived on farms — NOT," Sis says. Otherwise, they are silent until they get to town.

"Why are there so many drunks here?" Junior asks.

"We've really fallen away from traditional values," Mom explains. "Back then, the average American swilled 1.76 gallons of hard liquor. Now it's down to three pints."

"I'm thirsty. Let's stop at the soda fountain in the drugstore," Sis suggests. Junior observes that morphine and hemp are sold over the counter to all comers, and Sis comments on the potency of the Coca-Cola.

"That's because it had real cocaine in it," Dad says. "You know, it looks like this modern War on Drugs is an assault on Traditional Values."

"Dad, if you keep talking like that, I'll tell my school DARE counselor, and then they'll arrest you," Sis warns. "It's a family value now to turn in your parents."

The mecca of Tailfin Land lies ahead, the place where Mom could greet the children after school with milk and cookies because an ordinary working stiff like dad made enough to support the family. But to get there, they had to pass through a labor war between the militia and striking miners, and they got caught in the cross fire. They bled to death because they didn't have enough money with them — the triumph of another traditional American value.

HOW TO TALK REPUBLICAN
August 30, 1992

As BOTH a registered Republican and a student of our Official Language, I feel compelled by my sense of public duty to explain certain details of the Grand Old Patois.

The dialect usually is spoken in country clubs and corporate boardrooms. But the electoral process requires that, at four-year intervals, we peons get to see characters on TV who talk Republican as they read their scripts.

In its general syntax, Republican follows Official English with rare exceptions. Most notable of these is its refusal to employ the traditional adjectival form for the other party's name. Observe these examples:

Bad: "The Democratic Party"

Acceptable: "The Democrat Party"

Presidential: "The Other Side"

Excellent: "We have a two-party system — Democrats and Americans."

But it is in its diction and semantics — the selection of words and the meanings assigned to those words — that Republican can be most confusing to the novice. Here are some definitions to help you translate from Republican to Official English:

Special Interest Group. This does not mean the Federal Timber Purchasers Association, the National Association of Manufacturers, the American Medical Association, the Milk Producers of America or similar benevolent organizations dedicated to the public interest, as evidenced by their PAC contributions.

It refers instead to women, children, working people, unemployed people, people who want to breath clean air, citizens who weren't born rich and white, and similar grasping, greedy, selfish lobbies.

Soft on Crime. This applies to a bleeding-heart who questions the need for a sentence of life at hard labor for a hemp farmer.

Many other acts that might at first appear to be crimes — deliberately lying, subverting the Constitution, raiding the public treasury, operating a dangerous workplace — are, in the Republican dialect, known as campaigning, foreign policy, domestic policy and business as usual.

Get Government off Our Backs. This should be taken quite literally.

Government remains in your pockets — Reagan and Bush signed the largest and second-largest tax bills in history. And in your bloodstream and urine, where the federal government may require your employer to conduct controlled-substance tests, on pain of losing federal business. And in your bedroom, where the Republican Supreme Court has upheld state laws forbidding certain private sexual practices. And in a woman's womb, if the Republican platform becomes reality.

But it's not on your back.

Beltway Insider or Entrenched Incumbent: A person of the Democrat persuasion who has held office in Washington for a considerable period of time.

A Republican in similar circumstances merits a different locution, as with Ronald Reagan's description of George Bush as "a man who has devoted most of his adult life to the service of his country."

Space prevents me from continuing. But with this start, you shouldn't have much trouble figuring out the real meanings of such Republican phrases as Traditional Values, Family Values, Traditional Family Values, Strong National Defense and Cultural Elite.

IF THEY WANT TO BUILD THE BOMB, HELP THEM
November 15, 1992

DURING THE RECENT presidential campaign, there were serious charges that American credit and technology might have gone to a nuclear-weapons program in Iraq.

All the important people agreed that this was an outrage, but they obviously didn't think the matter through.

If whatever hurts Iraq helps the United States, then this was no scandal. It was a sensible and prudent policy, and America should provide more nuclear technology to Iraq.

This may sound foolish, but consider what happened to a former enemy, the U.S.S.R.

During the Cold War, the Soviets built thousands of nuclear bombs, all designed to kill Americans. Not a single American ever died from a Soviet nuclear bomb.

However, recent news from Russia reveals that there were thousands of Soviet casualties from the bomb program — not only the direct deaths that occur with any heavy industry, but shortened lives from radiation overexposure and associated cancers.

Further, vast areas of Soviet territory are permanently uninhabitable on account of radiation. The effect, so far as the Russians are concerned, is precisely the same as if these lands were occupied by American troops (perhaps worse, since soldiers spend money, while contaminated land just sits there). And certainly vast herds of sheep and cattle were destroyed by nuclear tests.

So our then-enemy lost personnel, livestock, territory, and productive capacity — not from any direct action of the American military, but from the activities of its own military-industrial complex.

The same holds true in this hemisphere. No American soldier or citizen ever died from a Soviet bomb. But America suffered in the same ways from its own nuclear program: cancer deaths, crop and livestock destruction, and effective loss of territory.

In short, most of the harm that an enemy tries to inflict in wartime is precisely the harm you'll do to yourself with a nuclear-weapons program. If you're building nuclear bombs, you don't really need an enemy to lay waste to your personnel, territory and economy. Nor do you need enemy propaganda to make people question the wisdom and veracity of their leaders.

Given that, the United States should immediately cut some deals with Iraq.

We're broke, and they want to build the Bomb. We want to eradicate Rocky Flats, Hanford, Pantex, and similar toxic facilities. They'd certainly be willing to remove these plutonic factories and clean the sites. The Iraqis might even be stupid enough to pay good money for that privilege, which would improve our balance of payments while reducing the deficit.

Once they had all this set up over there, then they, too, could enjoy soaring taxes, herd exterminations, soothing lies from the Defense Ministry, death and disease among skilled and productive workers, permanent loss of territory, national bankruptcy and the other blessings of a nuclear-bomb program.

It would do more permanent damage to Iraq than Desert Storm ever did, and the assault would continue day in and day out for decades, at no cost whatsoever to American taxpayers — in fact, there might even be a net profit.

So why are they looking for a scandal in the alleged diversion of technology to Iraq? They ought to be looking for some chests to pin medals on.

Rationing Could Improve Health Care
February 22, 1994

When public health care came up in days gone by, the physicians raised the ghastly specter of "socialized medicine," which couldn't be as good as capitalist medicine.

Then Medicare and Medicaid came along, and doctors discovered that socialism wasn't so bad after all. In 1959, the average physician earned 390 percent as much as the average household. In 1989, with tax money flowing into medical pockets, it was 508 percent.

Since doctors did better after the government got involved, we don't hear about the horrors of socialized medicine any more.

Instead, we're supposed to be afraid of "health-care rationing."

Here's some news for our protectors in the U.S. Senate — unlike you, with your excellent, government-funded health plan that covers everything, most of us already have rationed health care. It's rationed by what we can afford, or by how much our insurance companies will pay.

Beyond that, there might be good arguments for rationing health care anyway.

It's difficult to quantify health, but some numbers might help. It seems fair to assume that a country with a high life expectancy and a low infant-mortality rate is a healthy country.

The average life expectancy in America is 75.5, and our infant-mortality rate is 10 per 1,000 live births. Some countries do worse, like Russia at 68.5 and 31, and others do better, like Canada at 77.5 and 7.3.

To compare the general health of nations, I divided life expectancy by infant-mortality rate, providing a health index of 7.55 for the U.S. I then compared every country's health index to ours, which was set at 1.

By this measure, Japan's comparative health index leads the world at 2.63, followed closely by Iceland at 2.6. Many other nations exceeded America by a substantial margin — Australia, Austria, Belgium, France, Iceland, Spain, United Kingdom, etc. — and they all suffer from socialized medicine and its attendant calamity of "health-care rationing."

There's another interesting feature buried in these numbers. Most nations that exceed our health index do it with fewer physicians.

For instance, we support one physician per 404 people; Canadians manage to live longer and produce more live births with only one doctor per 449, while Japan is at 588 and Great Britain 611.

This indicates that there's a limit of diminishing returns on doctors. Once you exceed a certain ratio, health doesn't improve; it declines.

My rough data indicate that the turning point is somewhere between 500 and 800 — Costa Rica, for instance, is almost as healthy we are at one per 798.

Given that, rationing appears to be the easiest way to improve American health care. Bring us down to one doctor per 600, like the advanced countries, and our life expectancy should rise as more babies survive. That would mean eliminating about 200,000 doctors, but there's no choice if we're serious about improving our health care.

Time to Set Aside a Richard Nixon Day?
April 26, 1994

Conventional wisdom, as expressed in the acres of admiring prose published during the past week, holds that the late Richard Nixon was brilliant at foreign affairs and a failure at domestic affairs.

But where are these triumphs in foreign policy? The war in Vietnam dragged on and on through Nixon's presidency, and when it finally ended, the terms were substantially the same as Nixon could have obtained in 1969.

The opening to China? Suppose Hubert Humphrey had won in 1968 and then gone to China the way Nixon did. Patriots still would be denouncing Humphrey in the VFW posts and American Legion halls of this great republic for "cozying up to the Red butchers and betraying our faithful allies on Taiwan." A generation later, it's still a matter of argument as to whether we should be doing business with the people who brought us the Tiananmen Square Massacre.

Detente? If that was so successful, why the need for the immense arms build-up that began in the Carter years and continued through the Reagan regime?

Meanwhile, the Nixon-Kissinger Realpolitik often consisted of betraying people they had earlier encouraged — ask the Kurds.

If those represent triumphs in foreign policy, what could possibly constitute a defeat?

On the domestic side, much of his legacy is not that of the small-government conservative he sometimes claimed to be, but instead a list that a big-government, pork-barrel, tax-and-spend Democrat could point to with pride: Amtrak, the Environmental Protection Agency, wage and price controls, Harry Blackmun's appointment to the Supreme Court, and a guaranteed-income welfare-reform proposal far more generous than anything Bill Clinton would dare to propose.

Of course there were Watergate, and the Enemies List, and the phone taps, and Kent State and Jackson State, the first round of the War on Drugs — Nixon practiced a savage politics of exclusion. Either you sported a flag on your lapel and belonged to the Silent Majority, or you were an un-American traitor to be denounced and maybe killed.

He campaigned on the theme of "Bring us together," and then did more to drive us apart than any politician since Jefferson Davis.

Besides, I've always hated him because he drafted me in 1972. People told me not to take it personally. But the letter was addressed to me personally, and it contained "Greetings from the President of the United States." It sure seemed personal to me.

Anyway, all "nonessential" federal offices will be closed tomorrow. In essence, it's a national holiday, and perhaps we should make Richard Nixon Day an annual event.

After all, when I was a schoolchild, we learned about Valley Forge and Yorktown every Feb. 22. On Feb. 12, we learned about Fort Sumter and Appomattox.

So why not a Richard Nixon Day? A day set aside to ponder opportunism, hypocrisy, campaign shake-downs, brutal suppression of dissent — a day that would give schoolchildren a better idea of the real America than any dozen homilies about young Abe Lincoln trudging barefoot through 3 miles of snow to return a book.

Property-Rights Movement Could be a Boon to us All
March 5, 1995

The Fifth Amendment to the United States Constitution is most famous for its protection against self-incrimination, in that "no person ... shall be compelled in any criminal case to be a witness against himself."

That provision, along with its prohibition of double jeopardy and its requirement of due process, sometimes upsets the law-and-order types. But lately, some right-thinkers have celebrated the last clause of the Fifth.

It provides that private property cannot "be taken for public use, without just compensation."

Normally, that means that if the city wants to widen the street in front of your lot, then it has to pay a fair market value for your land.

However, a growing property-rights movement argues that any form of government regulation that limits the possible economic return from your property constitutes a "takings" and you should be compensated.

Here's the logic. Suppose you bought a 40-acre parcel in some low-down-payment, easy-monthly-payment, serene and rustic mountain development. You plan to put a cabin on it someday.

Meanwhile, some dangerous radicals take over the rural county's government. They observe that your cabin site is essentially a mudslide waiting for a good thunderstorm, and they don't want to be stuck with the mess. Further, that charming scenic access road has steep grades and hairpin curves, such that no fire truck or school bus can climb it.

So the county commissioners adopt a new zoning plan and forbid all residential or commercial construction in this area.

You've still got your land, but you can't legally do much with it, on account of a governmental action. The restrictions mean that your property is worth less. It certainly appears that a part of your property, its development rights, has been taken for "public use," and that the Constitution entitles you to "just compensation."

In essence, that's the argument of the emerging property-rights movement. Its proponents were excited last summer when the U.S. Supreme Court limited the ability of local governments to make real-estate developers set aside environmental easements.

At issue was the desire of a plumbing-supply store owner to expand her store and pave the parking lot. The city of Tigard, Ore., said she'd have to dedicate about 10 percent of the property to a storm-drain and pedestrian pathway. She said this requirement was a "takings" and the Supreme Court agreed.

The decision thrilled the rip-and-run crowd. If they can get the "takings" clause to cover any government regulation of property, then they'll have to be compensated every time a regulation affects them. Environmental regulations will become so expensive that no government could afford them.

Or at least, that's what my environmentalist friends tell me — that this whole property-rights movement is just a right-wing plot to insure that polluters and developers always have their way.

But it also could enrich the rest of us. The first "takings" lawsuit was brought in Kansas, a haven of virtue that adopted statewide prohibition in 1887.

Peter Mugler, who owned a brewery, sued. His mash tuns and wort kettles were worthless on account of prohibition, a governmental action that had put him out of business, and he wanted his "just compensation."

He didn't get it. The Supreme Court then held that "a government can prevent a property owner from using his property to injure others without having to compensate the owner for the value of the forbidden use."

However, that was essentially the same Supreme Court that created the "separate but equal" doctrine that was later overturned. So the Mugler precedent is certainly not carved in stone, and a more enlightened court could strike it down after hearing arguments from the well-funded attorneys of the property-rights movement.

If that happens, one friend plans to send the federal and state governments a bill for $100,000 a year. He has about 10 acres with decent water rights.

"I just read somewhere that a dedicated pot farmer can clear about $10,000 an acre every year," he said, "and so the laws that forbid marijuana cultivation are taking this much potential income away from me and my family. If that's not a 'takings', I don't know what is, and I want my just compensation."

I don't own any land besides some city lots, but they'd probably be worth considerably more if I could replace the current structures with casinos or bordellos. The laws that prohibit these uses, like various environmental laws that prohibit certain property uses, must be a form of "takings." Where do I file for my compensation?

Those noisy airplanes that the government allows to fly over your property, thereby diminishing its value — how much compensation do you deserve? If you're in the metro area, how much "just compensation" do you deserve for what the Brown Cloud costs you in lost property values?

With a good Supreme Court decision that upholds the arguments of the property-rights movement, we could all get rich.

FRANKLIN: THEY THAT GIVE UP LIBERTY FOR SAFETY DESERVE NEITHER.
April 25, 1995

ATTENTION Federal Anti-Terrorism Authorities: I, too, felt horrified by our government's actions at the Branch Davidian compound. It never before occurred to me that the way to prevent child abuse was to have the children barbecued by the FBI. Must be one of those lessons we learned in Vietnam — destroy the village in order to save it.

In addition, I have publicly supported various provisions of our Bill of Rights, among them the rights of free speech and press, the right to bear arms, the right to worship deities other than Mammon and the right to be secure in your home.

Further, my wife grew up in Michigan, home of one militia, and the last time I left this state, I went to Arizona, another militia hotbed. Last weekend I was in Gunnison County, where some Davidians may have fled. I live in Chaffee County, where the Fuqua sect allegedly was stockpiling arms.

Around my premises, I see equipment that could be used for, well, whatever. For instance, there's an old Tandy 100 laptop computer. Attach the primitive cassette-recorder connector to a relay wired to a detonator, program the computer to close the relay at a certain time, and presto, a big-time terrorist device, right up there with that VCR that didn't have tapes.

Having thus confessed, I expect to be questioned as our federal government, always eager to find an excuse to expand its power, cracks down on terrorist threats in response to the "attack on the Heartland."

The main result of the Oklahoma City bombing will be a further erosion of whatever "inalienable" rights we might still exercise. Put wiretaps on everybody. Outlaw cash so there's always a credit-card paper trail to trace. Install more undercover informers, and if they don't turn up enough indictments they can become provocateurs and justify their presence on the public payroll.

The focus on the Heartland angle has odd implications. One is that we might understand somebody setting off a bomb in an important place like New York, Washington or Los Angeles, but Oklahoma City?

Another implication is that the Heartland was a refuge, somehow immune from terror and violence until last week.

That must be why the Cherokee moved to Oklahoma from Georgia in 1839. Odd that they called their migration route the Trail of Tears, but maybe they did feel safer there after terrorists — no, make that hard-working American land speculators — attacked them.

Perhaps the Cheyenne and Arapaho also felt safer in Oklahoma after they moved there in 1867, a couple of years after terrorists — no, make that a joint anti-terrorism task force — attacked their homes in a pre-dawn raid and butchered women and children at Sand Creek in Colorado Territory. The children had to go because "nits make lice," and as for the women, their breasts and genitalia, once removed and tanned, made for distinctive tobacco pouches.

Even when you ponder only terrorist bombings, it's hardly a novelty in this Heartland sanctuary.

On July 6, 1904, dynamite exploded under the railroad depot at Independence in the Cripple Creek District. Thirteen men died and dozens more were seriously injured. A bomb killed the former governor of Idaho in 1905. In 1908, a mine manager's house in Telluride was bombed.

These actions, of course, were denounced roundly as acts of terrorism, and the perpetrators — as well as anyone who had ever expressed sympathy with the notion that there was something wrong with a system that paid men $2.50 for a backbreaking 12-hour day while the mine owners cavorted in their private railroad cars — were summarily rounded up, imprisoned and sometimes even tried.

The word terrorism does not describe a heinous act. Instead, it describes the actor.

If our government performs the act — say, mowing down women and children at Ludlow, or shooting down a civilian airliner in the Persian Gulf, or providing arms to thugs in Guatemala, or killing an unarmed woman with her baby in Idaho — then it's a matter of preserving national security, and we should all sleep better at night.

But if anybody else does such things, then it's an act of terrorism, and we should all feel fearful and ask that same government to protect us.

So, how should our government respond to the brutal and senseless act in Oklahoma City?

It could try cleaning up its own act. No more undercover informant-provocateurs. Quit contriving threats, especially at budget time. No more domestic raids with tanks and machine guns, sharpshooters and poison gas.

Do I want to live among dingbat, white-supremacist, gold-standard, tax-hating gun lovers? No. They frighten me, and I wish they'd go away.

But I don't feel nearly as threatened by them as I do by a superpower government that feels free to ignore its own rules in the guise of protecting us. As Benjamin Franklin once observed, "They that can give up essential liberty to obtain a little temporary safety deserve neither liberty nor safety."

If he was wrong, then the government should take his picture off the $100 bill. If he was right, then we should heed his words.

Let's Retire the Word 'Conservative' Since it Means Nothing
February 18, 1996

Let us count our blessings and thank the good people who attended GOP precinct caucuses in Iowa last week. Now it will be possible to watch the news without hearing Phil Gramm.

His campaign was so well-planned that last summer they were up here filming the Texas senator and his family rafting down the Arkansas for use in commercials this year.

Around here, we speculated as to how the footage would be used: "When Phil and Wendy get into whitewater, they do it the old-fashioned way." Or maybe a regular-folks approach: "Like millions of other down-home Texans, the Gramms enjoy summer vacations in Colorado." Could be they were just trying to position the senator as an active outdoorsy fellow rather than a bookish economic wonk.

Perhaps they planned some geographic fun: "Up here in Colorado, the Arkansas River runs fast and clean. When it gets to Kansas, Robert Dole's home state, it dries up. And we don't even want to talk about what happens to it when it gets to Arkansas, home state of the Evil Clintons who wanted to destroy the best health-care system in the world and replace it with one of those horrible socialist systems like they have in backward nations like France and Japan."

The Gramm family visit was all pretty mysterious. They were in and out before we heard anything about it.

Gramm had money, organization and something to say. There was even a time when I admired him. Last year he went before some family-values forum and possessed the courage to say that preaching was best left to the clergy; he was running on economic issues that were the proper concern of government.

Naturally, he had to recant his heresy in order to placate the pious mob, but it was refreshing to see a Republican with a backbone, no matter how ephemeral.

The problem with the "Conservative Revolution" is that "conservative" really doesn't mean anything. It's a fashionable term, so they all try to position themselves as "conservatives."

A few examples should suffice. William F. Buckley is a conservative. He has written that the War on Drugs is an immoral and unjust abuse of governmental power and an infringement on our constitutional rights. William Bennett is also a conservative, and he says the only thing wrong with the War on Drugs is that they haven't locked up enough people yet.

Phil Gramm is a conservative, and he believes in free trade. Patrick Buchanan is a conservative, and he believes in protective tariffs and other trade restrictions.

Bob Dole is a conservative, and he has supported food stamps throughout his congressional career. The House Republican freshmen are conservatives, and they say food stamps just cause us to be shiftless and lazy and they really hurt people.

Steve Forbes is a conservative, but he apparently sees abortion as a matter for women and their physicians, not as a criminal matter. Meanwhile, Buchanan and many others want a constitutional amendment; presumably, the death penalty would loom for any woman who goes horseback riding at the wrong time.

Conservatives lash out at broken families and divorce, yet make divorced George Will a prophet and worship at the shrine of Ronald Reagan, our first divorced president. They're horrified at the size of the federal debt — which more than tripled during the Reagan-Bush years.

They attack "academic elites," while Newt Gingrich and Phil Gramm were both college professors who never met a payroll before getting elected to office, where they got more room at the public trough.

No matter what the issue — Bosnia, the Gulf War, China trade or gay rights — usually you can find conservatives on both sides.

The confusion grows when you hear an aspiring office-holder define himself as "fiscally conservative but socially liberal."

Wait a minute. How can you operate liberal social programs without spending a lot of tax money? But it doesn't really mean that. It means that he's socially tolerant, thus following the traditional conservative principle of limited government.

Liberals oppose censorship on the Internet, but so does state Sen. Charles Duke, and nobody would call him a liberal. Conservatives oppose government regulation, except they trip over themselves to support V-chips and anti-porn laws.

More points of confusion emerge with further contemplation. If conservative means anything, it should mean "defender of the status quo." However, the "conservatives" in the House of Representatives also call themselves "revolutionaries," bent on uprooting status-quo programs like Medicare and Aid to Families with Dependent Children.

Since "conservative" doesn't mean anything, and it doesn't tell us where a candidate might stand on any issue from abortion to zymurgy, why don't we retire the word, at least for this election year? They're all "conservatives." But what are they, really?

Repeal the Child-Protection Laws
March 31, 1996

JUST ABOUT every time one of our governments proposes something truly draconian and stupid, the proposal gets support because "we need to protect our children."

Most recent of these imbecilities is the Communications Decency Act, which prohibits the computer transmission of racy images to any spot where a child might see them.

Both sides seem to agree that children shouldn't see certain things, and the question is which mechanism would provide the best shield for tender eyes. The question nobody asks is "so what if a child does see them?"

Modern America operates under the theory that exposure to sex or violence damages children irreparably and causes them to grow up to be serial killers or water diverters.

In the course of other work, I often read from diaries and memoirs of people who grew up in 19th-century America.

Most children then lived on farms, where barnyard couplings happened in plain view and where chickens were butchered daily, often with toddlers assisting.

Further, children frequently shared a bedroom, or even a bed, with their parents, and families of eight or nine offspring were common. The typical 18-year-old of 1896 had seen considerable live sex and violence, and yet we keep hearing from our Republicans about how much better America was during the days of William McKinley.

And if that direct exposure did not send my grandparents' generation into hedonism or anarchy, why would indirect exposure via electronic images do so?

The Communications Decency Act has nothing to do with protecting children, and everything to do with finding employment for more police, prosecutors and prison guards. Another example of the inanity of child-protection laws appeared a fortnight ago here. Five girls, aged 14 to 16, were injured when their vehicle rolled over as they were leaving a woodsy.

Now, if we didn't have laws to protect children from buying alcohol, and they wanted to get loud and stupid, they could have just walked to a saloon, where they would have been under the supervision of bartenders and bouncers.

After all, in the days of yesteryear so beloved by our modern moral guardians, 12-year-olds were routinely dispatched to the tavern to fetch a bucket of beer for dad or to the drugstore to procure opiates for mom's neuralgia. Yet those children somehow grew up to be productive adults.

But in these protective times, the thirsty teenagers had to sneak off to a keg party up a rough road, with predictable consequences. We butcher hundreds of kids every year in the guise of "protecting" them.

Attorney General Janet Reno's decision to barbecue the children in the Branch Davidian compound at Waco in 1993, in order to "save" them, is consistent with how America in general protects children. We use it as a justification for enlarging the Big Brother aspects of government and we really don't care what happens to the children we said we were protecting.

A society that truly worried about the welfare of children might have a minimum wage of such a level that one wage earner could support a family, thereby leaving another parent with time and energy for the children, rather than the corporation.

Such a society might insure that every family had access to affordable and decent medical care, or that kids didn't have to worry about getting shot on their way to or from school, or that the teachers in said school were competent and literate. It might insure that all children with the will and the talent would get higher education without indebting themselves for life.

That doesn't sound anything like America.

Since we really don't protect children, perhaps we should observe the words of Thomas Jefferson: "... all Men are created equal, that they are endowed by their Creator with certain unalienable Rights, that among these are Life, Liberty, and the Pursuit of Happiness — That to secure these Rights, Governments are instituted among Men..."

That is, a government exists to protect rights, not children. As matters stand, government destroys rights in the name of protecting children, and doesn't protect children from real threats anyway.

We'll never get rid of the people who make a business of minding other people's business. But if we got rid of the "child-protection" laws, at least we'd get rid of some pretense that gets more annoying by the day.

WHAT'S THE MOST FRAGILE ELEMENT OF MODERN SOCIETY?
August 5, 1997

GRANTED, summer isn't the best time for parlor games, but then again, you may need something to talk about around the campfire. Instead of "Twenty Questions," you could pose just one: "What's the most fragile thing you can think of?"

The easy answer used to be "white blood." The racist speakers of my youth used to allege that if a person's heritage comprised as little as 1/32 African-American ancestry, then that person's blood somehow was tainted.

Obviously, any substance that can be overpowered when it outnumbers another substance by better than 30 to 1 is a weak and fragile substance indeed.

Fortunately, that drivel has pretty well vanished from public discourse, and one might today nominate "the Ramsey investigation" for the fragility prize.

You name it — the publication of photos, the release of autopsy information that is normally made public, a glitch in the power supply to the computer room — and we get an immediate announcement from the Boulder Ministry of Public Information that "this could impede the investigation."

Such things happen frequently during the course of other criminal investigations, so one has to wonder, given the fragility of this case, how all those other criminals get arrested and convicted.

Another contestant in the fragility sweepstakes is the limited-sweepstakes gambling industry in Central City. Allowing big companies to gut the innards of old buildings and install one-armed bandits and blackjack tables was supposed to give the place a vibrant economy.

Apparently it's not all that vibrant, since its cash flow is threatened by neighboring Black Hawk. So Central City says it needs a new $35 million road — one that won't pass through Black Hawk first — to stay in business.

Somehow, I can't imagine Salida trying to build a road that evades Fairplay, Gunnison promoting a Poncha Springs bypass, or Saguache encouraging motorists to swing around Villa Grove.

Central City gambling must be fragile indeed. Perhaps the whole industry is — just by using the word "gambling" instead of the industry-preferred term, "gaming," I'll probably get a tart letter from a public-relations professional, concerned that the simple and accurate term "gambling" might tarnish the industry's image. They like "gaming" because it sounds like "game," which is what innocent children play and therefore carries a wholesome family aura.

My nominee for the "most fragile" award, though, is property values.

This was brought to my attention by a gay correspondent in Denver, who observed that merely by moving into a neighborhood and quietly going about his life, he could lower property values.

I responded that I, too, a practitioner of Traditional Family Values to a degree that should entitle me to an honorary seat on the Republican National Committee, could wreak havoc on property values just by going about my life: old cars, a clothesline, some wind chimes on the porch, asphalt shingles on the roof and a woodpile in the back yard.

All these harmless objects apparently damage those delicate and fragile property values, since many upscale venues, dedicated to the preservation of property values, employ restrictive covenants to ban clotheslines, wind chimes, non-cedar-shake shingles, etc.

Over the years, other threats to our dainty property values in this state have included pickup trucks, lawns of some plant other than Kentucky bluegrass, exterior paint of an inappropriate color, neighbors of an inappropriate color, etc.

The property-values lobby resembles the gambling apologists in another way — not only do they often attempt to protect their interests with legislation, but they deliberately obscure the issues.

The gambling industry wants you to say "gaming." The property-values crowd often says it's talking about "property rights."

Property rights and property values aren't the same. Property rights allow a woodpile or a clothesline or a partner of the same sex at your domain, no matter what effect that might have on some greedy neighbor's real-estate appraisal.

Now, I can't say for certain that property values are the most fragile element of modern society, since there are so many delicate contestants. But property values are so weak that they're certainly a strong contender.

The Culture Wars & More

In modern America, it's impossible to separate culture wars from political dis-putes. Perhaps this is an unanticipated consequence of the end of the Cold War.

Until the Berlin Wall and the Soviet Union fell, it was always safe to accuse your opponent of being "a little pink" or "soft on Communism."

But without the lurid specter of the godless international Communist conspiracy, those slurs became worse than useless. Campaign strategists had to come up with something else, like Family Values.

Not that any candidate for high office could really practice such values. If you care about your family and enjoy their company, you stay with them — you don't run all over the state and nation, eating bad food, enduring dull company and delivering inane speeches.

These tactics produce startling anomalies, starting even when the Cold War was going strong. Go back to 1972 and there was Richard Nixon, who had spent World War II as a liquor supply officer far from the front in the Pacific, running against George McGovern, a decorated bomber pilot. So guess which one got portrayed as the exemplar of courage and patriotism?

Or go back to 1980, where there was Ronald Reagan, a divorced Holly-wood actor, running against Jimmy Carter, a devout Baptist Sunday school teacher. Guess which one was portrayed as the avatar of American morality?

Beats me how they get away with this, but it sure continues. I can recall several local political races where one candidate for the legislature said he should be elected because he "shares our values."

I don't know about you, but one of my strong values is a total lack of any desire to spend six months of each year in Denver hanging out with lobbyists, journalists and right-wing windbags from El Paso County — and that's what service in the General Assembly means. A candidate who shared my values would do a horrible job of representing this district.

It's like hiring a lawyer. Do you want one who "shares your values" or one who will win the case? I know that if I needed legal representation, I would avoid the idealistic attorney in beads and sandals who might "share my values" in favor of some silver-tongued fellow who drove a Mercedes and was reputed to be the best fixer in six counties.

We'd have a better political system if we voted for our interests, rather than our values. The values hustle generally insures that we get screwed by the people who are supposed to look after our interests.

To move on, the major recent insult is "cultural elite." I have on occasion been accused of belonging to the "Colorado cultural elite."

That would be news to the many people who wrote angry letters when I wondered why rock or country fans should be taxed to provide symphony orchestras, but in some ways I suppose it's a compliment.

Here I am, an indifferent student who twice dropped out of college. I live in a rather isolated little town where the start of elk season is one of the year's major events. My taste in movies runs to the "Naked Gun" series. My literary contributions are mostly adult westerns under a pen name. My clothing style runs heavily to blue jeans, T-shirts and gimme caps. I am so poorly traveled that I have never crossed the Mississippi River, and my sole foreign visit consisted of an afternoon in Vancouver, B.C.

And yet, Colorado for Family Values will tell you that I'm part of an elite.

That's flattering, but it's also something of a disappointment. I had hoped that joining the elite would mean living in a house with more than one bathroom, that it would mean driving a car that is less than a decade old, and that it would mean spending Mud Season on some tropical isle, rather than enduring the slime and wind of April in the Rockies.

So the rewards of belonging to the "cultural elite" seem rather illusory. In fact, I can't think of any. But the culture wars have always been entertaining, even if they don't make much sense.

CONFESSIONS OF A PORNOGRAPHER
July 25, 1986

WHEN I was trying to get a degree from the University of Northern Colorado years ago, I sampled a rich variety of boring jobs: dishwasher, truck driver, sign printer, typesetter, hay hand, construction laborer. So I was thrilled in early 1974 when I landed a new part-time job that sounded interesting.

I became the weekend manager and promotion director of the Mini-Flick, a movie house on the north side of Greeley. If there was any socially redeeming value to our movies, it was that showing porn films at the Mini-Flick provided a few jobs. Some people — I am not among them — believe that holding a steady job improves one's character.

Clarence "Marty" Martin owned the Mini-Flick, as well as Cinema 35, a similar outlet in Fort Collins. If pornography provides vast profits to its purveyors, his accountant must have been a wizard at sheltering assets. Marty's mansion was a basement apartment next door to the theater.

We were drinking coffee in there one Saturday morning, trying to figure out how to persuade more people to pay $2 a head to watch dirty movies. The problem with porn, unlike other vices, is that it isn't addictive. Once you've smoked a few cigarettes or started playing solitaire, you can't quit. But our patrons just wouldn't get hooked.

So we had to find ways to draw new customers. An advertising blitz was impossible. The Greeley Tribune wouldn't accept advertising for X-rated films, and I had lived there for 23 years without ever meeting anyone who had listened to the local radio stations.

We hatched a publicity scheme. It was an election year in a conservative county. The district attorney might see some need to say that Weld County soon would rival Sodom and Gomorrah unless he acted immediately. In his voter-pleasing anti-vice campaign, he could denounce the city's only adult theater.

If that occurred, we'd get acres of free publicity from the same stodgy newspaper that wouldn't sell us ads. Preachers and politicians would get on the bandwagon. People would be curious; we'd sell theater seats.

I went to see District Attorney Robert Miller, who laughed when I explained our promotion plan that would bolster his re-election campaign. "I have real crimes to worry about — murders and rapes and robberies. Why would I care what movies people go to?"

So I never did figure out how to make porn attractive to more people. As for those who came to the shows, never did I sell a ticket to an old man in a raincoat. I saw a sprinkling of respectable types — businessmen who had enjoyed stag night at the VFW hall, or trendy couples who just wanted to say they'd seen "Deep Throat" or "The Devil in Miss Jones."

We attracted young customers, although many of them were turned away because they looked under 18 and said things like "Oh, I left my wallet in the car" or "I lost my driver's license." Most of the rest were college students. I liked them best because they devised witty dialogue as the movie ran, hollering their lines to the rest of the audience.

That was as interesting as the job ever got. I quickly learned why we didn't get many repeat customers. After you've seen two or three porn films, you won't see anything new in the next 200. That quarter, I got my best grades ever, because even reading Henry James in the lobby was an improvement on watching those movies. One night the show stopped because the projectionist had fallen asleep.

Maybe the Meese Commission is right, and such movies cause exploitation of women in an economy where working women get paid 64 percent as much as working men. Or perhaps pornography inspires a casual commercial attitude about sex in a society whose merchants use exposed skin to sell everything from blue jeans to computer software. Or maybe it leads to mindless violence in a nation that boasts an arsenal of 10,398 thermonuclear warheads.

But as a retired panderer, all I can say for sure is that dirty movies cause boredom. As for those few poor souls who get excited by endless sweaty renditions, where would you rather have them — in the theater or out on the street?

Why Can't Upper-Crust Music Pay its Own Way?
October 10, 1986

It always seemed logical that musicians and music-lovers would be more creative than the stolid bean counters who run major corporations. But when the musicians' union for the Denver Symphony Orchestra wants a new contract, the management sings the same tired tune played by distressed airlines and asbestos manufacturers: "Do It My Way, or I'll File for Chapter 11."

When word got out that Denver, which already lacks something that Cleveland has, a major-league baseball team, soon might lack something else that Cleveland has, a symphony orchestra, then came the predictable wailing about how the quality of metropolitan life would deteriorate to the quality of metropolitan air.

American symphony orchestras have never been profitable. Professional soccer and spring football weren't ever profitable, either, but nobody ever feared that Western Civilization would collapse if we didn't send money to the Colorado Caribous or the Denver Gold. When a public entertainment gets a reputation for being an aspect of high culture, though, it's a different story.

Our cultural betters not only insist that we ought to share their worries, but also that we boorish philistines should help pay for their symphonic entertainment — directly through taxes or indirectly through tax breaks received by those who do contribute. In the age of Reagan, this makes perfect sense: tax the poor to provide pleasure for the rich, but tell the poor that it's for their own good.

Even if you can't afford to dress for a concert, much less attend one or know when you're supposed to applaud, this theory has it that your life is better because there's a full-sized orchestra down the street, capable of performing unintelligible works by obscure composers. You've heard of trickle-down economics. This is trickle-down culture.

Both function pretty much the same way, but there is an important difference. When the money doesn't trickle down, those of us on the bottom don't have any. But whether or not the *haut monde* can enjoy a tax-deductible night at the subsidized symphony, those of us in the lower orders of American life would still have music.

The only real American contributions to music have come from saloons and churches on the wrong side of the tracks. Bluegrass, jazz, folk, blues, country, gospel, Dixieland, country and western, rhythm and blues, soul, gospel, rock and roll — those forms of music were invented, performed and perfected by poor folks, black and white. Most of them couldn't read street signs, let alone sheet music, many were in prison and few of them would have enhanced a corporate image.

American low-life music is immensely popular in the rest of the world, a fact known even to our national propaganda ministries; the Voice of America often plays blues or jazz, but seldom puts on a symphony.

In this country, blue-collar music is the only music that pays its own way. Peter McLaughlin has to devote considerable time and energy every year to organizing the Denver Symphony Run, because upper-class music can't support itself and must resort to this and other peculiar forms of financing.

Nobody has ever organized a Denver Country & Western Run or a Mile High Gospel Marathon, for the simple reason that no one has ever needed to. No one has ever come on my TV set to solicit charitable donations for the Colorado Bluegrass Festival or the Telluride Jazz Festival. As for rock festivals — the musicians sometimes raise money to support other causes, instead of relying on other causes to support the musicians.

People who like those forms of music are willing to pay for their pleasure; unlike symphony dilettantes, they don't expect the rest of the public to contribute. America is a nation of music lovers; even in my remote little town there are dance halls, churches, radio stations, home stereos, private instruments, bands, combos, choirs, glee clubs, automotive cassette decks, ghetto blasters and a summer series from the Aspen Music Festival.

If the Denver Symphony Orchestra cannot attract enough patronage to turn a profit, it doesn't mean that Colorado people are too uncouth to appreciate music. All it really says is that most of us don't have the same musical tastes as 18th-century Austrian aristocrats. Is there any reason why we should?

IF IT'S A RELIGION, WHERE ARE THE MISSIONARIES?
March 13, 1987

Is SECULAR HUMANISM a religion? A federal district judge thinks so. Last week, Judge Brevard Hand of Mobile, Ala., ruled that certain textbooks could not be used in the public schools.

The proscribed books — many of them also are used in Colorado schools — explain scientific disciplines like geology and biology. They advocate personal responsibility for personal actions. They recognize that not all children come from two-parent households.

In the judge's opinion, these 44 books do not represent sincere efforts to deal with objective reality. Instead, such books actually promote a system of religious belief — Secular Humanism.

Our Constitution requires the separation of church and state. That means that religious doctrines cannot be advocated in state-supported schools. So books that espouse or promulgate the doctrines of a religion cannot be used in the classroom.

If Secular Humanism is indeed a religion, then it certainly stands to reason that our schools should not promote Secular Humanism, any more than our schools should encourage students to sacrifice bulls to Zeus.

I've never been able to find out just what Secular Humanism might or might not be. But I do feel reasonably certain that Secular Humanism isn't a real religion.

For one thing, real religions send missionaries to enlighten heathen American neighborhoods. Many times I've raced out of an afternoon shower to answer the doorbell. My peace and dignity have been disturbed by Mormons, Jehovah's Witnesses, Pentecostals, Moonies, Baptists and Seventh-Day Adventists, but never by anyone who said he was a Secular Humanist and that if I didn't read his tracts, I would roast in molten sulfur.

For another, the people who follow real religions talk about their beliefs. You always hear things like "As a born-again Christian, I deserve your vote." Even the devotees of more exotic doctrines will corner you at parties and

82

babble interminably about their past lives and tarot readings. But have you ever heard a Secular Humanist discuss his creed? Does anyone ever say "As a practicing Secular Humanist, I wouldn't dare lie to you about how much you're going to like this car"?

Real religions have chapels, churches and cathedrals. At last count, Salida's 4,870 residents could pick from 19 congregations. However, there is no listing in the local Yellow Pages for "Churches - Secular Humanist." Of course, this is God's Country. But even in Denver, a worldly metropolis with churches of Krishna Consciousness and Spiritual Unfoldment, there are no listed Secular Humanist congregations.

Real religions have preachers on radio and television. Any time you drive, especially late at night, your search for music can be disrupted by the breathless opportunity to get a certified prayer shawl in exchange for a $25 free-will love offering. You can see the Rev. Pat Robertson command the hurricane to spare Virginia. You can watch Oral Roberts raise money to prolong his temporal life while explaining how it feels to grapple with Satan.

But I've never encountered "The Old-Time Humanism Hour" on any radio I've ever owned. My cable company doesn't offer the "Secular Broadcasting Network," and I've yet to turn on the TV and find some Secular Humanist beseeching the faithful to send money so that he could continue his vital ministry.

Real religions have bodies of doctrine. You can't be a Baptist unless you believe in total immersion, you can't be a good Muslim without visiting Mecca, and you must accept the Apostles' Creed to be a Roman Catholic. But where's the creed or catechism for Secular Humanism? What is it that Secular Humanists believe in that other folks don't? How does one define or recognize a Secular Humanist?

Along with doctrines, real religions have disagreements. Consider Catholics and Protestants in Northern Ireland. Or Shi'ites and Sunnites in the Middle East. Or Sikhs and Muslims in India.

Secular Humanists are said to believe in evolution, but when have you read of violence between Gradualists and Catastrophists? Where are those bloody wars between various branches and sects of Secular Humanism? How many infidels and heretics have the Secular Humanists stretched on the rack or burned at the stake?

I don't know where Judge Brevard Hand got the information for his decision. As nearly as I can tell, Secular Humanism isn't a religion at all. Not only is it impossible to define, it's nothing like any religion I ever heard of.

Who'd Miss Hispanic Culture, Anyway?
September 14, 1989

As IT TURNED OUT, 1988 was the last year that Colorado celebrated Hispanic Culture Week during September. Later that year, voters approved the "Official English" amendment to their state constitution. Outraged by this insult to them and their contributions to Colorado life, Hispanics said they no longer felt welcome. They acted quickly to remove themselves and all signs of their culture from what was thenceforth called the State of Red.

The effects were noticed immediately by miners, who no longer could speak of "placer" deposits, nor of "bonanzas." Many mines had to tear down their headframes, which resembled those first used in the Guanajuato district of Mexico, and all ore-grinding mills that traced their ancestry to arrastras were likewise dismantled.

Farmers felt a much greater impact. Not only were they deprived of much of their labor force for cultivation and harvesting, but they also learned that they could no longer irrigate their fields.

Some historians argued that irrigation was part of mankind's common cultural heritage, since the practice apparently was invented in China sometime before 2200 B.C.

But that didn't bring irrigation back to Red. Those citizens of Red who had a Chinese background quickly pointed out that their ancestors' experiences here hadn't been all that pleasant: In the Leadville of 1880, prominent signs announced that "All Chinamen will be shot," and that same year, an anti-Chinese riot erupted in Denver, resulting in burned buildings and at least one death.

Besides, the evidence was fairly convincing that the state's modern irrigation practices had been introduced by the Hispanic colonists of 1851 who laboriously carved out the acequias that carried water to their fields.

Thus, the farmers were forced to change crops. Again there were arguments that corn, pinto beans and potatoes were not really Hispanic contributions, but came from the Mayas, Hopis and Incas. But as Frederick Vickers, once a state official in Red, had commented, "The only truly good Indians are dead ones." While Hispanic and Indian scholars argued as to whose ancestors had introduced which crops to Red, the speakers of Official English were denied all use of those crops.

The daily diet changed radically in Red. No one could argue about the origins of tacos, enchiladas, tortillas, burritos, nachos, chili verde, huevos rancheros and other staples of Red cuisine. Upscale beer drinkers no longer displayed their bottles of Corona, and discerning tipplers greatly missed their

Negra Modelo. Those who enjoyed beef with their dark beer felt doubly deprived when they learned that it was the Spanish who brought the cow to America.

The Spanish also brought the horse, and the whole idea of herding cows on the range was invented by Hispanic vaqueros. Cowboy hats and cowboy boots, both developed for that enterprise, had to be abandoned; many residents of Red suddenly felt naked every time they went outdoors.

Further, no more rodeos could be held in Red. One of Denver's major conventions, the National Western Stock Show, was canceled forever in 1989 when its organizers realized that men who spoke Spanish also had brought domestic sheep, goats and swine to America. Without Hispanic culture, there wasn't any livestock industry.

Meanwhile, legal historians pored over the records of the state's constitutional convention of 1875-76, so that they could remove any sections, clauses, phrases, words or ideas that might have been contributed by Agapeta Vigil, Jesus M. Garcia or Casimiro Barela.

The biggest shock came when someone pointed out that the word "Bronco" came from Mexican Spanish. The law-abiding management of the football team quickly removed the bronco from the scoreboard. They changed the team's name to "the Denver Bronx." But even the South Stands fans had trouble learning the required "Bronx cheer."

When asked what she thought of all the complications she had wrought with her "Official English" amendment, Barbara Philips, a state representative from Red Springs, refused to comment. "The last poll we took, in the summer of 1988, showed that people still supported us," she said, "and I wouldn't want to do anything to jeopardize that."

WHAT AMERICANS DON'T NEED TO KNOW
January 29, 1989

JUST WHEN I thought it was safe to return to my rustic and culturally illiterate ways, a review copy of "The Dictionary of Cultural Literacy" arrived. It's a best-selling sequel to "Cultural Literacy," wherein E.D. Hirsch Jr. explained why all Americans need to know certain things. He even provided a 64-page list of what we should know.

This time around, the list has expanded to 586 pages, because it includes short definitions. It also includes things that just aren't so.

Here you can learn that James Butler "Wild Bill" Hickok "was a rider for the Pony Express in his youth." Hickok never rode for the Pony Express. His total involvement was tending horses for a few months at the Pony Express station in Rock Creek, Neb.

Or you might discover that the Santa Fe Trail was "an important route used by settlers moving west," and that it ran "from Independence, Missouri, southwest to Santa Fe, New Mexico."

In fact, few settlers ever took the Santa Fe Trail, which was a route of commerce. Settlers took the Oregon Trail. Despite what you read in the "Dictionary," the Santa Fe Trail didn't end in Santa Fe — the bulk of its trade continued south to Chihuahua, Mexico. Anyone here who trusted this "Dictionary" would be teeming with erroneous notions about his own culture.

You could also examine the curious logic employed by our cultural betters. On page 252, we learn that Gen. William Tecumseh Sherman "was known for saying 'War is Hell.' " On page 284, we are informed that "Sherman supposedly said this ('War is Hell') several years after the war."

Did Sherman say it, or didn't he? Why can't we get a definitive answer from this "Dictionary"? Isn't that what dictionaries are for?

Not this one. It tells us that the phrase "iron curtain," in reference to the Soviet bloc in Eastern Europe, "was coined by Winston Churchill." Winston Churchill coined many memorable phrases during his distinguished career, but that one isn't his.

Churchill said iron curtain on March 5, 1946, in a speech at Fulton, Mo. Its first use was apparently on Feb. 23, 1945, by, of all people, Joseph Goebbels, the Nazi propaganda minister: "If the German people lay down their arms the whole of Eastern and Southern Europe, together with the Reich, will come under Russian occupation. Behind an iron curtain, mass butcheries of people would begin."

One apparent virtue of Cultural Literacy is that you don't need to do any research. You are allowed to know about the Beatles, but you will find no entry for Chuck Berry, who merely invented the most popular form of music in the world.

The "Dictionary" doesn't improve when you leave history and popular music and enter real literary culture. Christopher Marlowe may been second only to William Shakespeare among English playwrights, but you can be quite Culturally Literate without knowing about Marlowe or "Marlowe's mighty line" that Shakespeare adopted — Marlowe doesn't rate an entry.

Historians of such matters declare that the world has produced only three great mathematicians since the dawn of reckoning: Archimedes, Isaac Newton and Carl Friedrich Gauss. But Gauss is nowhere to be found. Am I the only one who finds it amazing that a man can be one of the three greatest mathematicians ever, can have a unit of measurement named after him, can exert a major and continuing influence on the ways we measure and manipulate the physical world — and he isn't worth mentioning?

Cultural Literacy apparently means accepting dime novels as history, crediting people for quotations that they never said, giving the wrong people credit for memorable phrases, and ignoring people who did make significant contributions. That is a fair description of how American culture really works, but I had been expecting better from any book that presumes to tell us "What every American needs to know."

THEY'RE LOOKING AT THE WRONG DECADE
January 27, 1991

FOR A DECADE that accomplished so little, the 1960s attract considerable attention, most recently from the six-hour PBS series that aired last week.

In politics, the major effect of the 1960s was to launch Ronald Reagan's political career. Eminently popular, Reagan ran illegal wars, presided over widespread corruption, rebuilt the military-industrial complex, and launched the greatest transfer in history of wealth from wage earners to capitalists — the T-bill holders who get a chunk of your paycheck every week.

The other political effects of the '60s were just as opposite to the activists' goals. Again there are 400,000 American soldiers on the other side of the world. Despite all that civil rights work, the leading destinations for young black men are jail and cemeteries. Taking the mentally ill out of institutions just put them on the cruel streets, with no support. And of course, there is the War on Drugs.

One could argue that at least the '60s changed American culture, but it would be a foolish argument.

Clothing? My dad always wore T-shirts and blue jeans to work, and so do I. If you have the misfortune to toil in a corporate office, the modern Power Outfit can't be much of an improvement on the traditional Gray Flannel Suit.

Personal appearance? William Henry Quillen, my Populist great-grandfather, boasted more beard and hair than I ever will. Back-to-the-land movement? My maternal grandfather, Byron Wollen, homesteaded in the middle of Wyoming in 1919, and until his death in 1965 he lived 17 miles from the hamlet of Bill without running water, electricity or a telephone.

Anti-war protests? There were huge draft riots in New York during the Civil War, and people went to jail for opposing the Mexican War. General activism and domestic violence? What of 40 years of labor wars in our mining camps, the Wall Street explosion in 1920, Coxey's Army, the Bonus Expeditionary Force and the agrarian revolt a century ago? Rural communes? What of Brook Farm and the Union Colony experiment?

The more you look, the more it appears that the '60s were actually a fairly normal American decade. It was the '50s that were weird.

That was the only time in history when most Americans apparently believed that the entire world wanted to live in sanitized income-scale suburbs, that if you showed up for work every day then the company would take good care of you, that any dissenter was a Russian agent, that there was one right way for everyone to live, and you could learn it just by watching "Ozzie and Harriet."

Otherwise, America was always a nation teeming with agitators, drug abusers, malcontents, organizers, protesters, troublemakers, suffragettes, do-gooders, free-love advocates, rabble rousers, communards, socialists, pacifists, draft dodgers, crackpots, greenbackers, single taxers, anarchists, prohibitionists, libertarians, moralizers and reformers.

That has been gloriously true throughout the American experiment, except during one decade — the 1950s. There's the aberrant decade, and that's the one the historians should scrutinize instead of wasting more time on the counterproductive counterculture of the '60s.

Sensitive, Caring and Selfish
June 19, 1991

MARTHA LAUGHED hilariously Sunday morning as she read Contemporary. For once, it wasn't Dave Barry; it was the cover story.

"Can you believe this? In our decadent cities, men have apparently forgotten how to be men. So they go to the woods, strip naked, and get inside these steam-bath lodges where they sit close to each other. That's not exactly my idea of a stud."

I cautioned her not to say anything politically incorrect that could be interpreted as homophobic, lest the Virtue Squad raid us again. Last week they found undecaffeinated coffee in our pantry, but let us off with a warning.

"You're right," I continued. "If men have forgotten the traditional ways, we could open an academy in Salida and make some money. Most of what we need is here."

"There's the 'Men's Resource Center,' a.k.a. the Victoria Tavern," she agreed. "That's where you guys hang out, swill beer and swap lies."

"There's a problem with that," I said. "Our potential students wouldn't approve of hanging out and griping. They want to be caring, sensitive and nurturing."

"But that's crazy," Martha said. "Do women want to be caring, sensitive and nurturing any more? Or do they want power, fame, fortune and glory?"

"Nobody wants caring, sensitive and nurturing any more," I concurred. "Except for these sweat-lodge wannabes who think they can be GI Joe and Barbie at the same time."

"Right," Martha agreed. "Everybody knows a real man can hammer his thumb, engage in combat, fall off a scaffold, dig ditches till he drops, chug a pitcher, chain-smoke Camel straights, work under a bumper jack, eat a year's worth of cholesterol at one picnic, and clean a bathroom without touching the toilet, the sink or the floor."

"Those guys are idiots," I said, "if they think they can express their masculinity by sitting in a sauna."

"No, you've got that wrong," Martha said. "Isn't it just like a man to spend a lot of money to go off for a weekend with the boys and claim it will make him a better husband and father? Instead of taking his wife somewhere? Or doing something with his kids?"

"You probably think a man should waste his weekend by taking his kids and their friends to Chuck E Cheese's."

"At least that would show he has stamina and courage."

"I'd rather paint myself blue and howl at the moon."

"So would they. This is a great scam. When old-fashioned, insensitive men go off deer hunting with their friends, they don't dare claim that it will make them better fathers or more attentive husbands. If you ask me, these New Age males have the essence of masculinity all figured out, no matter what they do or don't do in their sweat-lodge rituals."

What Do you Get with Good Character?
March 29, 1992

When the experts are not analyzing the Bubba Factor or dismissing any Jerry Brown primary victories as deviations from the sacred script that requires anointed front-runners to have their nominations nailed down by April Fool's Day, they often mention the "character issue."

As nearly as I can tell, "character issue" actually means that George Bush is asking, "Aren't you worried about Bill Clinton because he dodged the draft and had a reputation for catting around?"

That may be a fair question, but it is rather hypocritical when it comes from the Republican campaign. Bush certainly has nothing against Vietnam-era draft-dodgers; he picked one to serve as secretary of defense and another to sit a heartbeat away. Bush has never been known to question the character of Ronald Reagan, who once complained that he was getting tired of waking up in bed with various women whose names he did not know.

One problem with the "character issue" in presidential politics is that a president can be personally above reproach, and still produce wholesale corruption.

For instance, President Ulysses S. Grant was a man of unquestioned personal probity; never did he pocket so much as a crooked nickel. But during his administration, corruption flourished in every federal office from remote Indian agencies to the vice president's chambers. In more recent times, Ronald Reagan was never for sale but many of his appointees were, and it will take generations to pay the bills. Personal financial integrity, one aspect of character, is no guarantee of an honest administration.

Other aspects of private character may be just as irrelevant to presidential fitness. Who betrays more people? The candidate who might have lied to his wife, or the president who says "No new taxes" and then agrees to new taxes?

The main problem with judging a public leader by private character is that it leads to some peculiar conclusions.

Consider one prominent 20th-century leader, a decorated war veteran. He abhorred smoking and drank only in moderation. Never was he known as a womanizer. A vegetarian, he despised any cruelty to animals. He liked to take long walks outdoors, and he encouraged his countrymen to become more physically fit and in tune with nature.

By enlightened New Age standards, this man was a paragon. He got in touch with the mystic forces of the cosmos by consulting astrologers from time to time, and he often considered promoting the indigenous religious beliefs of his people to replace the alien religions that imperialistic invaders had implanted long ago.

That is the private character of Adolf Hitler. By contemporary standards of character, Hitler was positively angelic in comparison to Winston Churchill, a hard drinker and youthful opium user who was never without a cigar, and Franklin D. Roosevelt, with his mistresses and his jaunty cigarette holder.

The current concern with character — that a person's vices or lack thereof are the paramount indication of that person's desirability as a political leader — would tell us that Hitler was a better person than Roosevelt or Churchill.

If you want to believe that, then the "character issue" means something.

CHILDHOOD TRAUMA: A PROFITABLE INVENTION
February 7, 1993

OTTO MEARS, Pathfinder of the San Juan, once held heroic status because he established toll roads, railroads, gristmills, newspapers and similar accouterments of civilization in southwestern Colorado.

Such deeds are not esteemed in these revisionist times, for they lead to the irreparable loss of pristine wilderness. Mears was also among the few whites who could speak Ute. This allowed him to negotiate the Brunot Treaty of 1873, which pushed the Nuche out of their ancestral homeland on the Western Slope.

(When I lived there, though, we thought that this was one time Indians came out ahead on a land deal. The Utes got 25,000 pre-inflation gold dollars, and we got frostbite, mosquitoes, skiers and the Denver Water Board. We wondered how much we'd have to pay the Utes to take back the Western Slope.)

By the standards of the time, though, Mears lived a productive life before he died in 1931 at age 91. However, this seems impossible in light of what we now know about Childhood Trauma.

Born in Russia in 1840, Otto was orphaned at age 3 and soon sent to relatives in New York. When he was 10, they forwarded him to an uncle in San Francisco, via the deadly Isthmus of Panama. The uncle never showed up — Otto made his way by hawking newspapers along the Barbary Coast.

Orphaned, neglected, forced to cope with companions dying of typhus and malaria in Panama, abandoned, exposed to frequent murders and every vice in the tenderloin of a wicked port — with such an overload of childhood trauma, it seems miraculous that Otto Mears didn't become a cannibal, or at least a serial killer.

No grief counselors, no trauma therapists, no child-advocate caseworkers, no truant officers, no nurturing, caring, supportive environment — how did he ever manage to get dressed in the morning, let alone build a railroading empire and enjoy a happy marriage for 50 years?

Nor is Mears unique. We've all read biographies of people who succeeded despite abusive parents, war-torn childhoods, family death camps and other horrors that should have left permanent scars on the inner child and created a permanently dysfunctional personality.

Childhood Trauma is apparently another proof of Quillen's Law of Commercial Success: The way to prosper in America is to invent a disease and sell the cure.

A generation ago, there was no Childhood Trauma. It was just assumed that everybody got some rotten breaks, and you were supposed to get over them and go on.

Thanks to the recent invention of Childhood Trauma, though, you won't recover from something as banal as witnessing an auto accident unless there's an expensive therapist at hand within minutes of this traumatizing incident, and even with prompt treatment you may never fully recover.

Poor children go hungry. Children die daily from drive-by shootings. Family-value Republicans believe corporate profits are more important than enabling parents to spend time with their children. The potent Gray Lobby insures that we spend much more on geezer comfort than on building a future. Our drug industry fights against universal childhood immunization.

However, whenever a bus crashes or a madman sprays bullets on a playground, we always find the money to rush in a brigade of therapists and counselors to the survivors to treat their Childhood Trauma.

These priorities seem peculiar to me, but of course, I might well feel differently if I shared in the profits of the therapy industry.

ARE BULLIES REALLY THAT IMPORTANT?
May 2, 1993

COLORADO schools may say they're hurting for money, what with Amendment One and a grasping teachers' union that values longevity more than competence.

It was tempting to believe that — until I read about a bully prevention program at some metropolitan schools, complete with inspirational videotapes, counseling sessions for students, sensitivity training for teachers, multicultural multimedia modules and related paraphernalia for holistic self-esteem enhancement.

There was no indication that this was an extra-curricular project running with donated money on the teachers' own time. Bully prevention thus must take time and resources away from classes like math, English, art, music, geography, history, science and other once-important disciplines.

Why does bully prevention matter so much? The educationists say that children can't learn if they're in fear. So, if you plan to teach grammar or chemistry someday, first you've got to get the kids in the mood to learn, and they won't be in the proper receptive state if they're worried about their lunch money.

This premise, that fear impedes learning, sounds good, but a moment's reflection will show it is quite dubious.

The fear of getting yelled at or grounded by my parents often inspired me to creative academic feats that seem amazing in retrospect — 20-page term papers cranked out overnight on a manual typewriter, complete with fabricated footnotes and fictitious bibliography.

The fear of losing face with my chauvinist chums, who were sure that boys were smarter than girls, sometimes propelled me to honest scholarship so that I might outdo one of the valedictorian girls who always got straight A's.

The fear of getting beaten up by the big kid who sat behind me in eighth-grade history and always copied off my tests was a major inducement toward sustained review of the material before the exam.

Indeed, to this very day, the fear of penury keeps me busy researching and writing.

Even so, it must be granted that schoolyard bullies are a nuisance at best, and should be controlled. But there's a big difference between control and elimination, and the future of the Republic will be jeopardized if they succeed in eliminating bullies.

Without bullies, where would we find the tough CEOs who delight in downsizing in order to make American industry more competitive in world markets? If there were no bullies, where would we find managers who insure that their subordinates are productive? Without bullies, we'd have no linebackers, few jailers, fewer federal cops, no Rush Limbaugh, no Donald Trump, no Arnold Schwarzenegger movies — American society as we know it would collapse.

And if we eliminated even the concept of bullying, the notion that "I'm bigger and tougher than you are and I'll make sure you know who's in charge around here," what would America do for a foreign policy?

It seems obvious that if our schools are determined to devote scarce time and money to bullying, and if they want their graduates to be successful and admired, then they should teach kids how to excel at bullying.

If they take that approach, and teach bullying with the same success they enjoy with algebra or rhetoric, then the happy day might dawn when there would be no bullies. Even the mean kids who had enthusiasm and talent for bullying would have it bored out of them.

They Missed One Ethnic Studies Program
May 3, 1994

It was surprising to read yesterday that the University of Correctness in Boulder had just decided to organize an ethnic studies department. I had just assumed that the University Office of Academic Trend Imitation had installed such a department years ago.

These departments are a good employment program. First you go on a hunger strike to get a major in Turko-Chilean cultural studies.

Now it may appear that such a degree is about as valuable, for job-seeking purposes, as a bad discharge from the Army. However, there are all these other colleges with new Turko-Chilean cultural studies programs resulting from student demands, and these programs desperately need faculty. You can pretty well write your own ticket and enjoy a lifetime of steady paychecks. Should anyone question your job performance, or even whether your job is necessary, the critic is a racist.

This is a tough world, and you can't really blame people for pressuring universities to create jobs that only they are qualified to fill.

One disadvantage, though, is that good material might get hidden inside these professor-of-color employment programs. For instance, I was exposed to a wonderful book, "One Hundred Years of Solitude" by Gabriel Garcia Marquez, in a regular college English class. These days, it probably would be found only in Hispanic Literary Tradition 401, and students outside the ethnic studies department would never see it or many other great works.

Such narrow disciplines also tend to increase segregation on campus, and that's another loss. In 1970, Martha and I were the only white tenants in a Greeley apartment house known as "the White House of the Black Student Union." They turned me on to Langston Hughes and Malcolm X; I turned them on to Lenny Bruce and H.L. Mencken.

It seemed as though college was doing what it was supposed to do — broaden one's horizons — and the current trend appears to go the other way. "Multi-culturalism" means "Study my own culture, and no others."

After all, if universities were serious about studying all cultures, especially significant American cultures, there would be departments of White Trash Studies.

Students would have to answer test questions:

"What are the two favorite White Trash outdoor sports?"

"Poaching and urination."

"Who are the leading manufacturers of White Trash yard sculptures?"

"Ford, General Motors and Chrysler."

The manifold contributions of White Trash to American life, from Davy Crockett to Tonya Harding, would be explored. There's the "Bubba factor" so important in presidential elections since George Wallace developed it; there are also presidential brothers like Billy Carter and Roger Clinton. Historically, White Trash have done most of the fighting and dying in American wars. There are important White Trash literary archetypes, like Pap Finn and Flem Snopes.

If CU really wants to be in the vanguard of ethnic studies, we'll see a major in White Trash. But don't hold your breath.

WHAT REALLY RAPPENED TO THE BEVERLY HILLBILLIES?
June 28, 1994

GENERALLY, my 16-year-old daughter Abby has the same rotten taste in movies that I do. Send her to the video store, and she returns with a no-brainer slapstick comedy.

Movies are for entertainment, and if I want to think, I'll read a book. Uplifting films of moral significance like "Schindler's List" and "Dances with Wolves" doubtless deserve their awards, but why should I spend three hours to feel angry and depressed when the paper can do that inside of 15 minutes, and for only a quarter?

Abby recently returned with "The Beverly Hillbillies," and even I, a devotee of the "Naked Gun" series, was ready to draw the line. But it was funny enough, although Martha observed that the plot was dated.

In modern America, Jed Clampett wouldn't strike oil, get rich and move to Beverly Hills. Instead, the Clampetts would be going about their lives — moonshining, poaching and spitting — in their scenic but remote mountain hollow.

Then the Upscale Land Development Corp. acquires the surrounding territory, and one morning, the Clampetts are amid trophy homes. Instead of them moving to Beverly Hills, Beverly Hills moves to them.

Jed discovers this one afternoon when he's out hunting cottontails and the new neighbors appear. How could he kill small furry animals? And that coonskin cap and leather coat? He returns home, but only after the animal-rights activists have doused his duds with red spray paint.

At the homestead, the Architectural Controls Committee is conducting an inspection.

They tell Granny to put out her pipe. Even though they're outdoors, the secondhand smoke could shorten their anticipated mean life expectancies by 0.7 of a second.

Trying to be hospitable, she offers them moonshine, but they want fruit juice or mineral water. Granny stomps off.

The clothesline has to go, since it's an esthetic affront and children might be permanently traumatized by inappropriate exposure to underthings in broad daylight.

Ellie May wonders how she'll do the laundry. The committee says she needs a $500 clothes dryer.

Jed points out that the dryer requires electricity, which they don't have. Only $8,000 to run the line, plus a $75 minimum monthly bill, he learns.

Jethro's truck is towed away, since the covenants don't allow pickups of any vintage to be parked in public view. The woodpile attracts rodents and vermin, and they can't use the stove anyway, because it might reduce air quality, and the development already has enough trouble with that because most people in it commute 70 or 80 miles a day to their career-track positions.

Finally the committee leaves to consult with social workers about removing Jethro and Ellie May from their deprived environment, and Jed gathers the family. "They made us a pretty good offer on our land," he says, "and I reckon we ought to take it and get out whilst we can, afore them new folks raises our property taxes any higher. Any notions where we might settle?"

Jethro, always a bit feeble-minded, says he thinks Colorado would be a great place to get away from these arrogant People of Money. They head west, but we'll have to wait for the sequel to see how that turns out.

READ THE NEW TRANSLATION, AND YOU'LL UNDERSTAND EVERYTHING
September 25, 1994

FOR THE FIRST 18 years of my life, I spent most Sunday mornings inside a Baptist Sunday school classroom. To the disappointment of my parents, most lessons failed to stick, but I did learn my way around the Bible pretty well.

So when I read the accounts of the recent Christian Coalition convention, I was rather surprised. Given the state of American society, I expected some impassioned jeremiads concerning avarice, materialism, bigotry and hypocrisy. Instead, most of their pronouncements and activities appeared to bear little, if any, resemblance to the Bible whose verses I once memorized.

For instance, I didn't recall any passage in the Epistle of Paul to the Romans where the apostle urged them to petition the tribunes and senate to require prayer in public academies.

Nor did I remember any announcement that the men of Rome should gather in the Coliseum to hear a trainer of gladiators encourage them to become keepers of promises. And if there was a gathering of the faithful in Ephesus or Corinth, and aspiring candidates for procurator or satrap spoke to those gatherings about shared goals, I missed that, too.

This was confusing, so I called a friend in Colorado Springs who has some connections with Focus on the Bottom Line, Californians for Phantom Values, Muscular Morality and similar right-minded organizations dedicated to the purification of our great Republic.

"Your problem, Quillen, is that you're still looking at the old King James translation," my friend said.

"It has beautiful prose," I said. "What's wrong with that?"

"Well, biblical scholarship has made tremendous strides in the past 380 years," he said, "especially in the last decade. The King James may offer majestic cadences, but that majesty often comes at the expense of accuracy in the light of modern theology."

He offered to send me the latest translation, approved by William Bennett for citation in the Book of Second Virtues and certified by Pat Robertson for use in private-school classrooms.

Much of it looked about the same as the familiar King James, although in Leviticus, the prohibitions against eating shellfish and wearing raiment made from more than one kind of cloth had vanished.

But when I got to the New Testament, I found a new book, the Gospel according to Danforth. Although its diction is as dated as that of the King James Bible, the new translation does provide a sound biblical basis for the inspired teachings of the Christian Coalition.

Since this version is apparently not in wide circulation at the moment, I thought I'd share some of its teachings:

"It is easier for a camel to pass through the eye of a needle than for a liberal to enter into the kingdom of heaven."

"When thou runnest for school board, hide thy light under a bushel and let it shine only after thou hast taken the oath of office."

"Judge often and harshly, lest ye be judged."

"Then Jesus came upon a woman who had been caught up in adultery, and a crowd of virtuous men gathered about, ready to stone her, for such was ordained by the law and the prophets. 'Let him who is most concerned about the rising rate of out-of-wedlock births to teen-age mothers cast the first stone,' he said."

"One day on the road to Cana, a scabrous, emaciated leper was lying in a pit beside the way. He approached toward Jesus, who said to him, 'Come not unto me, for thine own decadent and abominable lifestyle hath caused thine affliction, which is a punishment from Heaven.' "

"Though I speak with the tongue of men and of angels, and hath not a good direct-mail list, I am as a sounding brass or a tinkling cymbal."

"When thou prayest, do not go into a closet and shut the door, but instead thou shouldst utter thy prayers in a loud voice and before an assembled crowd, as the Pharisees do."

"Then the multitude began to grow restless, for they were without meat or drink in the heat of the day, and there were but five loaves and two fishes. 'Get me some air time on our cable network,' Jesus commanded his disciples, 'and soon the contributions will be pouring in.' "

"Take ye therefore great thought of the morrow and accumulate your treasures upon earth."

"Render unto Caesar that which is Caesar's, so that he may deploy more centurions, for a strong national defense is beloved and ordained by our father in Heaven."

"After the lame man had touched the hem of his garment and was healed, Jesus said unto him, 'Thou owest me twenty shekels, payable immediately in full or in easy monthly installments secured by thine first-born, for if I did not charge thee, it could lead to socialized medicine and the end of the finest health-care system in the world.' "

It would have been interesting to continue reading, especially the new version of Revelation with prophecies about God's gruesome wrath against the evil frauds who gain prominence in the end times, but the day was drawing on, and my friend wanted his Bible back.

When does the Decency Enforcement Administration Start to Work?
February 4, 1996

SINCE everybody important in Washington is in favor of a downsized federal government and reduced regulation, the latest version of the Telecommunications Act came as something of a surprise.

The bill does deregulate some things, such as cable TV rates. Under regulation, our struggling cable entrepreneurs have suffered the indignities of living in tiny, 10,000-square-foot houses and donating only $80,000 or $100,000 to select politicians. These terrible conditions will be righted.

The new law also allows more competition. Long-distance companies like AT&T, Sprint and MCI will be able to offer local phone service. Local providers like US West and PTI will be able to offer long-distance service. Cable and cellular companies will jump into the fray.

The family dinner hour — the time they pick for telemarketing because that's when they might find someone home to answer the phone — will be one long session of jumping up to "just say no" to yet another solicitor.

But they really are trying to protect "family values," at least in theory. Every TV set sold in America will have to be equipped with a V-chip that can block the reception of programs that someone labels as offensive.

If you truly cared what your kids watched on TV, you'd watch TV with them. You'd at least be around the house, so that if your 6-year-old's eyes were glued to adult material like "NYPD Blue" or C-SPAN, you could order some alternative programming.

So this V-chip obviously is designed for negligent and absentee parents who use the TV set as a babysitter. Yet we're all supposed to pay for it. This is fair?

The new Telecommunications Bill also addresses another major problem: porn on the Internet.

Why, just last week a neighborhood boy found an Internet Service Provider that would give him credit, bought a fast $200 modem, mastered the SLIP and PPP protocols, got Trumpet Winsock to run for more than two minutes without crashing, figured out how to run his news reader, discovered that every posting in "alt.binary.naked.cheerleaders" was from religious fanatics who warned him that he would boil in molten sulfur for eternity because he looked in that forum, eventually kept his connection going long enough (no mean feat with US West lines) to download something that sounded saucy from "alt. binary.licentious.pictures", and then discovered that his viewer would handle only TIF and GIF files, not the JPG format.

He threw his computer out the window, and it just missed hitting an innocent girl was who skateboarding down the sidewalk.

Clearly, society must be protected from this and similar menaces. Many boys don't get that far before acquiring repetitive motion strain injuries, and others, who finally manage to view a nude photo of Sandra Bullock, learn that it's a fake and develop cynical and distrustful attitudes that will forever prevent them from paying proper heed to teachers and employers.

Some might say that kids gazing at lurid images on computers at home are less of a problem than they would be at the local cigar store, sneaking peeks at Penthouse and High Society when the clerk isn't looking.

But the sanctity of the home must be preserved, and the inevitable consequence of the current Telecommunications Act will be the federal Decency Enforcement Administration.

The new DEA will have to work closely with the Customs Service. Stopping the importation of television sets without (or with defective) V-chips is only part of the job, and the easy part at that.

The DEA will also have to examine every one of the millions of sites on the Internet. After all, someone in some backward country like Sweden or Denmark, where they actually let people look at any picture they want to look at, might make a lurid digitized image available.

Then every communication link to the United States will have to be monitored to see whether anybody in the land of the free downloads the explicit material. Once the DEA knows where it went, agents can drop by to see whether minors might gain access to this material.

And if so, someone will be in trouble. Will it be the initial provider in Denmark? Probably not — U.S. jurisdiction doesn't extend that far. However, there might be a cooperative program in the future, with American military aircraft flying low with sensitive sensors to scan the low-intensity signals put out by computers. Bombs would then fall on the offenders.

Perhaps the communications carrier will be in trouble for being part of the process that made the stuff available to minors. But if we follow this logic very far, then Ryder Truck Rental will have to be a defendant in the Oklahoma City bombing trial.

That won't work either, and the other possibilities don't seem all that promising. But I have faith. If there's a way to spend billions every year while accomplishing nothing except the oppression of American citizens, our protectors in Washington will find it.

Taking Daughters to Work
Won't Solve Self-esteem Problems
April 28, 1996

On Thursday, I again strived to be an enlightened parent and entrepreneur, much to the dismay of our daughter at home, Abby, who was sipping her morning coffee.

"Okay, Abby, listen up," I barked. "This is Take Our Daughters to Work Day, and I don't want you to lose self-esteem. So you're going to stay home and work with me."

She started to splutter a protest, but I knew my duty and didn't let her interrupt.

"First we've got to get a column written for The Post. Then there are about a dozen people to call for a magazine article we're going to work on. There's about an hour of tedious scutwork where you get to piece out the phone bill. And the office needs cleaning — you want to start there?"

"Dad, that's sexist, making me clean while you do the exciting stuff."

"But you said writing is real boring work, and cleaning my office can be quite interesting, especially if you've been studying fungal growths in biology."

Abby offered her usual reply. "Dad, it's Take Your Daughter to Work Day, not Put Your Daughter to Work Day."

"But what are you supposed to do?" I asked. "Just sit there and look over my shoulder, I guess. I can't write with somebody looking over my shoulder, and so I can't do my usual work with you around, and that defeats the whole purpose, doesn't it?"

Abby agreed. "School's a lot easier than work, anyway." She further observed that since she's the only one in the household with an outside job, maybe she should ask her employer about Bring Your Parents to Work Day.

"It might be good for you, dad," she explained. "Nobody ever yells at you for being five minutes late, or tells you how to dress for work, and you can swear and smoke and belch all you want to while on the job — you ought to find out how the rest of the world works."

I told her I'd been there and done that, and I asked her if there was any merit to the logic behind Take Your Daughter to Work Day. The theory is that girls get less attention in school and lose self-esteem in adolescence, and if they get a special day in the workplace, then they'll get mouthy in class, just like boys, and do better in school and all that.

"But girls already do better in school," Abby pointed out. "We don't drop out as much as boys do, more of us go to college, we get higher grades — I don't know how they can say that schools work against girls."

"But what about math?" I asked. "I was in an accelerated math program in junior high and high school. When we started with eighth-grade algebra, it was about evenly mixed. But by my senior calculus class, it was all boys. The girls who dropped out along the way were pretty smart — there's got to be a reason."

Abby noted that "You were always worried about that, so you threatened to chain me and Columbine in the cellar, feeding us nothing but bread and water, if we didn't go all the way through on math."

Well, as a parent, you do what you must. Abby did agree that many girls lose self-esteem at the onset of adolescence, "but that's hardly our fault. Look at any magazine for teenage girls."

So I did — an old issue of "Young & Modern." Its scented and colorful pages teemed with articles like "How to attract an awesome hunk," "Getting an even suntan so guys will flock to you" and "Are you a good kisser?"

In short, the goal of a teen-age girl is to attract a teen-age boy, not to ace a calculus test.

Further, the magazine's theme is that the typical teen-age girl is ugly and repellent unless she invests in the proper perfume, cosmetics, nail polish, clothes, etc.

"The whole idea is to get you to think you're repulsive the way you are," Abby said, "but you'll be cool and popular if you just buy all this stuff that most girls can't afford. So of course we'll have self-esteem problems. These magazines are in business to give us self-esteem problems, which we can cure by spending a lot of money on Cover Girl cosmetics, Jordache jeans, Calvin Klein fragrances, Maybelline lipstick, Studio Line gels, whatever."

"There must be billions of dollars invested in promoting poor self-esteem in teen-age girls," I said. "It's a huge industry. Make girls feel inadequate, and then sell them some temporary feelings of adequacy with the right clothes or cosmetics."

"The Ms. Foundation folks can take daughters to work all they want to," Abby said, "but until they burn every copy of those magazines, teen-age girls will still feel inadequate. All the forces of Madison Avenue and Wall Street are organized to make us feel inadequate, and nothing's about to change that."

She took off for school, and I told her to kick some serious butt on her calculus test. But first I thanked her for "coming to work" with me to produce a column.

Let's be Grateful that Homer Wrote
a Long Time Ago
May 20, 1997

THE OVERNIGHT ratings haven't come in yet, so I have no idea how many millions of other Americans joined me in watching "The Odyssey" these past two nights.

It was required for a mandatory humanities class during my college days. Several hundred pages of iambic hexameter looked like heavy work, especially when contrasted with more important collegiate interests like beer and girls, and so I took a journalistic approach — Classic Comics and Cliff's Notes — and thereby passed the class.

But I kept thinking that I should read the real thing someday, and the opportunity came when our daughters were about 10 years old. Although they read quite well, they still wanted me to read to them at bedtime, and complained loudly if I didn't.

Thereby forced into spending quality time, I looked for reading matter that I could stomach. We enjoyed E.B. White and C.S. Lewis, but eventually we ran out of talking spiders, car-driving mice, trumpet-bearing swans and Narnia chronicles.

Then a no-lose proposition dawned on me when I found a prose translation of the Iliad.

I could read that to them. If they hated it, which seemed likely, I could get out of my evening duty with a clear conscience — after all, I'd tried.

If they liked it, I'd get it read, and read in a good way — slowly, taking time to look things up, discussing it as we went along. Further, the girls would acquire some classical lore.

And so we read "The Iliad" and "The Odyssey" before the girls became too old for bedtime stories. The effects linger to this day — we still have a tomcat they named "Hector" back then when he was a kitten. (Aptly named at first, since he fancied himself a great warrior despite his emasculation, but after an ocular injury in battle, he should be "Cyclops" now.)

I commend these classics to any parent who has trouble finding suitable bedtime stories. But then again, Homer's tales reek with sex, violence, magic, sorcery, deception, butchery, pagan rituals — in these enlightened times, if Social Services found out what you were exposing your children to, you might well never see them again.

Indeed, I wonder what would happen if Homer appeared at a publisher's office today to discuss the Iliad and the Odyssey with two editors — one a family-values right-winger and the other sensitive and politically correct.

"Mr. Homer, we like your work — good characterization, generally fast pace, plenty of action — but I have a problem with the relationship between Achilles and Patroclus. We can't have gay or bisexual warriors — Colorado for Family Values would boycott us in a minute."

"Well, I don't see a problem there. But having Achilles sulk for years because Agamemnon won't let him keep a captured person of the female gender — more patriarchal objectification of womenkind, and it's got to go."

"I can live with that. But there's too much sex here. Is it really necessary for Hera to lure Zeus into intercourse so that he'll fall asleep afterward and the Achaeans can prevail for a day against Troy?"

"That's just a fair comment on how men always fall asleep afterward, instead of cuddling. Let's move on. Is it right for Odysseus to cat his way around the Mediterranean while faithful Penelope waits at home? Talk about perpetuating gender stereotypes. You've got to fix that, Mr. Homer, or we'll have pickets outside the office, and I will be among them."

"There are other passages you must change first, Mr. Homer. The drug references must go — that lotus stuff with Odysseus, and then you've got Telemachus, a mere boy, taking opium — just because you call it nepenthe doesn't fool me. The last thing we need is an attack from William Bennett or DARE for glorifying drug use. Cut that stuff."

"Well, I am not fond of the way you portray Odysseus, Mr. Homer. Here he is, trying to get home, and everything is working against him — the sea, the wind and the follies of his crew. Yet he's in denial. He refuses to see himself as a victim, and so he refuses to get the support and therapy he so obviously needs. What kind of message is that?"

"There are even worse messages in there. This Odysseus fellow often tells flat-out lies to get himself out of predicaments — telling the Cyclops that his name is Nobody, for instance, or duping the Trojans with that wooden horse. We simply can't allow such a character to be a hero — what kind of moral example would that set for today's impressionable youth?"

The two editors continue their heated dissection of Homer's work, with one upset because of all the pagan deities and the other angry because goddesses like Aphrodite and Artemis should play larger roles.

Despairing, the blind bard sneaks out of the office and throws his manuscript into the river. He had toiled for years, but he knows now that his work is totally unfit for modern Americans.

READING HUSTLER COULD LEAD TO MICKEY MOUSE COMIC BOOKS
July 1, 1997

OVER THE YEARS, I've heard hundreds of jokes, some of them even printable, based on the stereotypical traits of various religious adherents, from Mormons to Mennonites. But as a lapsed Baptist, I felt excluded until I ran into Jerry Swingle of Durango one night in a Gunnison saloon.

"You want to hear a Baptist joke?" he asked. Of course I did, since the only one I could remember came from my father, a Baptist deacon, to the effect that if you put two Baptists in a room and let them talk religion, you'll get at least three theologies, four millennial sequences and five eschatologies.

"Why don't Baptists have sex in public while standing up?" Swingle asked, and I pressed for the punch line.

"Because it could lead to dancing," he replied.

After the boycott resolution passed by the Southern Baptist Convention in Dallas last week, this joke could be revised:

"Why don't Baptists let their kids go to skin flicks?"

"Because it could lead to Disney movies."

I can understand boycotting products that result from processes you find morally reprehensible, although in Colorado, it's pretty hard to live without gasoline or diverted water.

But if the 15 million Southern Baptists in this country are henceforth going to engage in boycotts on moral grounds, they've certainly got some curious priorities.

The Disney Corporation may suffer from scores of ethical flaws, but so far as I know, it does not actively persecute Christians.

The same, alas, cannot be said of China, where the government has been arresting Christians because they attend "unlicensed churches," and there are credible reports of torture and the like.

I've never heard that Disney even reprimanded its employees for going to church, let alone imprisoned and tortured them.

If there are good Baptist reasons for boycotting Disney, then there are excellent reasons for boycotting China and its ubiquitous exports, but the Baptists, so good at seeing the speck in Disney's eye, somehow missed the bridge timber sticking out of China's.

Or if the Baptists cared about the biblical injunction that "The laborer is worthy of his hire," they might propose a boycott of Nike and its $150 sneakers. Here's a company that can find millions of endorsement dollars to pay sporting celebrities who are already quite wealthy, but has trouble paying more than a few dollars a day to the Third World workers who actually make its products.

This troubles at least one Protestant denomination, the United Methodists, who hold Nike stock and have asked the Nike corporate directors to investigate its labor prices.

The Baptist boycott of Disney apparently is based on two main factors:

1. The company offers benefits to partners of homosexual employees.

2. The company promotes degenerate and immoral lifestyles with programs like "Ellen."

As for the first, the Baptists might have real cause for complaint if Disney canceled benefits for heterosexual partners in favor of supporting extralegal unions.

But that's not the case. Instead, the company has extended its benefits to people that many other companies don't include, and it takes a truly jaundiced eye to see evil in generosity.

Regarding the second concern, the presentation of abominations to impressionable children, well, what of the Bible, which is often promoted by Baptists as good family reading?

There's Lot, the only virtuous man in Sodom, committing incest with his daughters. And Lot's Uncle Abraham, father of the chosen people, offering his devoted wife, Sara, to the pharaoh of Egypt to get himself out of a jam.

And Jacob, swindling his brother Esau out of his inheritance. And David, a man after God's own heart, arranging for the death of Uriah, the husband of Bathsheba, a woman he covets.

Nor should we forget horrors like the Spanish Inquisition that were perpetrated by people who professed to follow the Bible — how many "Ellen" broadcasts would it take to match that?

The only obvious conclusion is that the Southern Baptists, like most of the rest of America, are on a selective-morality binge.

Outside the Baptist convention, it's fashionable to decry adultery while celebrating avarice and usury. Inside, boycott Disney for its minor vices and ignore China, where the Baptists couldn't even hold services, let alone a convention.

'Tis a Privilege to Live in Colorado

One problem with being a Coloradan is that nobody believes you. I noticed this in college at the University of Northern Colorado in Greeley. I was born in Greeley; the building that was then the Weld County Hospital stood at the corner of Eleventh Avenue and Sixteenth Street, just north of the campus and less than a block from my apartment the year I was editor of the campus paper.

It was there that I got a telephone call one day berating me for some left-leaning editorial (isn't that what college newspapers are for?), and among my flaws was that I was "some radical from the East."

Patiently I pointed out that I was standing just a few yards from my birthplace, that I had attended Greeley's public schools, and that Greeley itself was founded as a sort of commune in 1870 by a bunch of idealists.

"Don't go trying to put one over on me by making stuff up," the caller warned.

Well, being from Colorado isn't something that anybody would make up. It does you no good whatsoever. Look through the chief executives of the state's biggest companies, peruse the biographies of the General Assembly and the congressional delegation, search where you will among the birth certificates of the movers and shakers of this state, and you'll find precious few of them are from Colorado.

When I was a kid, Colorado seemed to have about the same reputation that, say, North Dakota has today — a backwater that talented people fled as soon as they were graduated from high school. Colorado may have been growing, but it wasn't anybody's idea of the "leading edge," and it was assumed that if you wanted to amount to anything, you'd leave.

During the 20 years I've lived in Salida, the town has undergone a similar transformation in reputation. I liked it from the first because it was so much like the Colorado I grew up in — somewhat backward and isolated, I suppose. Of late, the gentrifiers have come, and occasionally I hear someone concerned about protecting or enhancing Salida's "image."

That means it's probably time to move on, but I fear that Colorado has about run out of places to hide in. My spies on the High Plains report that trophy houses are sprouting even in those bleak realms.

There are cycles in what's trendy, though. Colorado was cool during the "back to the land" '70s. It was pretty depressed and unhip during the '80s, when the *zeitgeist* favored a Fifth Avenue penthouse. In the '90s, Colorado is again a cool place to be, what with all this great outdoor recreation and a chance to have your very own 35-acre ranchette surrounded by BLM and Forest Service land.

And so I figure that in the '00s the trend has to change, and Colorado can go back to being a place to live and work, rather than a lifestyle statement.

As to why I've stayed in Colorado, I suspect it's mostly sloth. Moving is hard work. It's easier to stay in place and put up a fight against all these folks who, merely to enrich themselves, are bent upon destroying everything I like about my home.

In other countries, they call this an "invasion" and the government may even enlist on the side of the people who'd like to be left alone. In this democratic nation, it is known as "progress" and the government is always on the side of the invaders.

Trying to maintain a livable home is probably a lost cause, but, well, I was educated in this state, and thus can't be reasonably expected to act all that intelligently.

But at Least they Appear to Know Who They Are
March 8, 1985

THE RIVALRY between Colorado and Texas shows no signs of abating. Governor Lamm continues to apologize for stale jokes. With each campaign, the annual Twin Lakes Tomato War attracts more splattered soldiers. The Denver Post even devoted several Sunday columns recently to the relationship between the Centennial State and the Lone Star State.

No one seems to know how this started. Perhaps it was with the Adams-Onis Treaty of 1819, which set the boundary between the United States and the New World possessions of Spain. After several revolutions, that boundary — the Arkansas River and a line north from its source — separated America from the Republic of Texas. Texas visitors thus may represent something beyond tourism. They could well be pilgrims, visiting lost portions of their ancestral homeland; 60 percent of Colorado, including the major portion of the mountains, was part of Texas until 1846.

Not one Colorado resident in 20 has heard of the Adams-Onis Treaty or the Battle of La Glorieta Pass. Texans are pumped full of lore about the Alamo and San Jacinto and Sam Houston, and can spout it interminably whenever primed with a six-pack of Pearl. A Colorado resident who knows of "Bloody Bridles" Waite or the Grand Lake War is a historian.

That's why I find it difficult to hate Texans. As a Colorado native, I'm supposed to loathe turkeys, flatlanders and all those loudmouth, whoop-it-up Texans.

But instead I am jealous. For better or worse, Texas has an identity and Colorado doesn't. You can close your eyes and envision a Texan. The stereotype will be as inaccurate as stereotypes must be, but the important thing is that there is a shared image of Texans. A bit of reflection, and you'll almost hear "Heidi, yawl?" and feel your back being slapped.

Now turn to Colorado: You'll find it's simpler to imagine a great city than it is to envision a Coloradan. You can't even make up jokes about Coloradans. We can't decide how to spell "Coloradan" (some newspapers insist on "Coloradoan"), much less figure out what one might be. Someone in a mud house with a dirt floor in the San Luis Valley, whose family has been there since time began? A laid-off miner in Leadville, hoping he has enough beer, pinto beans and firewood to get through another brutal winter? A cocaine importer in a $350,000 white-on-white palace in Boulder? A sodbuster on the High Plains, praying for rain and getting it during hay harvest?

Judging by articles in national magazines about Gary Hart's candidacy, the Colorado stereotype may be the white wine and Perrier yuppie joggers who devise software and go skiing on those weekends that they aren't networking in fern bars. But there is nothing specifically Colorado among the experience-sharing Volvo set; Colorado is just another rung on the career ladder.

Texans cherish a sense of place; someone from the Staked Plains who never sees a tree or a Republican until he is well past majority comes from a different place and is thereby a different person than if he had come from the Gulf Coast or the Hill Country.

Coloradans seldom hold any sense of place. It's nearly impossible. Our places change continually, always toward some homogeneous mellow experience, almost as if someone sold franchises. Mountain towns used to present differing characters: Leadville was a mining town, Aspen a cultural mecca,

Durango a railroad center. Now they're all after tourism, and it gets harder and harder to tell them apart. Greeley, Boulder and Fort Collins all once had identities. Now they all have downtown malls and development commissions bent on attracting more high-tech business.

My envy of the sense of place and identity held by Texans would not necessarily make me like them, of course. There are lots of people I envy whom I don't like. But I have come to like Texans, more or less. Of all who come here, they're the easiest to tolerate; I have finally realized that they come to Colorado because they like Colorado just the way it is.

Our other invaders, intent on subdividing valleys, establishing world-class enterprises and making a billion by next week, are worse — much worse. They're missionaries who see native Coloradans as heathen savages who must be forcibly converted. During my employee days in assorted Colorado towns, I often received clothing lectures from ambitious Wisconsinites and speech lessons from transplanted New Englanders. Never has a Texan informed me there was anything untoward about being a Coloradan or dressing or talking like a Coloradan. Never has a Texan tried to make me ashamed of my origins or told me to overhaul my personality.

Being surrounded by *auslanders* is one of the prices one pays for staying in Colorado. But if we must be invaded, let it be by Texans. They're so happy and secure being Texans that they'll let us be Coloradans.

Pay So that Others Might Prosper
March 7, 1986

Every announced candidate for governor has stressed economic development. In their view, the state government has an obligation to gather money from Colorado citizens and use that money to attract more tourists and more in-dustries. The promised result is more jobs and more prosperity for the Colorado citizens who forked over the money.

If it really worked that way, I'd be all for it. I'm never against spending money if it will benefit me. But if economic development works the way it has worked before, then if I help pay for it, I'm either generous or stupid.

I grew up in Greeley, a farming town that didn't have a lot of jobs. If you wanted to make something of yourself, you got out of Greeley the day after you graduated from high school. This exodus distressed the civic leaders.

So they promoted the area. Industries like Kodak and Hewlett-Packard moved in, lured by mountain views and slick brochures and all the other tools of industrial promotion. Suddenly there was an expanding local economy with jobs.

The jobs, however, seldom went to those of us who grew up there. At one time, I almost had a job lined up at a Fort Collins newspaper, until another applicant appeared. He had a journalism degree from Missouri and had written for the Wall Street Journal. I was a kid from Greeley. Guess who got the job.

Nothing in my education had prepared me to face the kind of competition I'd have to face, thanks to economic development, if I tried to follow my chosen career in the area I grew up in. Economic development gave us world-class competition without world-class credentials.

During this boom, my high-school friends didn't fare any better. The last time I visited the Greeley area and saw two of them, one was tending horses and the other ran an antique shop. Neither held a position that hadn't existed long before the benefits of economic development. Both told me that although there were good jobs around, those jobs always went to people from Connecticut and New Jersey.

None of us benefited in the slightest from all that economic development. Even so, we all paid. There are direct costs, like increased taxes on properties whose values were driven up by speculation, as well as the need to pay for more law enforcement and the ever-increasing costs of moving water across the Continental Divide.

That's only money. The indirect costs are in some ways harder to bear. Longs Peak used to be visible from Greeley, and it has vanished in the murk that passes for air on the Front Range. You might not have made much money if you lived in Colorado, but the mountains always offered cheap and uncrowded recreation.

Thanks to economic development, there still isn't much money to be made if you had the misfortune to grow up in Colorado, and you can't enjoy much cheap and uncrowded recreation in the mountains any more.

We mistakenly believed that more water, more industries, more tourists would make us prosper. We never saw a dime of that prosperity. And we lost most of those intangible qualities that made Colorado a pleasant place to live. It's one thing to sell your birthright for a mess of pottage, but quite another when you don't even get the pottage. We gave it all away so that people from Connecticut and New Jersey and everywhere else could have the good jobs while they befouled our sky, crowded the mountains and fished out the creeks.

Now the candidates are at it again. They want Colorado citizens to pay for more economic development, even though, the best I can tell, economic development doesn't benefit Colorado citizens.

Maybe it's just middle-aged greed creeping over me. But I don't want to be taxed so that more people from elsewhere can come here and occupy all the good new jobs and such scenery as remains. What I spend money on ought to do something for me — and economic development has always worked against me, my family and everyone I grew up with.

We may be sadder and wiser, but we're also a minority. The cycle of stupidity will continue. We'll end up with a new governor. Whoever he is, he'll be a shill for Colorado. Our taxes will rise as new industries move in. The resultant "opportunities" will attract new herds of ambitious, greedy people. They'll get the money. We'll get dry rivers and browner skies.

All we Need are Speech Lessons
December 5, 1986

Roy Romer hasn't even taken office yet, and he already has fulfilled a campaign promise — a summit conference, aimed at improving the Colorado economy.

From what I read of this conference, the summiteers meant well, but they never discussed a sure-fire way to put Coloradans to work. By Coloradans, of course, I mean those of us who grew up in this state.

Many Coloradans are capable people who can adapt quickly to the new high-tech age in some respects. Anybody at can do a roadside brake job on a Studebaker pickup during a blizzard finds it easy, even pleasant, to work with computers. After all, it's indoors, there's no heavy lifting and you can find the parts you need.

Our problems come when we have to deal with the imported management of these New Age enterprises. We can't understand them, and they can't understand us. The Blue-Collar English of the native Coloradan and the High-Tech English of his employer are two different languages.

Let me illustrate with some translations of common workday expressions (please note that this is a family publication, so some of the Blue-Collar renditions are not quite accurate).

Blue-Collar: First thing tomorrow, I'll see the foreman and line out the day's work.

High-Tech: My current mentor and I will network and implement immediate optimization strategies when we do a power breakfast.

Blue Collar: We're going over to the Elks tonight. Wanna come along?

High-Tech: We've just been accepted for membership in the exclusive Club Wapiti. Could you consult your personal scheduler to see if you're free to share the experience with us this evening?

Blue Collar: I catch you walking the dog on company time again, and you're history.

High-Tech: You haven't reached maximal participation in our enhanced productivity environment. Perhaps you might attain greater self-actualization while performing in an alternative career framework.

Blue Collar: I worked my butt off.

High-Tech: Through the duration of the project, my aerobic cardiac monitoring indicators were substantially in excess of target levels.

Blue Collar: He's a jerk.

High-Tech: He/she has difficulty transitioning into our corporate culture, and further, he/she does not exhibit sensitivity toward the interpersonal needs/attitudes of his/her co-workers.

Blue Collar: We got our butt handed to us on that job.

High-Tech: Despite a temporary negative direction imputed to the overall cash-flow posture resulting in unavoidable dilution of the corporate equity position, the project provided invaluable experience while climbing the steep segment of the learning curve of state-of-the-art technological innovation.

Blue Collar: I'd like to get me a bag job someday, where I could just supervise.

High-Tech: My priority five-year career objective is the attainment of a management position wherein my unique matrix of developed skills, innate talents and acquired experiences would be deployed at optimal utilization.

Blue Collar: Yeah, me and the old lady had a good time on vacation, but it's kind of nice to get back to work.

High-Tech: My significant other and I experienced an awesome transpersonal growth experience while sharing a unique ambiance during my annual personal leave. Returning to my career arena, however, fully energizes me while enhancing my confidence levels.

Blue Collar: Draw your time, and don't let that door hit you in the butt on the way out.

High-Tech: A cyclical market downturn has adversely impacted you and certain fellow members of our performance team whose quarterly productivity evaluations reflect submaximal levels. Your cumulative severance benefits are now available in the corporate outplacement office.

See what I mean? No matter how skilled you are at the actual work you do on the job, you'll probably lose that job if you can't understand that the boss means "Do this first" when he says "This procedure follows from implementation of the optimal prioritization strategy."

Revitalizing our economy so that Coloradans have jobs might be much simpler than improving colleges, sending emissaries to Japan or building a new airport. Just find some way to teach us how to talk.

From the Town of Exit in the State of Red
January 9, 1987

Whatever happens in Colorado happens first in California: from campus rebellions to holistic materialism, from hot-tub karma to far-right politics, it all starts in the Golden State and migrates to the Centennial State.

Thus it came as no surprise to hear serious talk of making English the official language of Colorado; California recently approved such a law. I'm all for it, because once English becomes our official tongue to the exclusion of all others, life here will become immeasurably simpler.

For example, we've never been able to agree on what to call a resident of our fair state. In the Denver papers, you're a "Coloradan," but in Pueblo or Fort Collins, you're a "Coloradoan."

Once English is official, we'll all live in the state of Red; the geographic name will echo our fiscal reality. And that will make all of us, even the right-wing crazies from Pass (nee El Paso) County, into Reds. The mayor of Denver will no longer be Federico Peña, with that troublesome un-American tilde; he'll be plain old Fred Rock, or perhaps Fred Flintstone.

We won't have to put up with newly arrived TV announcers who can't pronounce "Costilla" or "Conejos," because our state will contain Rib and Rabbit counties, as well as the jurisdictions of Orphan, Table, Cow, Soul and Pain.

Our map will display an enchanting variety of Saxon nomenclature: Silver, Snake and Tooth among our 14,000-foot peaks; the principal city of the Saint Lewis Valley will be Cottonwood, on the Grand River, and about 30 miles south of Red Springs will be the city of Town; various small towns will be called Little Anthony, Gulch, Ox Driver, Small Box, Unruly, The North, Lame and Red Apple; we will visit the Blood of Christ and Saint Ian mountain ranges, crossed by such passes as Spoon, Vein and Mole.

Of course, once we become the state of Red, we'll have to change more than just Spanish names. Beulah, a Hebrew term, will become Married. The Ute-named peaks and towns of Antero, Pagosa, Saguache, Toponas, Uncompahgre and Tabeguache shall be Graceful Walker, Stinking Water, Blue Spot, Sleeping Lion, Red Lake and People Who Live on the Warm Side of the Mountain. Fred Rock won't have to contend with that Latinate Aurora any more; the treeless maze of shopping malls to the east will be called Sunrise.

The French also passed through here, way back when, and the place names they left — Platte, Cache La Poudre, Laporte, Bellvue — will become the Flat and Gunpowder Storage rivers and the towns of Exit and Pretty View. However, the Spanish-named municipalities of Salida and Buena Vista will also become Exit and Pretty View as soon as English is official, so there's likely to be some arguing as to which towns get the Anglo-Saxon versions of their traditional names and which ones have to change entirely.

For several years, I have argued that Salida's name should be changed to indicate its current condition; that is, from "Exit" to something like "Dead End," and this will be the opportunity to replace boom-days romance with contemporary accuracy.

The legal requirement of English will provide benefits far beyond those of a simplified map here in the state of Red. Both my daughters, for instance, are taking piano lessons, and they often find themselves mystified by the Italian terms they encounter: largo, staccato, battuta, lento, mezzo forte and crescendo.

Dealing with various professionals will become much easier, too, once English is mandated by law.

No longer will educators be allowed to call classrooms "affective domain instructional modules" and libraries "multimedia learning resource centers." Children can be stupid or smart, instead of "developmentally disabled" or "cognitively gifted." Doctors will have to say "I don't know what's the matter with you" instead of telling you that you suffer from a "chronic idiopathic condition."

Nowhere is English less evident than in our legal system. The score or so of thick books that make up our revised statutes will have to be rewritten, at tremendous expense, to get rid of alien terms like recuse, concomitant, replevin, covenant, situs, et al. Once ordinary people are able to understand state laws and legal documents, hundreds of attorneys will find themselves out of work.

No reasonable person could be against that. So here's hoping that the General Assembly moves quickly to make us into the state of Red.

RAISE THE GAS TAX TO $10
May 1, 1987

COLORADO'S gasoline tax of 18 cents per gallon is already among the highest in the nation. It might rise to 23 cents if the General Assembly finishes passing a bill that has received preliminary approval.

For once, our state legislators are on the right track. But they're not going far enough. They ought to set the tax at a more reasonable figure, and $10 a gallon is reasonable.

There are those who would object, arguing that tourists might shy away from Colorado if gas sold for $10.72 per gallon.

But tourists still go to Europe, where fuel runs $3 or $4 per gallon. Did anyone ever visit Texas 20 years ago just because regular was 18.9 at Lone Star pumps? Obviously, gas prices bear no relationship to a region's ability to attract tourists.

We might lose coast-to-coast traffic to Interstate 80 across Wyoming, but those aren't the people who stop and spend money, so we wouldn't be losing much. People traveling on the cheap probably would shun Colorado, too; again, we wouldn't be losing much. And a high gas tax means that the remaining auto-borne tourists would necessarily leave more money in Colorado, which is precisely what we've always wanted.

Most of the other seeming problems with a $10 gas tax would likewise turn into benefits, albeit with some adjustment.

People who commute great distances to work would suffer at first. But they would soon form car-pools, which would give them closer relationships with their co-workers. That would improve communication on the job, and thus raise overall productivity. Colorado would gain a better business environment.

Or the commuters would move closer to work. When people live and work in the same neighborhood, they get more involved in its activities; we'd see more interest in local government and service organizations. Our communities would benefit.

Or they would demand better public transportation. As long as public transportation is the swaying long-distance bus full of crying babies and drooling drunks, or the lurching city bus hauling bag ladies and sweaty collectors of aluminum cans, then the political constituency for mass transit is nearly powerless.

But if the gainfully employed middle and upper classes started relying on mass transit, we'd see efficient, clean public transportation.

A high-tech revolution is already underway; you can prepare your work on a home computer and send it in over the phone. That's how this column gets from Salida to Denver. High gasoline prices would encourage more of this, making Colorado a leader in "telecommuting." That means a growing pool of skilled labor, and again a more attractive business climate.

Then again, many folks would walk or bicycle to work. Both are healthy activities, good for the heart, lungs and general disposition. Lives would be saved immediately, since cars kill about a dozen Coloradans every week.

People walking or pedaling to and from work at all hours of the day or night would mean a vast increase in the number of decent, law-abiding people on the streets. A nearly empty street means any pedestrian is easy prey for a mugger or rapist; a bustling sidewalk is by and large a safe sidewalk.

Making gasoline very expensive would abolish needless driving. No more rowdy teenagers dragging up and down some preferred thoroughfare: West Colfax in Lakewood, F Street here, Main Street in Longmont, and so on around the state. People along those afflicted boulevards have been asking for a solution to this problem; here it is.

Consider the enormous decline in metropolitan air pollution with a $10 gas tax, or elimination of the need to construct new highways, and the substantially reduced maintenance that would be required of existing highways.

The state budget would show a magnificent surplus; we'd likely be able to abolish the sales and income taxes — another improvement to the business climate, and that's something everybody from the governor on down has said we need.

It isn't often that our legislature gets the chance to improve the business climate, make neighborhoods more cohesive, encourage mass transit, promote high technology, strengthen public health, reduce street crime and highway carnage, eliminate adolescent cruising, cut down air pollution and slash much of the tax burden.

Raising the tax by a nickel won't even be a good start, though. Get it up to $10 a gallon, and see how Colorado prospers while becoming a vastly better place to live.

They Never Return to the Plow
March 25, 1990

To improve our governance, State Sen. Terry Considine has proposed that representatives and senators be limited to 12 years in office. In theory, they will be more sensitive to the needs of us commoners if they know that upon a stated date, they will lose their exalted status and return to normal life, wherein they must endure the laws they enacted.

This sounds good, but the Considine solution is based on a fairy-tale premise — the story of Cincinnatus.

As the Roman legend goes, Lucius Quinctius Cincinnatus served a one-year term as consul, then retired to his small farm. A few years later, in 458 B.C., the republic faced a crisis. Aequi invaders had surrounded a Roman army at Mount Algidus.

Desperate for a leader, the Romans found Cincinnatus at his plow. He gained victory in one day and celebrated a triumph in Rome. He then immediately resigned the dictatorship and returned to the plow.

Although scholars agree there was once a prominent Roman named Cincinnatus, the rest of the story is deemed fanciful. You can see why. Consider the past 20 years of displaced Colorado federal office-holders. Precious few of them ever returned to the plow.

Peter Dominick was defeated by Floyd Haskell and became an ambassador. After losing to Bill Armstrong, Haskell opened shop as a Washington lobbyist. Mike McKevitt hired on to lobby after Pat Schroeder beat him. Ray Kogovsek left Congress and started lobbying. Ken Kramer wangled a high-level job in the Defense Department. Gary Hart maintains an international law practice, which means he utilizes the foreign connections he made during his Senate days.

From what I could tell, only three — Jim Johnson, Gordon Allott and Don Brotzman — went back home to do what they did before they went to Washington. The rest either found other means of staying on the public payroll, or became well-paid lobbyists. On a local level, about 30 Statehouse lobbyists are former legislators. Unlike Cincinnatus, they don't return to normal life.

Forcing people to leave office sooner will not make them think "Gee, I'll be just another grunt in a few years, so I'd better work on some fair and sensible laws."

More likely, they will think "Just another couple years, and I can start making $500,000 for lobbying. But they won't pay me that kind of money unless I show I can deliver. So I'll ask the bagmen how they want me to fix this bill so their clients get subsidies while avoiding taxes."

The problem really isn't that people stay in office too long; it's what they generally do when they leave office — gain a private profit as a result of public service.

There are better approaches than the Considine plan. One is that whenever someone leaves office, he should be barred for life from any contact whatsoever with his former colleagues.

That would be hard to enforce, though. So we should try the opposite of Considine's plan, and elect for life on good behavior. We might thereby get senators and representatives who are content to serve us.

Otherwise, limit or no limit, we'll continue to see hustlers who treat Congress like an $89,500-a-year apprenticeship. It gives them connections that they can use on that glorious day when they leave office and start bringing in the big money.

SHEEP IN POPULIST CLOTHING
June 26, 1990

ONLY 25 YEARS AGO, candidates boasted about how "liberal" they were; nowadays most office-seekers would rather be accused of sodomy than liberalism. Nobody was a "populist" then, but now Gov. Roy Romer says he's "probably the most populist governor in 50 years," while John Andrews, his Republican challenger, says his stands make him more of a populist than Romer is.

So what's a "populist," besides this year's political buzzword?

About a century ago, the Populists were a potent third-party movement. They were not happy people. Consider this excerpt from the national Populist platform of 1892:

"We meet in the midst of a nation brought to the verge of moral, political, and material ruin. Corruption dominates the ballot-box, the Legislatures, the Congress, and touches even the ermine of the bench. The people are demoralized .... The newspapers are largely subsidized or muzzled, public opinion silenced, business prostrated, homes covered with mortgages, labor impoverished, and the land concentrating in the hands of the capitalists.... The fruits of the toil of millions are boldly stolen to build up colossal fortunes for a few ..."

Makes you proud to see how far America has come in the past 98 years, doesn't it?

The Populists did win elections in the Midwest and West. In 1892, they got control of the Colorado Senate, and the state elected a Populist governor, Davis H. "Bloody Bridles" Waite.

His nickname came from a flaming speech where he announced that "it is better, infinitely better, that blood should flow to the horses' bridles rather than our national liberties should be destroyed."

In 1893, the miners of Cripple Creek went on strike for an eight-hour day. Waite did not do what most Colorado governors do — call out the militia to shoot workers. Instead, he ordered the militia to keep the peace, and personally negotiated a settlement that favored the miners.

For those and similar reasons, Waite was widely perceived as a dangerous radical; there was great fear that no one would invest in Colorado as long as the state government was in threatening Populist hands.

But Roy Romer travels the world to get people to invest in Colorado, and he's busy with government/business partnerships when he's in town. John Andrews comes from a conservative think tank where they're still trying to discredit parts of the old Populist program, such as the eight-hour day and the graduated income tax. No politician this side of Czechoslovakia has the courage to stand on a platform that sounds anything like the old Populist platform.

Romer is a millionaire businessman, and Andrews a professional right-wing apologist. If either is a "Populist," then the word is meaningless. And the campaign has just started.

SHED NO TEARS FOR ROCKY FLATS
January 29, 1992

PERHAPS we could persuade the American dairy industry to increase production of the milk of human kindness. My supply is running short.

Did I exhaust it last fall, when I was supposed to feel sorry for a $9-million-a-year profligate who caught an incurable disease? Perhaps, because there just wasn't any sympathy left for the American auto executive who gets $4 million a year while his company loses money and closes plants.

So I couldn't come up with any deep and heartfelt concern for the 7,500 workers who might lose their jobs at Rocky Flats, now that the plant's only customer is no longer buying the once-popular W-88 hydrogen bomb.

The most preposterous reaction came from Sen. Tim Wirth, who said the Rocky Flats workers deserve a "GI Bill" for retraining because they "are veterans of the Cold War like any other veterans."

Let's get real here. The real veterans were in the military, where they underwent certain privations. For one thing, they often lived in ships, barracks and tents; they weren't billeted with their families in suburban homes. During their service, real veterans couldn't just quit their jobs, a right enjoyed by the Rocky Flats Employment Force.

Some real veterans faced hostile fire, and all ran that risk. What risks did the Flats Force face? The chance that plutonium might leak — in other words, incompetence. And the risk of driving on Colorado 93 after hoisting one too many at the bar across the road from the plant gate — stupidity.

The hazards and sacrifices of military service presumably entitle real veterans to benefits from the public treasury because most of us don't have to face hostile fire or obey orders without question.

But we all have to contend with incompetence and stupidity; what's special about the Flats Force? If working in an industry that contributes to the national defense makes you a veteran deserving of public largess, then every coal miner, roughneck, farmhand, teamster and gandy dancer also qualifies for a slot at the public trough.

We have a group of comfortable people who made no sacrifices. They were paid well for something they freely chose to do — produce weapons of mass destruction. In the aftermath of other wars, similar activities have been adjudicated as "crimes against humanity," and the offenders were steered toward a gallows, not a job-retraining program.

Besides, there's no real reason to worry about their employability. The United States has announced it will hire about 2,000 former Soviet nuclear workers, lest these folks sell their plutonic knowledge to Iraq or Libya. This means there are jobs aplenty out there somewhere for the people who learned their trade at Rocky Flats.

WILL THEY CORRECT OUR MAP NEXT?
April 27, 1993

Now that the offensive Redskins no longer represent Arvada on fields of glory, we can assume that the purification of Colorado nomenclature will advance. But where will the crusade turn next?

Perhaps to Pitkin County, named for Frederick W. Pitkin, who was elected governor in 1878 after he made a simple campaign pledge: "The Utes must go."

It must be conceded that Pitkin came much closer to keeping his campaign promises than most of his successors in the Statehouse, and thus his name should be enshrined among the oddities of American political history.

But the Nuche probably don't see things that way. A compromise might be possible — restore the original name of Ute City to Aspen, the county seat.

Colorado also has a Custer County, named for the Butcher of the Washita who was once court-martialled for abandoning his men in the field. Whether you judge George Armstrong Custer by a martial or humane standard, he comes up short, and we will hear that the Wet Mountain Valley is much too pleasant a place to be besmirched with such a name.

Out on the high plains, there's Kit Carson County. For some reason, the Navaho still hold hard feelings about how Carson betrayed them, starved them by destroying their farms and livestock in Canyon de Chelly, and then brutally marched them to the Bosque Redondo concentration camp.

Taken as a group, though, our county names are fairly balanced here, since we also honor Indians with Arapahoe, Cheyenne, Kiowa, Ouray, Saguache and Yuma counties.

However, what will happen when feminists look at the list of 63 county names and see men everywhere: Alva Adams, Antonio D. Archuleta, William Bent, Jerome B. Chaffee, John H. Crowley, James W. Denver, Stephen A. Douglas, Samuel H. Elbert, John C. Frémont, James A. Garfield, William Gilpin, John Gunnison, George Hinsdale, Andrew Jackson, Thomas Jefferson and William Larimer, just for a start? Many of these men were racist, chauvinist, homophobic or otherwise undeserving.

The only woman honored with a county is the Virgin Mary; Dolores County came from the Dolores River, originally Rio de Nuestra de los Dolores (River of Our Lady of Sorrows).

This could raise questions about separation of church and state — if there are Dolores, San Juan and San Miguel counties, why not Sinawaf and Coyote Trickster counties?

At any rate, Colorado offers not even a pretense of balance between male and female namesakes, and we will someday hear that this a shameful performance.

And that will be just a start. Our map offers many offensive or elitist names: Son of a Bitch Hill, Cannibal Plateau, Squaw Pass, Harvard, Superior and Victor. There's even a "Stoner," clearly an impediment to the War on Drugs.

Will the purification come one battle at a time, as it has so far? Or will there be a wholesale renaming convention? Either way, I can't wait.

SPIMY AND PSIEN COULD SOLVE THE NIMBY PROBLEM
December 19, 1993

MANY WOULD AGREE that Thomas Jefferson was the greatest political philosopher this continent ever produced. But few have noticed that, among Jefferson's other contributions to our political discourse, he invented NIMBY: "Not In My Back Yard."

The Jefferson connection is that our third president was an urbane fellow who much enjoyed products of cities like books and music. However, he didn't want any cities in North America; as far as he was concerned, all of the urban needs of his agrarian commonwealth could be met by the cities of distant Europe.

Thus did Jefferson father NIMBY. The products of cities were welcome, but as for the cities themselves, "Not In My Back Yard."

It may be of some comfort, then, to realize that modern NIMBY protesters are not merely hypocrites who want certain benefits without paying the real price, but are instead continuing an American political tradition.

The main problem with NIMBY is that it shifts costs and benefits unfairly. Consider Los Angeles, which has air pollution problems so severe that no new coal-burning power plants can be built.

Does this mean that Angelenos find ways to live with less electricity? No, it means that the power plants get built in the Four Corners area. Other people, generally poor, get to suffer the strip mining and pollution, while Los Angeles gets the electricity. L.A. wants the power, but as for the messy work of generation, "Not In My Back Yard."

That's just one example, and it could be indefinitely extended. It might be fine to have a homeless shelter in Denver, but NIMBY objections in lower downtown and at Lowry mean that there's no site for one. Jefferson County homeowners may enjoy solid concrete foundations under their houses, but they'll block any effort to dig gravel for making concrete. Most of us burn gasoline, but we prefer that the refinery be in Casper, Wyo.

Further, "out of sight, out of mind" comes into play. Nobody will pay much attention to the homeless, or to pollution, or to mining methods if they're all sequestered, thanks to NIMBY.

We should adopt two new models: SPIMY and PSIEN.

SPIMY means "Sure, Put It in My Yard." If you want electricity, you install solar panels or a natural-gas cogeneration unit. If you want food, you grow it. If you eat meat, you butcher it. If you care about the homeless, you take one in. You compost your organic garbage and make arrangements to recycle the rest.

Under SPIMY, we'd all assume full responsibility for everything we consumed.

However, SPIMY wouldn't be practical or efficient for most of us. Thus PSIEN: "Put Some In Every Neighborhood."

Under PSIEN, the local government would make a list of necessary but undesirable operations, and these would be parceled out to each neighborhood as appropriate.

Do rich folks in Cherry Hills consume more than poor folks on Capitol Hill? Then put the landfill in Cherry Hills. Do commuters in Douglas County burn the most gasoline per capita? Then the refinery should be in Castle Rock. Do Evergreen homes use plenty of concrete? They get the regional gravel pit. Do downtown Denver developers raze old SRO hotels and thereby eliminate affordable shelter? Then they can install a few low-rent floors in their skyscrapers.

The big objection to PSIEN would be that "it hurts property values." But since undesirable uses would be spread around, everyone's property values would suffer, and relative values would remain about the same.

Further, the wealthy and well-connected — generally the major NIMBY protesters — would apply their energies to monitoring whatever PSIEN allocated them. A Cherry Hills landfill would never leak and the quiet, upscale Castle Rock refinery would smell sweeter than roses.

Of course, neither SPIMY nor PSIEN will ever be adopted, and we'll be stuck with NIMBY hypocrites for eternity. Of all of Jefferson's concepts, why is it that only the worst one remains in force?

COLORADO'S OWN WINTER GAMES
February 27, 1994

EVERY TIME the Winter Olympics dominate sports coverage, we must endure a regional chorus complaining that we were really stupid in 1972 when we voted not to use tax money to subsidize the 1976 Winter Olympics, and that Colorado ought to host some future winter games — presumably, it's our duty to help promising young athletes get multimillion-dollar endorsement contracts, and we've shirked that obligation.

I remember arguing with my father just before the 1972 election. "Dad, if you vote for the Denver Olympics, the mountains west of Denver will get totally commercialized — tawdry, garish strips of fast-food joints and motels along I-70 all the way from Golden to Vail. Summit County will turn into a franchise mecca that looks just like every other freeway exit in America. The mountains will develop all sorts of urban problems like traffic jams and air pollution."

Despite my anguished pleas, he voted for the Olympics, and that's exactly what happened.

Except we didn't have the Olympics. However, modern politics consists of placating those vocal pressure groups that can conjure up some way to demonstrate that they are marginalized and oppressed. Thus it is inevitable that someday we will have to please the Survivors of Colorado Winter Games Deprivation, and maybe our own set of Colorado Winter Games will do the job:

— Floyd Hill Grand Slalom. A fast, exciting course through a dozen jackknifed semi-trucks while being pursued by an overloaded runaway. Other obstacles include frightened flatlanders turning doughnuts and people trying to flag a tow while standing outside stuck cars.

Contestants are judged on both elapsed time and style — how close can they come to an obstacle without actually touching it.

— Beater Jump-starts. When it's 20 below or colder, the contestants — dressed only in T-shirts and jeans because they like to show how tough they are — sort through a pile of fishing tackle, oilcans and jack handles behind the seat of a pickup. As soon as they find the jumper cables in the mess, they've got to untangle them, always a challenge when the cables are about as flexible as bridge timbers. Then it's a race to get the cables connected — they'll be gigged if they follow the safety rules, and a battery explosion is no disqualification — and the winner will be the first one to get his '58 Dodge D100 started and slid into a deep, snow-filled ditch at least 100 yards from the starting line.

In future years, we could add ether sniffing and Stupid Tow Tricks (i.e., a dog chain and a pot-metal come-along for a three-ton pickup sitting at a 45-degree angle) to this exciting competition.

— Snowboard Biathlon. In a normal biathlon, cross-country skiers carry rifles and shoot at targets as they ski the course.

The first Colorado variant was pioneered by Claudine Longet, who used a pistol and remained stationary while the target was a skier.

Now we can move into the 21st century by inviting snow-boarders to participate. Since this is just a game, we'll give them paint guns, and score them not only on shredding style, but also on how many overbearing ski patrollers they can shoot while zooming down the slopes.

— Men's and Women's Tire Chain War. Put a couple in a two-wheel drive car. The road is slick and it's snowing. She says it's time to stop and put on the tire chains. He says there's no need, even though the car is fishtailing.

The winning woman will be the first to get her partner to chain up. The winning man will get to the finish line without ever leaving his seat, with the prospect of extra points for changing a cassette tape, drinking coffee and lighting a cigarette all at once while the car is swerving out of control.

— Going for the Gold. This seemed like a natural for Summitville, but the mining company dropped out. So now it's up to the Colorado Republican Party — will Bruce Benson come up with the most gold and get the nomination for governor? Or will someone outbid him? This could be a marathon, so keep watching.

WE'RE THREATENED BY MIGRANTS, TOO, AND NEED PROP 781
November 20, 1994

JUST A DOZEN days ago, California voters approved Proposition 187 because they were upset by increased immigration, primarily from Mexico and points south.

It appears that California is getting a new kind of migrant these days. The old ones ventured north to harvest crops under the hot sun or to toil in sweatshops that pay low wages and offer no benefits.

Anyone who complained or tried to organize a union got deported, so Republicans understandably spoke favorably of those immigrants — an excellent supply of cheap and docile labor for their farms and factories.

But the new aliens send their kids to school instead of to the fields, and even worse they go to doctors when they're sick. Clearly they're a threat to the good life in the Golden State, and so it's no wonder that California responded by passing Proposition 187.

But California isn't the only state that suffers from migrants who threaten its established culture and institutions.

In Colorado, too, we face an invasion of folks who sneak past the border stations, plant themselves in our defenseless communities, and then start making expensive demands on our political, social, health and educational systems.

To cope with this incursion, which threatens all that we hold dear, we must adopt Proposition 781, which is similar to Proposition 187, but reversed because our migrant problem isn't quite the same as California's.

The main source of our migrant problem is California. Every week, we see announcements that myriads of Californians have fled the miserable conditions prevailing in their homeland, searching for a better life in the Mountain West.

And when the People of Money get here, they can cause all kinds of problems. Thus Proposition 781, our way to protect ourselves.

For instance, Colorado schools used to be cheap because they trafficked only in multiplication tables and sentence diagrams.

As soon as the aliens move in, they demand that our schools enhance pupil self-esteem and impart holistic refusal skills while promoting multicultural awareness. All of this costs money.

The resulting graduates may feel good about themselves because their urine is pure. They may even respect and appreciate all cultures except the fundamentalist rural redneck culture their parents migrated into.

But they have trouble counting change or writing a simple declarative sentence. Proposition 781 would forbid Californians' children from attending Colorado schools, thus removing the malign influence of their parents.

Another problem with these migrants is their terrible effect on real-estate values. We used to have funky, ramshackle towns like Salida, Aspen and Durango where the people who worked there could also afford to live there.

Come the emigrés, and these once solid and stable communities immediately start to deteriorate. The desperate aliens will pay almost anything for real estate. Prices soar and the indigenous employees get pushed out. To keep their jobs, they're forced to commute great distances, adding to the pollution and congestion on roads that were already dangerous.

Proposition 781 addresses this problem by requiring that all purchasers of property be documented Colorado citizens.

As with the United States itself, a five-year residency period will be required before citizenship is granted. Prospective citizens will also have to pass tests in their knowledge of Colorado language and law.

By requiring a long residency before citizenship, we can also cut our taxes because these non-citizens will not be allowed to vote or organize the public.

As it is, People of Money will buy property in remote locations and erect trophy houses that are vacant most of the year. Then they start demanding services, like 24-hour sheriff's patrols, and the rest of us, who feel lucky if we own one house we live in all the time, are supposed to pay for the costs these parasites incur on our local governments.

No matter where you look, you find migrant aliens clogging our highways, infesting our forests, skiing our slopes, always taking things that rightfully belong to real Coloradans.

Proposition 781 should also protect us from being infected by the perverse political ideas these migrant aliens bring to Colorado. Need I mention where Doug Bruce came from? Or that almost every lunacy on our ballot, from Official English to term limits to the tobacco tax to the very length of the ballot itself, had its origin west of our border?

Just how much longer can we, the simple, hard-working people of Colorado, be expected to tolerate this invasion that threatens the very foundations of our society?

Controlling the borders is a fundamental function of any government, and since the federal government refuses to protect us from this invasion, we have no choice but to adopt Proposition 781.

COLORADO: THE GREAT STATE OF HYPOCRISY
January 29, 1995

ROY ROMER, who never met a growth he didn't like, just got re-elected by a handsome margin. That says one thing about Coloradans.

Then you read surveys, which inform us that growth has replaced crime as the leading worry of Coloradans. That says something else.

You feel as though you've just met a man with a drinking problem. It really worries him. It concerns him so much that he chugs Mad Dog 20 for breakfast, red-eye for lunch, rotgut for dinner and Sterno for snacks. In his few lucid moments, he tells you that he's quite disturbed by all this alcohol in his system. Then he takes another swig.

That's basically what you read in all the whining about how growth is ruining Colorado. Some woman worries that she can't smell the sagebrush any more. Other folks complain that they can't see many stars at night.

In 1919, one of my grandfathers homesteaded 17 miles from Bill, Wyo. I visited the ranch often in my youth. The stars at night were big and bright, for there was no artificial light as far as the eye could see, and it was easy to smell sagebrush if you were upwind of the privy and the corral.

Grandpa Wollen was willing to pay a price for that: no electricity, no running water, no natural gas, no telephone, no paved road.

And if the worriers were willing to give up those conveniences, they, too, could even now find places of lustrous stars and the redolence of sage. It's just not as important to them as it was to him. They don't want to pay (in the currency of poverty and isolation) for what they want, and so why should we listen to them? What makes them different from any other beggars?

Growth in Colorado seems to follow what Boulder cartoonist and writer Rob Pudim once called "the Evergreen Syndrome."

You move to the woods to get away from it all. But those kerosene lamps are a lot of work, and a major fire hazard to boot. So organize an electric co-op. Paying the new bill is tough on a rural income, so you start commuting to a city job, which means you want better roads. Your neighbor's septic tank is too close to your well, so you organize water and sanitation districts. Pretty soon you're living in a place that has it all, not a place that's away from it all.

If you really had cared about keeping those woods pristine, you wouldn't move to them and import the accouterments of civilization. You'd stay in town and admire the woods from afar.

If we really wanted to avoid the many adverse effects of growth in Colorado, we wouldn't look to government or to any blue-ribbon commissions. We'd change the way we conduct our daily lives. We vote with our pocketbooks. Buy a house in some sterile suburb, accessible only by freeway, and you're voting for more of what we say we don't want: traffic, pollution, etc.

Buy a house within walking distance of work and shopping, and then actually walk, and you're voting for more of what the surveys say we want: better neighborhoods, tighter communities, etc.

Now examine the real-estate sections of today's paper. If there really was a demand for those walking-distance houses with swings on the front porch, you'd see big ads for such homes. You don't.

Every time you get into the car and go to a shopping mall, you're deciding what kind of place you'll live in, and it isn't the place people say they want: the place where you walk to the ma-and-pa store, where they know you and the proprietor is a pillar of the community. If we wanted such businesses to thrive, we'd patronize them; despite our noble words, we actually want franchise freeway-ramp outlets that export their profits.

We may say it's important to preserve agricultural open space, but do we support it by looking for local produce?

This analysis could go on indefinitely, but the point should be clear by now. We make moral decisions every time we spend money, and the power to change things is in our pockets, not in the state capitol.

If we wanted to spend our money thoughtfully, we could have all the things we say we want. Real-estate developers would build pedestrian-scale small towns with commercial centers and diverse housing, rather than malls and income-segregated covenanted tracts. Independent merchants would flourish, as would farmers in the open space outside town.

If we created markets for these things, then the "invisible hand" would hasten to supply them.

That this invisible hand moves in other directions says that we say one thing, but act in other ways. We're too lazy to change our daily routines, or to give much thought to the moral decisions we make with every purchase.

If you're serious about the vital importance of bright stars and sage aromas, you starve on two sections in the middle of nowhere and forgo electricity. Otherwise, it's not that important to you.

And if you're serious about a better life in Colorado, quit worrying about growth and start paying attention to how you spend your money. The power is in your pocketbook.

If You're Not Along the Front Range, You're Not in Colorado
December 5, 1995

Various dark rural suspicions that official Colorado consists of the Standard Metropolitan Statistical Areas along the Front Range were confirmed last week by, of all people, the Colorado Historical Society.

A society review panel decreed that the first gold strike in what is now Colorado occurred on June 22, 1850, along Ralston Creek in what is now Arvada.

Previously, this official honor had been held by William G. Russell, who panned gold in 1858 near today's site of Cinderella City.

News of Russell's discovery reached civilization, where folks in the Mississippi Valley were suffering from the Panic of 1857. Having the farm foreclosed often inspires a man to abandon plowing for prospecting, and thus the 1859 "Pike's Peak Rush" came about.

Geographers have a useful term: "first effective settlement." It means the permanent arrival of the dominant economy and culture of a region.

To understand it, consider the voyage of Christopher Columbus in 1492. Many Europeans — Vikings, Irish monks and Phoenicians — may have reached the "New World" before then.

But Columbus brought soldiers and put the Americas into international commerce. That's why Columbus is significant in a way that Leif Ericsson isn't.

That's also why the Russell discovery is significant. It brought in a horde of prospectors, along with real-estate speculators, lynch mobs, militias, massacres, taxes and the other blessings of American civilization.

Previous gold discoveries did not do that. Ralston's gold discovery is well-documented, but it didn't make anything happen. Gold-seekers bound for California did not swing south from Fort Laramie. The Arapaho and Cheyenne still camped and hunted along the Front Range. Ralston's discovery changed nothing.

Even if the first documented discovery of gold, rather than the discovery that mattered, is what the historical society cares about, Ralston is not in the running.

Doubtless the Utes noticed gold nuggets over the centuries. But gold was too soft to be of much use to them, and they didn't leave written records, since Ute wasn't a written language until 1977.

Spanish expeditions into the northern frontier of the empire also leave no record of gold discoveries in what is now Colorado — just legends, as well as mysteries like Caverna del Oro in the Sangre de Cristo range.

As for the first written record, I will crib from the research of Steve Voynick, as printed in his wonderful book, "Leadville: A Miner's Epic."

In 1758, a French chronicler named Le Page de Pratz wrote a "Histoire de la Louisiana," wherein he mentioned a "rivulet whose waters rolled down gold dust" at the headwaters of the Arkansas near present Leadville. Steve told me yesterday that, to the best of his knowledge, this is the first written reference to gold in Colorado.

That reference is vague, though. For a specific discovery, we can move to about 1801, when an American trapper and trader named James Purcell ventured west from St. Louis. He spent two years in South Park, where, Voynick writes, "near the future site of Fairplay, [Purcell] had dug into the gravels and discovered placer gold."

Purcell eventually fell into the hands of Spanish authorities, who did not like foreigners in their domain. He was ordered to stay in Santa Fe, where another American under Spanish arrest saw him in 1807.

That American was Zebulon Pike, who included Purcell's gold discovery in his government report issued in 1810.

So we have a discoverer of gold, James Purcell, as well as a place and a date, all on record. And all ignored by the Colorado Historical Society in favor of Arvada.

Now, I have nothing against Arvada. I have heard considerable praise for its performing arts center, which encourages local productions with local talent, as opposed to Denver's arts center, which offers touring Broadway shows.

But for some urban arrogance, ponder the words of Lois Lindstrom, the city historian who argued for the designation of the Ralston site: "I'd say this is where Colorado history begins."

Not at Mesa Verde — those cliffside condos near Cortez were ruins long before Ralston stopped along the Front Range and began Colorado's history.

Nor at Bent's Fort, where American commerce began its invasion of the Southwest in 1832. The old trading post is documented and all that, but it's between Las Animas and La Junta, not in a Standard Metropolitan Statistical Area, so Colorado's history couldn't have started there, either.

Lindstrom can't have it both ways. If we're talking first documented gold discovery, then it's Purcell. If we're talking first effective settlement, then it's Russell. In neither case does anything start in Arvada.

Expecting accuracy in historical boasting is perhaps expecting too much. But we could ask for accuracy in nomenclature, and have a Front Range Historical Tourism Promotion Society instead of the currently misnamed Colorado Historical Society.

LOCAL CONTROL REALLY MEANS 'CONTROL THE LOCALS'
March 5, 1996

PICK UP a pile of GOP propaganda, and you will eventually read words to the effect that "the Republican Party is committed to local control."

In Colorado, that means "we believe in local control as long as we control the locals."

More than 20 years ago, the legislature gave Colorado counties strong zoning powers with HB 1041. Counties could enact strict zoning, or take a *laissez-faire* approach, or steer some middle course — this was local control, and if you didn't like it, the decision-makers were as close as the courthouse.

However, Colorado Springs and Aurora wanted to grab some water from Eagle County with the Homestake II project. Eagle County zoning halted the project.

The cities of the plain took Eagle County to court, arguing that the county exceeded its authority. The Colorado Supreme Court upheld Eagle County's HB 1041 zoning powers.

Did the Republicans in our legislature hail this victory for local control?

Not exactly. They have a problem with local control if it interferes with the ability of Front Range developers to amass money for campaign contributions.

When the cities didn't get what they wanted in court, they turned to the legislature, where Sen. Tom Norton, a Greeley Republican, got SB 48 passed in the Senate.

In essense, SB 48 removes zoning powers from rural counties if the zoning interferes with the divine rights of Front Range cities.

There is the argument that HB 1041 is good for strictly local matters, but something that interferes with a water diversion is not strictly local.

This is somewhat sensible, but if distant cities get to interfere with rural zoning when it affects the cities, then rural areas should have a say on urban zoning when it affects the hinterlands.

For instance, every time El Paso County approves another development, or Aurora sprawls farther toward Kansas, that means more people to clog Chaffee County's back roads, campgrounds and fishing holes on a given weekend.

When crime or congestion or smog gets more intense in urban Colorado — that is, whenever a Front Range city grows — more people are tempted to move to 35-acre ranchettes in the boondocks.

So, when the House takes up SB 48, I hope that the representatives amend the bill so that both sides are represented. It would be only fair if a rural area could veto an urban development by noting that "Another 10,000 people there means 700 more ranchette owners, which exceeds our school capacity, so we have to turn this down."

This will never happen, of course. Sensible proposals get as far in the Colorado General Assembly as I would in a marathon.

For instance, the legislature just killed a proposed bill that would have required warning notices on new houses whose water comes from diminishing aquifers. If it had passed, the proud owner of a new house in Douglas or Elbert County would have due notice the area has only a 100-year supply of water.

(The result of failing to give the warning is predictable: Thousands of people will build there, and their heirs and assigns will form a potent political force to grab water from some other drainage when their wells go dry.)

One opponent, Sen. Dave Wattenberg, said homebuyers have the sophistication to ask about their water supply, and so a warning is unnecessary.

How sophisticated are Colorado homebuyers? Let us ponder Durango, where coal-burning locomotives have been in continuous operation since about 1881.

Coal smoke isn't like underground water — you can see it and smell it without any special effort. You'd think that anyone who considered moving to Durango would be aware of locomotive smoke, and if the fumes were troubling, the prospective Durangan would move somewhere else.

But such thoughts would miss the imbecility of the South Durango Homeowners Association, which on Feb. 28 asked the Colorado Department of Health to investigate the Durango & Silverton Railroad because coal smoke perturbs their delicate sensibilities.

The coal smoke was there long before they were. If they missed it while inspecting their homesites, they must be so insensate that they'd miss a three-alarm fire at a creosote plant. They're the same kind of people who buy houses by an airport and then complain about noise.

So Wattenberg is dead wrong about homebuyer sophistication. If these latter-day Durangans are any indication, the average Colorado homebuyer has the IQ of a turnip, and our legislature should look into requiring an intelligence test of prospective Colorado residents.

Given current trends, that should solve our growth problems, and we wouldn't have to worry about SB 48. There would be plenty of water to go around if we restricted Colorado residency to IQ's that at least reach the double digits.

Checking Up on Colorado's Heart and Soul
November 12, 1996

Sometimes my other literary efforts demand that I give Colorado some character. That is heavy work. What character can you give a state that is hell-bent on establishing a generic American landscape of big-box retailers, limited-access freeways, outlet malls, fast-food strips, condo collections and cookie-cutter houses?

But people pay for creativity, not honesty, and so I can employ a rhetorical trick and pretend that Colorado has a soul and a heart, and that you can find the soul at San Luis and the heart at Leadville.

Leadville and San Luis are a good pair in this regard. San Luis is the state's oldest town; farmers moving north founded it in 1851. It's still rather pastoral.

Leadville is heavy industry set 2 miles above sea level. It was for many years our state's wickedest city (it hasn't been that long since the Pioneer Club closed), and it was founded by miners moving west.

Two streams of migration and two approaches to the landscape, as reflected in the farmer's shovel and the miner's pick on our state seal.

Granted, neither town sits along the Front Range, where the majority of Coloradans live, but you can't cover everything with a literary device like personification, and if it did become necessary to assign a body part to the source of the Brown Cloud, I'm sure I could think of something.

Our Colorado soul, San Luis, seemed in good condition on a visit there as last summer was winding down. We stayed in an old convent, now converted to a bed and breakfast. Raised as a Baptist, I found the convent exotic and fascinating, but the lapsed Catholics said it felt kind of creepy.

We were there to learn about San Luis's efforts to acquire "La Sierra" — the huge Taylor Ranch east of town. We even got to visit part of the ranch.

For that tour, I boarded a car driven by Felix Romero, the ultimate Colorado native — he owns and operates the R&R Market in San Luis, which was founded in 1857 by his great-great-grandfather and has been in the family ever since.

There were three other passengers, and I was the only one not fluent in Colorado's unofficial language. So it took me a while to catch on that we were pretty much lost on the back roads of Costilla County.

"Felix, this is going to be a major scandal if I ever get out of here to write about this," I finally interjected.

"*Gringo turista* kidnapped and taken for a ride?" he asked.

"No, that the town of San Luis wants the Taylor Ranch, and one of its leading citizens can't even find the place," I replied.

Eventually we got there, though, and Colorado's soul seems to be in good shape.

But the state's heart is about to stop pumping. Leadville's last operating mine, the Asarco Black Cloud, is closing down.

Leadville's silver boom in 1879 made Denver into a city — Leadville capital built mansions on Capitol Hill and the city's first substantial retail center. Leadville helped build the fortunes of Marshall Field and the Guggenheim family.

Over the years, while other mining camps either decayed or tried the Aspen route, Leadville steadfastly continued to mine. It offered a gritty reality — if you saw two guys waving guns at each other on a Saturday night on East Second Street, you took cover because this wasn't some show for the tourists.

But Climax began shutting down in 1981, and now the Black Cloud is closing, and central Colorado no longer pulses to Leadville's cadence.

Leadville is now more or less a bedroom town for the resort belt along Interstate 70. That's an awful fate for what was once Colorado's second-largest city, and as someone who cherished rough-and-tumble, ramshackle Leadville during the Shining Times, I've given considerable thought to how to save Colorado's heart.

Close Tennessee and Frémont passes. Blocking these arteries would keep the virulent I-70 pathogens from spreading to Leadville and points south, and this would certainly discourage commuters from settling in Leadville.

If the resorts needed hired help, they could pay wages sufficient for their workers to live nearby. And our state department of transportation, always strapped for money, could save the high cost of maintaining these two snowy crossings. It's a win for everybody.

Unfortunately, my sensible proposals never catch on in Colorado, and we'll have to try something else. The servant commuter population will grow — they might even ride a train to work someday — and eventually the EPA will certify Leadville as lead-free.

In which case, change the name to something modern and appropriate, like SouthVail or SummitWest, and forget there ever was a Leadville — it was just too damned rough and honest to fit into modern Colorado, anyway.

COLORADO PROBABLY CAN'T FLUSH AWAY ITS PROBLEMS
August 10, 1997

MANY OF MY FRIENDS HERE, like me, live in old houses that were erected back when plumbing and electricity were novelties. You get the idea that, around the turn of the century, there was a domestic conversation:

"Clara, we've managed to set aside a little of your egg money. Reckon we ought to try some of that new-fangled electricity stuff? An' mebbe an indoor flush toilet, too?"

"Well, Jake, it's up to you. But for my part, trimming and filling those coal-oil lamps can get mighty tedious, and our privy is in sore need of an overhaul anyway."

And so they tacked on a lean-to addition for an experiment with progress; over the years, the pipes and wires extended ever further into the house.

So you'd think that new construction would accommodate these utilities more comfortably, but that wasn't the case when I visited a contractor friend in his brand-new house. (He's been in it nearly six months now, thereby breaking the world's record for "contractor living in a house of his own construction." Usually they get one sold before they even start packing to move in.)

The need arose to visit the commode, where, to put it delicately, certain matter stayed around after it should have departed. I discretely mentioned this.

"Damn new water-saving toilets," he explained. "The feds outlawed the manufacture and import of the old 3.5-gallon toilets, so we're stuck with these 1.6-gallon tanks that you have to flush about five times."

This works out to eight gallons per visit, we figured, and thus the new water-saver resulted in twice the consumption of the old water-waster it replaced.

Even if these contraptions worked properly, though, just how much water would they save?

In an average year, about 100 million acre-feet of water will fall on Colorado. Of that amount, 85 million evaporates or is transpired by plants, leaving 15 million to flow in our streams. About 8 million of that flows to downstream domains, mostly as required by interstate water compacts, leaving 7 million for in-state consumption.

Of that, 88 percent is used by agriculture, 6 percent by industry, and the remaining 6 percent goes to municipal or domestic purposes. So, of the 100 million acre-feet (32.5 trillion gallons) we started with, we're down to 6 percent of 7 percent (0.42 percent or 136.9 billion gallons) for all household use.

At an average home, 54 percent goes to the yard and 18 percent for showers and baths, 1 percent to the dishwasher, 2 percent to leaks, and faucets and laundry each take 7 percent. The remaining 11 percent flows through the toilet.

In other words, all the toilets in Colorado consume 15 billion gallons a year, or only 0.03 percent of the water in the state. If we eliminated flush toilets entirely, it wouldn't make much difference, and even if low-flow fixtures worked properly, the savings aren't enough to matter, even in a desert like Colorado.

The trend is going the other way, though. Custer County just announced it plans to eliminate all traditional no-water-consumption-at-all privies by the end of this year.

They're still allowed, but only in rare special cases, in Saguache County, which has been getting suspiciously civilized of late. Just last week I got hustled into attending a chamber-music performance there — harpsichord and viola da gamba — and to my shock I enjoyed it.

(I'm hoping this forthright confession will keep me from getting thrown out of the Regular Guy Association, which can be brutal. They come by and confiscate all your gimme caps, beef jerky and grease-stained, low-hanger, moon-is-rising blue jeans. Then they break your left kneecap so you can never again double-clutch when downshifting a five-speed crashbox.)

Anyway, it appears that replacing low-flows that don't flush with privies that don't need to flush is not the wave of the future.

But there's another possible solution. Colorado toilets altogether consume the same amount of water as 126,000 people — the approximate population of Douglas County.

Rounding them up and deporting them would solve many problems, aside from allowing the rest of us to use flush toilets that actually flush.

Open space would be preserved between Colorado's two largest cities. The departure of all those commuters would reduce the need for new highway construction and expansion, so we wouldn't need that gas tax increase now being touted by the Asphalt & Gravel Lobby.

Our future would be more secure if we didn't have thousands of people relying on wells that will go dry within a century, and our politics would be more competitive without the solid GOP bloc of Douglas County.

Since we may have to endure an election this fall anyway, let's put the question on the ballot: Given that Colorado is supposed to limit its water usage, do you want people in Douglas County, or a toilet that flushes?

Mountain Towns & Public Land

————◦———

I can't remember a time when I didn't want to live in the mountains. Longs Peak was quite visible from our backyard in Evans, just south of Greeley, and we often took Sunday drives to the mountains. They seemed so interesting compared to the section-line monotony of the country around Greeley.

The mountains I found most interesting were the old mining areas up Boulder and Clear creeks, as opposed to the more pristine drives up St. Vrain, Big Thompson and Poudre canyons. Trees and rocks and creeks quickly started to look pretty much the same, whereas old mines, mills and railroad grades fascinated me.

This was especially so after a trip to Cripple Creek in 1959 when the Golden Cycle Mill and a couple of its gold mines were still running. I was so intrigued that my parents bought me a copy of Muriel Sibell Wolle's "Stampede to Timberline" for my birthday that year, and I devoured it, dreaming about a day when I could live in the mountains.

That day came in 1974 when I finally got offered two real newspaper jobs — one in Sterling and the other in Kremmling. Off to Kremmling we went, my dream coming true.

Kremmling, in those days, was a rather lively place. Amax was drilling the Henderson Tunnel, with Kremmling the base for the west side, so it was a mining town. Two sawmills ran day and night, so it was a logging town. Vast ranches spread around that end of Middle Park, so it was a cowboy town.

Saturday nights often involved brawls, shootings, broken glass — the Old West come to life, and not for the benefit of tourists, either. While that had its enchantments, I was essentially a quiet, bookish fellow, and I had trouble figuring out where I fit into this.

About four years later, we landed in Salida, where we've been ever since. Salida was then a lunch-bucket town whose handsome old brick buildings had survived, not on account of any historic-preservation movement, but because nobody could afford to replace them, and there wasn't enough regional trade to support some hideous shopping mall on the edge of town that would have destroyed downtown as a commercial center.

In short, poverty made Salida a pretty good place to live. Nobody made much money, but nobody needed much.

Salida was "discovered" by People of Money along about 1992, and as some of these columns chronicle, things haven't been the same since.

Although I like living in the mountains, I have no desire to live in the country. I'd rather write than divine the mysteries of wells and septic systems, and though I'm not all that "green," I believe it's better for me and the environment if I live so that the post office and the library and the stores are within walking range, rather than at the end of a 15-mile car trip taken two or three times daily. If we want "open space" around us, we need to live in "dense space" and work with our neighbors to make that space decent and livable.

You can't reside in the mountains without paying attention to their landlords — primarily the U.S. Forest Service and the Bureau of Land Management. They were created during the heyday of "scientific" management theories, as though one could calculate sustainable yields of timber and forage, and then operate that way as though there were no market or political forces.

So I try to keep an eye on what they're up to, and I see a trend emerging. Our public lands used to be managed for commodity production, which paid the freight, and recreation was a by-product that got to freeload.

Now recreation has become the focus, which means it's going to have to pay the bills. The days of just walking and camping freely in the woods are numbered. After all, we could be recreating at some taxpaying cineplex, whose campaign-contributor owner will argue that our strolls in the woods amount to subsidized and unfair competition.

Exciting times loom, along with a dismal outcome. Enjoy the public lands while you can. The feds probably won't sell them to private owners, but they will start charging, and charging well — the logic of the times demands it.

Confessing the Sin of Omission
May 18, 1988

Now that summer tourist season is almost upon us, we can expect the usual deluge of publications that guide the vacationer toward choice spots — lakes, campgrounds, fishing streams, hiking trails, etc.

However, no matter which "Guide to a Significant, Awesome and Secluded Rocky Mountain Experience" you decide to read, you should know that the best places have been deliberately omitted.

Why? I'll explain from my own experience. A decade ago, newly arrived in Salida as managing editor of the local daily, I discovered that one of my duties was assembling the annual special edition for tourists, "Summer Fun."

So I extolled the diverse attractions of this area, giving great attention to the places that I liked myself, to those that my colleagues enjoyed and to spots I heard other local people talking about.

"Summer Fun" came out at the end of May, and by the middle of July, I was about as popular as an IRS auditor among those very people.

The publisher wondered why I had to mention Xxxxx Creek as a spot where brookies teemed. "It was shoulder-to-shoulder fishermen last weekend," he complained. "I could barely find a place to cast from, and the creek has been fished out anyway. It'll take me years to find another place as nice as Xxxxx Creek was."

A friend in town moaned that the Xxxxx Trail, a scenic delight that had been his favorite getaway because he had the whole place to himself, now looked like the marching route for a mass migration of Boulderites in backpacks. "You'd have a better chance of finding peace and solitude if you went to a disco," he growled.

When I ventured to my own favorite camping spot, a secluded little glen just off the Xxxxx Road, I discovered it had three tents, two pickup campers, several Winnebagos, lots of trash and no firewood.

Since the place had always been empty in years before, I inquired of one of the campers. He pulled out a copy of "Summer Fun" and showed me my very own words, about how there was this wonderful camping spot about 4 miles up the Xxxxx Road from Xxxxx, which offered a tumbling creek, superlative views, etc.

I had learned my lesson. That was the last time I ever tried "full disclosure" when putting out a tourist publication. Every year thereafter, I polled my friends and the newspaper staff as to whether they had any favorite haunts in the nearby mountains.

Those places were of course omitted. It's not that I had anything against serving the tourist public, but we gave our visitors ample information about dozens of attractions. It only seemed fair that we reserve a few for ourselves.

Policies may have changed at "Summer Fun" since my departure five years ago, but the practice is reasonably widespread. I discovered that last month. I had written an article for a mountain magazine that must remain nameless.

The editor had some questions. As we were talking, I mentioned Xxxxx Pass as possibly worth an article someday.

"Oh no," he said. "That's one of my favorite places, and as long as I'm here, there won't be word one about it in this magazine. We're keeping that to ourselves, and I'd sure appreciate it if you never wrote about Xxxxx Pass for anyone else."

I said I understood perfectly, although this leads to mixed feelings. You enjoy montane tranquility and so you want to keep your discoveries to yourself. But as a writer, you have to keep finding new things to write about if you're going to make a living. And there's nothing that many editors like more than an article about some new and "undiscovered" spot.

On that account, I used to worry whenever I picked up a tourist guide, or visited the bookstore and saw some new "Guide to 3,714 Previously Unpublicized Trails, Campsites, Creeks, Passes & Peaks."

But so far, my fears have been groundless. My favorite spots haven't appeared in print. When I have a chance to ask the authors, they will confess that they started out with good intentions. They planned to be honest and forthright.

Along the way, though, they learned the same lesson I did 10 years ago. Self-interest got the better of them, and they left out the truly good places. For that we should all be grateful.

REAL MOUNTAIN DRIVERS
November 30, 1988

NOW THAT WINTER has arrived, it's time to consider a severe seasonal problem: persuading a reluctant vehicle to start when the sun has barely risen and it's so cold that the snow squeals under your feet. It's colder than the proverbial well-digger's rump, colder than a banker's heart, even colder than your wife's feet.

In the civilized areas of Colorado, this is an infrequent occurrence, but in the mountains it happens daily for six months of the year. Thus has evolved a group of cold-start experts: the Real Mountain Drivers.

Real Mountain Drivers will concede that the certain way to a morning start is to install a tank or dipstick heater and plug it in every night. But Real Mountain Drivers also consider that cheating, unless they find a way to connect the 200-foot extension cord to a neighbor's electrical outlet.

The Real Mountain Driver first walks around his vehicle. Although he squints carefully as he makes this circuit, he couldn't tell you what he's looking for. It's a ritual to placate the Turnover Deity.

The Turnover Deity is not in any way connected to football; it is the mysterious power of the universe that allows the engine to crank on some mornings but not others.

Holding his breath so as not to fog the windows, the Real Mountain Driver slides the key into the ignition and turns the switch to "on." Not to "start," because first he checks that everything is off. He doesn't want the radio, wipers or heater motor to drain precious electricity from the battery. Many Real Mountain Drivers avoid the need for this step by owning vehicles that lack radios, wipers or heater fans.

Satisfied that the starter faces no electrical competition, the Real Mountain Driver pulls the choke. On more modern vehicles with automatic chokes, he opens the hood, removes the air cleaner, and fiddles with the carburetor until he's sure the choke is shut. A sharp tug generally suffices to remove his fingers from the frozen metal.

Back behind the wheel, he pumps the accelerator precisely four times. Any less, and the engine won't start. Any more, and it will flood. Then he depresses the clutch so that a cold, stiff transmission won't be added to the starter's burdens.

Now the Real Mountain Driver is all ears. He must hear every grunt and groan from the engine compartment. Invariably at this moment, a dog will start howling or a semi will roar down the nearby highway, its Jake Brake® barking.

When silence finally arrives, he turns the key to "start." This is the moment of truth.

About once a week, it starts. The rest of the time, he must resort to:

— Jump starting. This presumes that someone will happen along with a set of cables, and that the cables aren't too short or missing a clamp. The other common complication is that the cable-bearer might also be toting a bottle of schnapps; after several warming gulps, no one can remember whether red is positive or negative. The cables melt if one or more batteries don't explode first.

— Mechanical assistance. Someone comes by who's willing to push or pull. If it's pull, the chain snaps in the cold, and both drivers spend the rest of the day shoveling their vehicles out of a ditch. For push, there's always a mating problem, and tailgates, bumpers and grills get smashed, as do friendships when the argument begins as to who's responsible for what.

— Ether. My brother Kurt, a certified diesel mechanic, insists that those spray cans of ether are meant for diesel engines and do not help gasoline engines start. But what does he know?

The truth is that spray-can ether is the same chemical that surgeons use to keep you from feeling the knife when they're cutting on you.

No matter what the mechanics say, ether is effective if you use it properly, the way Real Mountain Drivers do.

Just get under the hood with the spray can. Within 10 seconds of a short squirt, you lose all interest in the visible world.

You slither indoors. When you revive, you realize that you really didn't need to go anywhere that day anyway. Your job was a bore, and anyway, why contribute to resource depletion and air pollution? A bracing morning jolt of ether gives you severe attitude problems, and that's how Real Mountain Drivers handle the travails of winter.

ROADWAY FAUNA OF COLORADO
August 23, 1989

MILLIONS of trees have died so that we might educate ourselves about "The Roadside Geology of Colorado" and "The Roadside History of Colorado."

However, our authors have been devoting all their attention to the roadsides, and lately the most useful guidebook would tell you about what you'll find on the road, not beside the road.

Then you'd know about these species of highway wildlife:

— Macho 18-Wheeler. Preferred habitats include west side of Eisenhower Tunnel and Floyd Hill, but it can emerge wherever there's an extended stretch of twisting 7 percent downgrade. Its call is "Hey, man, downshifting is for sissies, only a candy-ass would use a Jake Brake™, and if you can't drive for 38 straight hours, you're a pansy." Track consists of long skid marks, blood and remnants of squashed passenger cars. Can be discerned from Sensible 18-Wheelers by their smoking wheel brakes. If you see one in your rear-view mirror, the best response is prayer.

— Arrogant 18-Gear Cyclist. Ranges throughout state. No matter how wide the shoulder or congested the traffic, always stays in main thoroughfare — except in parks, where it takes over all pedestrian paths. Ignores traffic signals and signs. This species is quite gregarious and generally migrates in flocks of 50 or more, thereby insuring that no other traffic will pass.

— Cellular Wizard. Most drivers find it sufficiently challenging to maneuver two tons of moving machinery. But that's just a start for the awesome talents of the Cellular Wizard, who can also adjust plumage, eat breakfast, absorb an oral version of a best-seller — and run up two hours of billable time in a 45-minute commute, thanks to its in-car telephone. Found only in densely settled areas, its call is "Let me get back to you on that."

— Country Mouse. In its home habitat, Country Mouse is relatively harmless. No one cares if it drives on the left side of the road, refuses to signal for turns, or, when it sees another Country Mouse in the other lane, pauses in midstreet to indulge in half an hour of gossip. Unfortunately, Country Mice are sometimes carried off by predators or economic forces and dropped into the Metropolitan Rat Race, with dire consequences all the way around.

— Four-Wheelers. The original habitat of this species was the back country, where they explored old wagon roads with their distinctive calls: "Let me put the hubs in." "Your winch working?" "Punched out my oil pan." Recently, growing numbers of Four-Wheelers have been spotted in upscale suburbs, but this is apparently an entirely different species, on account of its dissimilar call: "I just spent $24,000 for a new Wagoneer, and you think I'm going to take it off the pavement, where it might get scratched or something?"

— Rural Pickup. Easily spotted, thanks to its cloud of blue oil smoke and trail of empty tall boys. Moves erratically, either because its tie rods are bent or because the driver is under the influence of a controlled or uncontrolled substance. May have calls, but these are generally drowned out by the hole in the muffler or by the tape player blasting out country music (Redneck Rural Pickup) or blues (Ex-Hippie Rural Pickup).

— Metro Roadhog. Generally goes by in a flash, weaving across three or more lanes. Utters call — a protracted horn honk — only when forced to go less than 65 mph. Believed to be ancestral species of Cellular Wizard.

That's just a start. There are seasonal species, like the Rubbernecking Flatlander and the Hellbent Skier, as well as the widespread Grim-Faced Commuters, who migrate on weekday mornings, and Cruising Kids, who appear on weekend evenings. One once-common species, the Polite Driver, is endangered and may even be extinct, since no sightings have been reported for at least five years.

Marfies vs. Yupscales, and the Fate of the West
September 23, 1990

Now that the specter of godless international Communism does not haunt mankind, it might be possible to discuss class warfare without getting on some list of subversives.

The fate of the American West may depend on the outcome of a struggle between two social classes, Marfies and Yupscales.

Marfie is an acronym for "Middle-Aged Rural Failure." They live in the boondocks. Marfies are not especially educated, but they are reasonably skilled at blue-collar occupations like carpentry and welding. Their politics are unpredictable, although you can count on them to vote for friends or relatives seeking local office, in the hope of getting a cushy government job.

Yupscales don't need much explanation. They are educated, make good money and live in Standard Metropolitan Statistical Areas. As for politics, they're very concerned about the environment. Think of a Josie Heath supporter, and you've got a Yupscale.

Most current controversies in the West may look like environmental issues on the surface, but they're really class warfare between the Yupscales and the Marfies.

The great spotted owl debate in the Pacific Northwest is one example. Marfies are lumberjacks and sawyers who won't be able to find other work in their hometowns if logging is stopped. Yupscales want to stop the logging, supposedly because they're concerned about the environment.

But how many Yupscales refuse to produce or consume paper, which comes from wood, which comes from logging? Did you ever see a Yupscale manor without cedar shake shingles and a redwood deck? Yupscales commute 80 miles a day at a horrendous environmental cost. They like to ski, and ski resorts displace a great deal of wildlife.

So it can't be the environment that Yupscales really care about. The only other explanation is that they despise Marfies and want to impoverish them.

This makes sense in other controversies. Most opposition to mining comes from Yupscales — they're not going to be the ones who have to live on Food Stamps if the mine doesn't go in. The anti-fur movement is led by Yupscales, who have ample pity for animals but none for the Marfies who used to make their living by trapping.

Why would Yupscales want to make Marfies even worse off?

For one, Yupscales are the major consumers of expensive recreation, which would be even more costly without cheap labor to make beds and sauté mushrooms. If Marfies can't get $15 an hour for mining or logging, they'll have to commute to the world-class destination resort and smile at Yupscales while drawing Third World wages.

For another, if Marfies get poor enough, they'll be so desperate for income that they'll eagerly accept things they don't want, such as toxic waste dumps. Witness Lind, Wash., and Edgemont, S.D., both depressed rural towns where prosperous America — the land of Yupscales — wants to deposit its toxic trash.

In essence, Yupscales are saying, "In the name of the environment (which we don't really care about), give up the only job you know how to do. In return, we'll poison you or you can work for rotten wages." If that's not class warfare, it will do until the real thing comes along.

Salida: the Leading Edge
February 2, 1992

Well-meaning people have often told me that I should consider moving because Salida is a remote backwater, far removed from the mainstream of contemporary American life.

At first I argued that the mainstream rat race was a perfect place for rodents, who were welcome to it. But then I discovered that Salida might have taken over California's job of cultural and economic leadership.

The saying was that "Whatever happens in America happens first in California," but in truth, things happen first in Salida.

Is the rest of America now suffering from plant closings and layoffs that affect industrial workers? That happened here 10 years ago in 1982, when Climax Molybdenum and CF&I's Monarch Quarry shut down. It also happened in 1955, when the railroad closed its local shops and roundhouses. As for any new jobs, do they pay minimum wage? Welcome to Salida, America.

Are real-estate prices now declining nationally? Does it take just this side of forever to sell a house? That trend started here about 10 years ago. And even though prices dropped, we still faced a shortage of affordable rental housing — a problem that is hitting the rest of America now.

Nationally, banks were failing left and right in 1989. Three years earlier, the Buena Vista Bank & Trust failed on account of speculative loans, as did a local credit union. Our area led the way.

Is "cocooning" now fashionable in mainstream America? We might have invented it here in about 1985, when we couldn't afford to go out anyway.

In the middle of the 1980s, we often used to sit around someone's kitchen table, drinking beer or coffee while we gleefully exchanged pernicious gossip:

Teacher X and Administrator Y, both married to other people, had gone to an out-of-town workshop and didn't even bother to get separate motel rooms. But delivery-driver Z said Y's car is more often over at Secretary W's house these nights.

Wasn't that the same W who starred at a notorious hot- tub party thrown by Merchant V? She was also coming on to everybody at the big party where Lawyer U was found swiving under the pile of coats on the bed with Clerk T, who's the second cousin once removed of Waitress S, who was seen up at the Hot Springs enjoying a nude romp with County Official R.

I used to be rather embarrassed about talking of such frivolous matters, for this gossip seemed to exemplify all that was stupid, mean and petty about small-town society. I presumed that people in more enlightened regions found higher and nobler things to talk about — trade deficits, capital formation, decaying infrastructure, educational reform, etc.

But now, thanks to our great organs of public enlightenment and how they have handled the allegations about Arkansas Gov. Bill Clinton's activities, I realize that once again we Salidans were on the leading edge of American culture.

Perhaps I should be thrilled, because it means that just by living here, I've got an excellent view into the future. But actually, it's rather frightening to realize that important, sophisticated people in New York, Los Angeles and Washington have become just as stupid, mean and petty as we are.

Unintended Consequences of Public Land Fees
March 28, 1993

Most towns in the West began as centers for exploiting public lands. The nimble towns manage not by halting the exploitation, but by changing the means — Aspen from silver to skiing, or Moab from uranium to mountain bikes.

The West is a vast commons that underwent several waves of exploitation. Each earlier wave — mining, farming, grazing and logging — followed a pattern. Places boomed while folks grabbed the cheap and easy stuff, generally with the help of a government subsidy (Sherman Silver Purchase Act, etc.) But at some point, Washington proposes to make exploitation more expensive.

Now it is recreation's turn. A Leadville could once boom by selling powder, whiskey and sex to miners who used the public lands at minimal charge; a Moab or a Salida can survive now by serving cyclists and floaters who use public lands at minimal charge. Thus the recent administration trial balloon: user fees for recreation on public lands.

Recreation is not exactly struggling. At $257 billion in 1990, recreation is bigger than logging ($32 billion), mining ($80 billion), and cattle and sheep ($61 billion), all put together.

Outdoor recreation is heavily subsidized. Fees cover only 7 percent of the cost of national parks; a day at Disneyland costs $35 per head, while a week at Yellowstone is only $10 per carload.

From a national perspective, it does seem fair to bring public-land recreation fees up to market rates. But problems will come because people get demanding after they're forced to spend real money.

It's one thing to miss Old Faithful when you're just passing through; it's quite another to pay $15, stand in line outdoors for six hours, and discover that the geyser merely percolates during your 10 minutes.

Imagine this scene, a decade hence, in a regional office of the Interior Revenue Service.

"We'd like a total refund of our 14-day Western public-land recreation fees. Our vacation was a disaster."

"Could you explain your problems, so that I can get you the proper forms for you to fill out?"

"When we first pulled into Denver, we paid the Scenic View Fee, but the smog was so bad that we couldn't even see Lookout Mountain, let alone Mount Evans or Pikes Peak."

"Sorry. We don't have any control over atmospheric conditions, but we have to charge anyway, just in case somebody gets a breathtaking glimpse of the Front Range."

"Okay. We went camping after that, and it rained. When it wasn't rain, it was mud. We didn't even take our mountain bikes out, so why should we pay the trail fee?"

"But you could have used the trails, so we have to charge. I'm sorry, but we just don't have enough personnel to examine your tires on entry and exit and then calculate an appropriate trail mileage charge based on wear."

"Dad, tell 'em about the missing marmot."

"Right. The campground brochure said we'd see these furry creatures called marmots and not to feed them. Our little Sally looked and looked, but she never saw even one."

"Wrong time of year. You can't expect a bunch of trained woodchucks."

"For $160 a day for our family, damn right I expect it. Kids, we're going to Disneyland next year. Might cost a little more, but at least Mickey always shows up on time."

So our public lands will be managed somewhat differently as they become competitive, recreation-based, federal revenue centers. But it probably won't do any more damage than logging, mining and grazing.

Preventing Rural Gentrification
May 4, 1993

When I run into people from other mountain towns, the conversation often turns to rural gentrification and its dismal effects: ferns and smoke-free environments in what had been comfortable saloons, hardware stores turning into boutiques, workers priced out of housing, self-esteem instead of multiplication tables in school, etc.

Apparently, the best way to ruin a community is to have it discovered by people with taste and money, who like the town so much that they move in and change everything they liked about it.

149

How to preserve traditional mountain culture? An informal seminar at the Cattlemen's Inn in Gunnison recently came up with some innovative public-policy proposals:

— Destructive Covenants. Upscale folks put restrictive covenants in their deeds to enhance property values by forbidding wind chimes, artificial flowers, porch swings, children, etc.

The same legal technique could also keep property values low, so that people could afford to live near their work. Members of a neighborhood association could adjust their deeds to require that all yards contain a clothesline, privy, woodpile, four mongrels, two porch appliances and a minimum of three unlicensed vehicles.

— Appalachia Zoning. To extend and formalize the new covenants, the state legislature should require counties to create an Appalachia Ring Zone around every municipality. Along with the lawn-free downscale estates (25-year-old mobile homes would get special tax incentives, with flower beds and fresh paint strictly forbidden), the Appalachia Zone would also contain scrap yards, slag heaps, goat farms, wood lots, roadhouses, shooting ranges, gravel pits and other enterprises that will offend the sensitivities of the politically, environmentally and economically correct.

They'll be disgusted every time they come into town, and if they try to build above town, their deck panorama will always include jarring reminders of reality.

— Vacancy Tax. An Aspenite assured us that his town was a real community before the Big Money arrived in the '80s and built immense palaces that are occupied perhaps four weeks a year.

Meanwhile, the town suffers a severe shortage of employee housing. To finance the Appalachia Zone for affordable shelter, local government will levy a vacancy tax. The rate would need some fine-tuning, but for starters, let's say you'd pay $500 for every night that you didn't stay in your $500,000 house, or $750 for a $750,000 house.

And if that didn't work, there's always the possibility of Squatter Rights — if you don't use your 17 bedroom suites and 24 gold-plated baths, somebody else will.

Fairness requires that I make it clear that these concepts are not all mine. However, my colleagues at the seminar assured me that they would not be distressed if my name, rather than theirs, is associated with the public presentation of this innovative policy proposal.

What if They're Not Crying Wolf?
August 15, 1993

THE SAFEST prediction on this earth is that ranchers will whine. Read regional history, and you'll see predictions that allowing nesters to settle on the Great Plains would "drive all the stockmen out of business."

The same dire forecasts appeared when Herefords began to supplant longhorns, when shepherds tried to push their flocks into cattle country, when the cavalry didn't exterminate Indians with sufficient dispatch, when bleeding hearts insisted on due process for rustlers, and when compound 1080 was banned.

So it's hard to take the livestock lobby seriously when we hear that thousands of ranchers will be forced out if fees for grazing on public lands are raised from $1.86 to $4.28 per animal unit month.

But suppose there really is a wolf this time and that ranching actually did fade. What would that mean?

For consumers, next to nothing. Of the 98.2 million American cattle in 1990, only 1.2 million ever defecated on our public lands. Eliminating them means a 1.22 percent decline in beef supply that might be reflected in prices. Beef prices already fluctuate a lot more than that.

For a rural economy, not much would change, either. Or so I gather from Randy Russell, a friend who is a rural economic development specialist now practicing in Utah.

"When people tell you that you're in a ranching town," he once said, "they're talking myth. The major share of rural individual income comes from transfer payments — pensions, Social Security, disability, welfare. Throw in government jobs that pay decent wages — Forest Service, Postal Service, teaching. That's what supports a community. Ranchers are seldom much of a factor, even if it looks like a ranching town because you see muddy four-wheel-drive pickups with gun racks."

But there's still the environment to consider, even if the national environmental groups all favor raising fees.

Would the West be a better place to live if working 35-acre ranchettes and clusters of chipboard condos replaced ranches? If ranch water rights were diverted to more sprawling metro suburbs? If snobbish Gore-Tex™ mountain bikers and llama packers replaced cattle and sheep on public lands?

Apparently the national environmental groups are of that mind, given that they support the fee increase rather than a grassroots plan recently developed in Gunnison County — broader representation on grazing councils, and no fee increases if the land, especially riparian habitat, is restored.

Further, of all who plundered the West — slash-and-gouge loggers, rip-and-run miners, plow-a-dust-bowl sodbusters — only the ranchers stayed around to sleep in the bed they made. Continued overgrazing and environmental degradation can't be in their long-term interest, and they do seem interested in the long term.

Perhaps, then, the "environmental" aspect of grazing-fee increases is just a smokescreen. Behind the scenes, the real game could be dispossession followed by gentrification.

This happened 200 years ago in the Scottish highlands. The English gentry wanted a place to hunt grouse and fish for salmon, and that place was infested by crofters. These small landholders were expelled on political grounds, for supporting the Jacobite rebellion. The gentry got a playground. For something closer in time and place, read a John Nichols novel like "The Magic Journey." You see the same process at work, except the rationale there is economic, rather than political or environmental.

Those redneck ranchers may be all that prevents the West from turning into an extended Boulder-Aspen-Santa Fe — places that praise "cultural diversity" but have room inside only for the politically correct, smoke-free, white wine and tofu culture of appropriate conspicuous consumption.

If that's the case, forget grazing-fee increases. We should instead be grateful to the ranchers for the valuable service they provide in keeping the West truly diverse and livable, at the trifling expense of a few cows in the woods.

Why the Need to Import Environmentalists?
March 22, 1994

Last week, Interior Secretary Bruce Babbitt announced yet another formula to reform grazing on public lands.

A 15-member resource advisory council will supervise each former grazing district. Five council members are ranchers, five are other public-land users, such as outfitters or recreationalists, and the other five must be environmentalists.

Although the first two gangs of five must live nearby, the five environmentalists can come from elsewhere.

Putting environmentalists on grazing councils is a good idea, and if it had been done a long time ago, we might have prevented some of the problems we face now.

But why not use local environmentalists?

Could there be a shortage of environmentalists in rural communities surrounded by public land, and thus there's a need to import green thinkers to provide an informed perspective, lest the unwashed heathen go astray?

If there is such a shortage, I haven't noticed it. In any mountain town, even those amid overgrazed pastures of rapacious Herefords (a landscape so devastated that it remains good only for subdividing into 35-acre ranchettes), it's easier to find a health-food emporium than a feed store, and outdoors shops far outnumber implement dealers. At every public hearing in recent memory, local members of the Sierra Club, Greenpeace, Audubon Society, etc., have made themselves heard, often to good effect.

That fact means another possible Babbitt assumption is invalid — that there might be some environmentalists in rural Western communities, but they're scared to speak up on account of all those violence-prone, gun-toting rednecks, so they stay in the closet.

Intimidation certainly occurred in many places 15 or 20 years ago — but rural Western environmentalists, like rural Westerners in general, continued to say what they had to say. It took fortitude to make an issue of sloppy uranium milling in Moab 20 years ago, or of formaldehyde fumes from the sawmill in Kremmling a decade ago — but there were people in those towns who had that courage.

Obviously, there's no environmental need to import people from cities to serve on grazing advisory boards.

There is a political need, of course. The Wilderness Society (290,000 members whom Babbitt is attempting to placate) says that "local control is the problem, not the solution," and that any grazing reform should "give all Americans an equal voice in management decisions."

Indeed. So why aren't they lobbying to give all Americans an equal voice in other significant management decisions — say, for example, the operation of the federal reserve system, or the New York City transit system, which doubtless collects more federal subsidies than all the ranches in the West?

In a sensible world, if an urban environmentalist felt left out of range policy matters, he could move to the cowtown of his choice and take a seat at the table. Perhaps the move would hurt his career and income, but that's fair; he's dealing with other people's careers and incomes.

But under the latest proposal, all the concerned urban planet-saver needs to do is pack his carpetbag for an overnight trip. And still the national environmental groups whine that the secretary of the interior has somehow sold out to "the lords of yesterday."

ALL ROADS LEAD TO ROME
— AND EVERYTHING THAT COMES WITH IT
January 8, 1995

ON a couple of occasions last year, I attended meetings of an informal body called the "Colorado Cooperation Conference." The idea is to improve rural-urban relationships, and it's pretty interesting.

However, I never learned the ground rules for press coverage. As someone experienced in the art of finding sensational statements and publishing them out of context (as Bob Ewegen of The Denver Post often observes, "Journalism is the art of relentless oversimplification"), I can understand why people are reluctant to speak candidly when they might be quoted in the public prints.

So I'll avoid any names. Big City Mayor observed in meeting with his colleagues, "We've seen a pattern. Gang activity, and crime in general, tends to follow the interstates."

Half an hour later, Western Slope Politico announced that four-lane highways installed to every hamlet would solve most economic and social problems in Colorado.

When it was my turn to talk, I wondered if I was the only one there who saw the connection: better roads bring crime, not prosperity.

That's heresy in Colorado. As soon as the General Assembly gets into gear this year, they'll find ways to put more money into the highway fund, and the governor will go along with it. He'll probably take credit for it.

But I'm not the only heretic. Writing in the San Juan Almanac, Ken Wright argues that the San Juan region would be better off if it were more isolated, especially from highway traffic.

At home, I read that Salida is in a state of mortal terror and that we're all now shaking in our boots and locking our doors on account of a murder of a convenience-store owner Tuesday night in Poncha Springs, the "Crossroads of the Rockies."

Give people good roads, and they'll use them to find places to commit crimes, and then to flee. After shooting Richard Ellis, did this murderer head east or west on U.S. 50, or north or south on U.S. 285? Was this killer properly grateful to the Good Roads Lobby for the ease of his getaway?

What else happens when we get better roads?

For one thing, more long-haul commuters. I just read about someone commuting from Hartsel to Denver — about three hours each way. Does the phrase "get a life" come to mind? More than half of Park County commutes to another county, as does much of Lake County.

You get a population of people whose loyalties have to be divided, since they work in one place and live in another. And how much energy can they put into the place they live when they're gone so much?

While the presence of good commuter roads improves the chances of selling lots in some subdivisions, it doesn't improve much else. We get developments full of tired people and their latchkey children.

A drive along the Interstate 70 corridor between Denver and Vail reveals another "benefit" of an improved highway: commercial strip development, along with air pollution and congestion.

Every time a new metro highway is opened, we hear pronouncements that traffic will henceforth move smoothly. That actually happens for about a fortnight. Then the traffic flow magically adjusts so that the new highway is just as crowded as the others. Millions of dollars get spent to no discernible benefit — except, perhaps, to EPA bureaucrats who have more bad-air readings to help justify their existence.

As for the general arguments about prosperity, where are the highest real-estate values and per-capita incomes in Colorado? Aspen, at the end of a wretched two-lane road backed up against a wilderness. Crested Butte, at the end of a miserable two-lane road backed up against a wilderness. Telluride, at the end of a shoddy ... do you see a pattern here that doesn't have much to do with four-lane, limited-access highways?

Last summer, some history buffs based in Monte Vista began to organize the Old Spanish Trail Association. The trail, designed to connect Santa Fe to Los Angeles, represented a deliberate effort by the colonial office in Madrid to establish a route that would hold Spain's faltering empire together. The famous Dominguez-Escalante expedition of 1776 was part of this effort.

Reading about the Old Spanish Trail inspired some contemplation. Rome held its empire together with roads. So did the Incas. They needed roads not only for commerce, but to dispatch troops for quelling provincial disorders.

Then recall that our interstate highways were originally promoted as a "defense" measure for military transportation.

So when we hear talk about the need for "better roads," maybe we're missing the real question when we address things like crime, congestion or air pollution.

Perhaps we should realize that roads are actually instruments of empire, and ask ourselves "What imperial power wants this road, and why?" Not that our answers would matter, but we'd have a better idea of what's going on and why.

Here Come the Planners; There Go the Residents
May 28, 1996

How do you destroy a laid-back and ramshackle little mountain town? Easy. Just add money.

A decade ago, Salida wasn't worth anything, and so nobody cared what it looked like. You just lived here without worrying about resale values.

Now, alas, Salida seems to be worth something. People care about preserving property values. They care so much that we're getting a vision statement and a master plan, prepared by consultants: the Leland Consulting Group of Denver and Portland.

To put it charitably, the consultants have trouble reading a map or figuring out where they are.

In their acknowledgements, they thank our mayor, Nancy Sanger, as well as the Salida city administrator, the local volunteer planning committee, and "The Town of Crestone Board of Trustees and Mayor Kent Murray" who "supplied critical information about the Crestone community early and throughout the process."

Crestone is a charming town and, like many Salidans, I have friends there. But I still can't figure out why its mayor and town board should have anything to do with Salida's "Comprehensive Plan and Implementation Strategy."

In the appended maps, the main highway through town is identified as "I-50," as in "Interstate 50," rather than its accurate title of U.S. Highway 50.

Perhaps this confusion between an interstate and a federal primary route is an accident, but it could mean that the planners want us to have a genuine four-lane limited-access interstate highway, so that we could get the associated blessings of improved transportation: more noise, higher crime, franchise strips and outlet malls.

They seemed to imply that much at a public hearing last week. One of the planners explained that they had worked in Grand and Summit counties, and we should be aware that the big developers were looking southward at us, since they had pretty much run out of land to improve up there.

Now, if I were a planner who had anything to do with Summit County, I'd deny it unless I faced a perjury sentence, and even then I'd think twice before confessing to such a fact.

Before the interstate invaded, Breckenridge was a pleasant place where dogs slept on Main Street, everybody important drank breakfast at the Gold Pan, and people lived in cabins, tepees, old mine tunnels and converted school buses.

Now Breckenridge aspires to join Aspen as a stop on the Euro-trash circuit. Few who work there can afford to live there. Summit County has franchise strips, traffic congestion and air pollution.

If that's what planners can do for a place, why bother? We're perfectly capable of trashing out a valley all on our own, without any help from consultants.

If we need consultants, it's to find out how to keep Summit County from happening here.

The general thrust of the plan is to beautify and gentrify a gritty old railroad town.

Very little of the proposed zoning concerns legitimate issues like health and safety. Instead, most of it proposes to elevate local esthetics: "the elimination of blight-causing influences," "prohibit the use of materials associated with lower-quality industrial areas such as chain link fencing," "control the character and visual impact," etc.

Naturally, the plan addresses "affordable housing." The idea is to elevate housing standards. Those who already struggle to pay the rent certainly would have more trouble paying for the improved housing.

But the plan says there are federal subsidies. Hasn't anybody heard that the great federal subsidy machine is drying up? Or that no one has yet come up with a planning mechanism to save little mountain towns from People of Money?

Here's what will happen. Salida will adopt this plan, or something quite similar. It will become very difficult to be poor here, whereas it used to be fairly easy to live here without much money.

If rising real-estate prices in general aren't enough to drive us out, then the higher standards will force us to spend money we don't have in order to eliminate our "blight-causing influences."

And if we're resistant, there will be fines, inspections and similar municipal harassment. Eventually, we'll either join overregulated, live-above-your-means Mainstream America, or we'll move on.

Either way, the People of Money will triumph. They'll either chase us out or convert us. The city government, which we elect to defend and promote our interests, will be totally in their hands.

This happens all over Colorado, all over the Mountain West. It's happening here, and it's galling to realize how powerless you are when the People of Money, after their conquests along the I-70 sacrifice zone, decide to invade your territory.

Perhaps We Should Study What Lies Behind
the New Place Names
August 18, 1996

Place names always have fascinated me, perhaps because they offer, in a word or two, a whole bunch of history.

For instance, I grew up in Evans, just south of Greeley. It was named for John Evans, second territorial governor of Colorado and a major promoter of the Denver Pacific Railroad, which in 1870 linked struggling and isolated Denver to the booming main-line city of Cheyenne, Wyo.

Evans, who operated in Chicago before heading west, left his name in that area, too — Evanston was his real-estate development. Political patronage gave John Evans his job here; his appointment came from Abraham Lincoln, an Illinois politician.

This all seems to demonstrate that, during and after the Civil War, modern Colorado was taking form as part of the Midwest — politically, economically and culturally.

Other place names can be just as informative. Breckenridge was originally Breckinridge, named for John Breckinridge, vice president under James Buchanan. The goal was a post office — what politician could refuse to extend mail service to a place named in his honor? But when Breckinridge sided with the South (he became Confederate secretary of war), the town fathers changed the spelling.

That appears to be an early form of "geographic political correctness," and the process is still with us.

Minnesota recently attempted to erase "squaw" from its map. High-school students there traced the word to a term for vagina. One county complied with "Politically Correct Creek" and "Politically Correct Bay," but the state rejected those new names.

If this purification campaign spreads, future students will have trouble finding the site of the 1960 Winter Olympics: Squaw Valley, Calif. In Colorado, there's Squaw Creek, where Zebulon Pike's party celebrated Christmas in 1806. It flows 8 miles north of town, and I wonder when it will become "Native American Woman Cusec-Challenged Watercourse."

And if it's improper to name features for female body parts, what's to become of the Grand Tetons in Wyoming?

Early Colorado settlers often prevented this problem. Before they came, the 14ers above Crestone were the "Trois Tetons," but then became Crestone, Crestone Needle and Kit Carson. West of Walsenburg, the old name "Wajatoya" meant "breasts of the earth," but now they're the "Spanish Peaks."

But the pioneers didn't always leave us a PC map. There's still Nipple Mountain up by Turret and Granny's Nipple near Kremmling.

Cleaning up the map will take a while — just the research to find all the offensive names will require years, followed by hearings to determine more acceptable nomenclature. In my dark and cynical moments, I suspect this crusade is merely an employment program to provide publicly funded lifetime careers for enlightened geography majors, who might otherwise have to find honest work.

Devil's Tower in Wyoming is another recent target. Critics argue that it was a sacred place to whichever tribe had it last (we took it from the Sioux, who took it from the Crow, who took it from, etc.), and our infernal nomenclature constitutes insensitive blasphemy, at best.

We'll be busy in Colorado if the Devil must also be exorcised here: Devil's Slide on Rollins Pass, Devil's Thumb east of Fraser, Devil's Backbone west of Loveland, Devil's Nose in Clear Creek County and Devil's Point near Durango are examples.

That's merely a possibility, though. Other forms of renaming are underway.

A rural mailing address used to be of the form "Route 3, Box 456, Backwater, Colo." This was meaningful only to the Postal Service.

If you had to drive there yourself, as I did in learning my way around Kremmling's environs years ago, you learned to navigate by the directions you got: "Go up the Back Troublesome a couple-three miles till you get to the old Wheatley place where they had the fire in '56, then hook the next right, just down from where George Henricks got caught in the slide ..."

In other words, you had to acquire a considerable amount of local lore to go anywhere off the pavement. This was annoying at first, but I got used to it and realized that it served a noble purpose — keeping out people who wouldn't bother to learn their way around. If people refuse to learn Front Troublesome from Back, or where the old Wheatley place is, they have no business being there.

Now, however, mainstream America is overlaying the established rural geography with standardized addresses. "Route 3, Box 456" becomes "78901 Generic Lane." I've been told this is to accelerate emergency response for imported 911 dispatchers and the like, but it also simplifies matters for process servers, outside police agents, real-estate speculators and other strangers who are seldom up to any good.

History shows us that conquerors exercise their right to put the names on maps, and I must confess that even if I don't approve, it is fascinating to see the process at work right before our eyes.

New Theories May Explain the
Disappearance of the Ancient Ones
December 3, 1996

MILLIONS OF AMERICANS must share my mild interest in the Anasazi — the "Ancient Ones" who inhabited the Four Corners region about a millennium ago. They erected hundreds of buildings, some of them huge even by Park Meadows Mall standards, and then disappeared.

Some argue that the Anasazi were the ancestors of today's Pueblo tribes and others that they were the Utes' forebears. Frequently you see a Hopi claim of descent from the Anasazi.

Nobody seems to know for sure, but there's no lack of theories — one just appeared in print yesterday, concerning the precise north-south alignment of three major Anasazi centers at Aztec Ruins, Chaco Canyon and Casas Grandes.

During my formative years in this state, the most powerful politician from Colorado was Rep. Wayne Aspinall, chairman of the House Interior Committee. Aspinall never saw a river that didn't need a dam, and, right or wrong, he represented Colorado attitudes in that regard.

And so in grammar school, when it was time to learn about Mesa Verde and other Anasazi remnants, our teacher would explain the marvels of dendrochronology — building time-lines from tree rings.

The rings on the timbers used in Anasazi structures also indicated that there were decades of severe drought before the Anasazi moved out, we heard. The teacher would conclude that if the benighted Anasazi had just had a Bureau of Reclamation to build dams, diversions and canals to get them through the dry years, they could have stayed there. And so we should be grateful that we lived in an enlightened era.

By the time the Anasazi appeared in my college curriculum, we had just celebrated the first Earth Day, and dams were out of fashion.

Thus we learned that the Anasazi probably had multiplied beyond the carrying capacity of the land around them. As they stripped the canyons and mesas for firewood and food, the land became less productive, an ecological catastrophe caused a famine and those who survived moved on.

Obviously, we were supposed to learn a lesson from that example of ecology and human population dynamics.

But what I have really learned is that theories about the Anasazi tell us a lot more about the theorizers than they do about the Anasazi.

Every Native American tribe with a remote claim on the Southwest also claims descent from the Anasazi. Among the white-eyes, the Water Buffalo Tribe uses the Anasazi as an example of what happens if you don't build dams, and the Earth Day People cite the Anasazi as an object lesson about the results of overpopulation.

This leads me to believe that soon we will see other theories about the disappearance of the Ancient Ones:

— From the Colorado Cattlemen's Association. For centuries, the Anasazi thrived as their turkey flocks roamed the mesas. But then the Evil Central Government in Acoma, concerned about the alleged effects of so-called overbrowsing on the acorn crop, started charging market rates for fowl forage permits, which put the poultry ranchers out of business, and the Anasazi starved to death.

— From the Colorado Board of Realtors. The Mesa Verde complex was originally built as an apartment house, but its owners realized they could make a fortune in copper bells and parrot feathers if they took it condo.

So they evicted all the residents and started selling units, some on time-shares. Unfortunately, the Pecos Pueblo Savings & Loan, which had been financing the project, got overextended just as interest rates began to climb. It collapsed, and the developers, unable to get alternate financing on account of Onerous Government Regulations, had to leave the area. Without developers to provide jobs, the Anasazi had to leave, too.

— From Club 20. For many years, the Anasazi thrived by trading pigments, made from uranium ores on their plateaus, to other cultures. However, that market collapsed, and meanwhile, the Unheeding Regional Government at Chaco Canyon refused to build more long and smooth roads, which the Anasazi believed were essential to their prosperity. Despite fervent prayers and offerings to the Caterpillar, a common petroglyph believed to symbolize their road-building deity, the Anasazi were denied and just faded away.

— From the most recent scientific research. We wandered through some of Anasaziland on a vacation last spring, and at every stop, there was this annoying New Age flute music playing in the background.

Upon inquiry, I learned that this worse-than-Muzak was the kind of music that some Anasazi rock-art flautist might have played. If that's the case, the Anasazi, unable to eliminate this noxious and omnipresent noise from their environment, committed mass suicide.

The Right Signs Could Produce
a Truly Educational Trail
July 15, 1997

At first I was appalled at the notion that some segments of the Continental Divide Trail might be financed by corporate donations, acknowledged by signs along the route.

I presume the messages on these signs would resemble the "noncommercial" announcements on public radio: "The next 8 miles have been made possible by a generous grant from the International Grain Cartel, proud provider of the raw materials that make up your gorp."

This prospect seemed to negate the very reason one might go for a getaway-from-it-all stroll in the mountains — I suspect that most of us don't head for the high country to see billboards, even tasteful billboards, of any size.

Then again, in modern America, it's pretty difficult to escape commercial messages. Public schools sell advertising along their hallways, coaches and athletes at state universities sport corporate swooshes to indicate their true loyalties, humble bus benches are festooned with gaudy promotions and shopping carts carry placards. Ads appear even on the walls above urinals where we used to read advice like "Why are you laughing? The joke is in your hand" and "For a good time, call Candy at 555-1234."

So why should the Continental Divide be any different?

But even at that, I'm not too sure trail sponsorship would be a good deal. When you're above timberline and a dozen miles from pavement, you're not in a position to make an immediate purchase.

The trail sign is thus a form of institutional advertising, designed to make you think "Well, next time I need a pair of hiking boots, I'll buy some Hobstompers, since they're such caring people who share my interest in establishing and maintaining back-country trails."

I don't know about you, but when I'm at 12,000 feet and up, hypoxia means that I have trouble thinking, let alone reading and remembering some brand name. The last time I climbed a 14er, I dumbly sat and enjoyed the supernal fireworks of an electrical storm headed ever closer. Only when my skin began to tingle as my hair stood straight out did it dawn on me that I'd best hasten down before I got a real big charge from the expedition.

So I don't know that the trail-sponsorship signs would do much toward enhancing the sponsor's revenue stream, but there could be some educational possibilities if anybody, not just a corporate external-affairs department, were allowed to put up signs along the trail:

— The next 9 miles of sunny, open meadow laced with skidder trails and punctuated by stumps, formerly a gloomy forest, was made possible by the routine activities of the Louisiana-Pacific Corporation, which has since shut down its local mill and moved on. Please report any lingering formalde-hyde vapors to the state health department.

— Fill your canteen now. Water in the next 4 miles of Wightman Fork contains cyanide compounds and high concentrations of heavy-metal ions, due to a generous chemical donation from Galactic Minerals, a Canadian corporation beyond the reach of United States law.

— Your easy hiking in the next 12-mile stretch, where you will not need to fret about bogs, swamps or the perils of fording a raging torrent, is the result of bountiful diversions by the Aurora Water Department, the Northern Colorado Water Conservancy District and the Colorado Springs Utility De-partment.

— The next 160 miles of gentle grade, complete with trestles and tun-nels, was made possible by a major abandonment from the Union Pacific Railroad Corporation, which has been avoiding Colorado since 1869.

— Convenient willow-free access to the creek for the next 21 miles has been facilitated by the National Park Service, which encourages overpopula-tion of elk, since visitors like to see big herbivores and the more visitors, the more money for the Park Service. The elk eat all the willows and you enjoy a better view of the creek. Another service from your federal government, pro-tecting our environment.

— As you overlook the valley for the next 3 miles, the brilliant glares that temporarily blind you have been made possible by the Acme Steel Roof Company, proud providers of high-snow-load, high-reflection covers in the high country since 1958.

All manner of other possibilities come to mind — severely eroded "single-track" ruts created by the mountain bike industry, begging marmots made possible by the dried-fruit processors, fire-blackened ruins in the Stupid Zones resulting from our hard-working rural real-estate developers.

So I've come to terms with this commercialization of a public trail, just as long as they're not too restrictive about signage.

Draining Lake Powell Would
Continue the West's Traditions
November 16, 1997

THE SIERRA CLUB received considerable criticism this fall after its president, Adam Werbach, proposed that the government consider opening Glen Canyon Dam and draining Lake Powell.

The benefits would include more available water in the arid Southwest, since Lake Powell loses more from evaporation than it gains by storage. It also traps sediment that once built beaches in the Grand Canyon, and the reservoir cools the Colorado River to the detriment of endangered native warmwater fish.

Removing the dam is hardly an original idea.

I first saw it 20 years ago in an essay by Edward Abbey, who bemoaned the loss of the gorgeous canyon now inundated, as well as the consequent industrialization of what had been wholesome, challenging and useless desert. The remnants of the dam, he suggested, should be named Floyd Dominy Falls, after the commissioner of the Bureau of Reclamation when the dam was built in 1960-64.

For my part, when I finally visited Page, Ariz., in March 1996 during the artificial flood, I was prepared to despise the dam, like a good Abbey fan.

But instead, after riding to the bottom where I could gaze up at its immensity, as the huge generators throbbed and great jets of high-pressure water plumed out toward the river, well, I felt rather proud to be of a species that could even imagine such a project, let alone build it and keep it running.

Perhaps the West's congressional delegations felt the same way, though they expressed it differently: just the usual denunciations of absurd schemes from tree-hugger idealists who aren't real Westerners, or they'd understand how important it is to balance the federal budget while continuing federal subsidies for anything that might benefit real-estate development in the West.

Further, what point is there in building this huge dam — 710 feet high, 4,901,000 cubic yards of concrete, 27,000,000 acre-feet of storage — at a cost of 272 million pre-inflation 1964 dollars, only to tear it out just a few decades later?

That sounds like a good question, but it's one that no Western representative or senator should ask. The history of this part of the world is pretty much a story of building things at tremendous expense (from the public treasury if possible, but from private sources if necessary) and then abandoning them.

Within an afternoon's drive from Salida, I can easily find at least $272 million in wasted capital spending — that is, money invested in projects that looked like good ideas at the time, but now are abandoned or mothballed.

At the top of Frémont Pass, for instance, sits the Climax Molybdenum Mine, where hundreds of millions of dollars were spent in the past 75 years — and the only current activity is in the water-treatment plant. Even during the Shining Times, private enterprise was just as talented at waste as government — a $20 million oxide-recovery mill opened with great fanfare, only to be scrapped within the decade.

All around here are old railroad routes — Marshall Pass, Trout Creek Pass, Alpine Tunnel, Hagerman Tunnel — that good men died to build and operate. Right through town there are rails, laid and maintained at tremendous cost over the past 117 years, which the Union Pacific Railroad plans to abandon — more millions down some rathole in the West.

For that matter, the Union Pacific itself was the result of federal subsidies right after the Civil War. The idea was to move goods across the continent. At last report, the UP was hopelessly snarled, unable to do the job it was created to do — more millions, perhaps even billions, wasted in the West.

What of all those abandoned silver mines and smelters, built when the federal government subsidized silver mining and discarded after the subsidies quit in 1893? Or more recently, the toxic residues of a uranium boom financed 50 years ago by taxpayers of this great republic?

Or the nuclear-weapon fabrication plants and facilities — Hanford, Rocky Flats, Los Alamos, Yucca Flat — billions of dollars invested in the West, all worse than useless now?

Go as far back as we want — even a millenium, to Chaco Canyon and Mesa Verde — and we find little but ruins from vast investments that later turned sour.

By those standards, $272 million Glen Canyon Dam is a mere drop in the bucket, another one of those propositions that seemed like a good idea at the time, but didn't turn out quite so well.

As I mentioned, Glen Canyon Dam and Lake Powell awed me, so I'd be just as happy if they stayed in place.

But if it turns out that the dam wasn't such a good idea after all, it wouldn't be the first time. Considering how the West teems with the ruins of everything from cliff houses to missile silos, forlorn farmsteads and decaying ghost towns, Floyd Dominy Falls would fit perfectly in this land of expensive failures.

THE INVASION OF THE KILLER TREES
Published in Empire January 18, 1998

THE SKI-INDUSTRY PROMOTERS have had their work cut out for them recently, attempting to persuade Americans that alpine skiing remains a relatively safe activity despite two fatal accidents involving prominent people — Michael Kennedy and Sonny Bono.

The industry is right, of course. As leisure activities go, skiing is fairly safe — about one fatality per million skier-days. Figure the average skier's day involves six hours in lift lines, riding the lift, or even actually skiing, and that works out to one fatality every 6 million hours.

For every six million hours that Americans spend in their cars, 36 die in accidents, so the actual skiing is much safer than the journey into the mountains to reach the slopes.

Of course, that statistic won't help the ski industry's current image problem. It's hard to imagine ads that proclaim "Once you get here, you're 36 times safer than you were on the trip. Good luck on the trip home — and honest, it really doesn't take six million hours to get back to Denver from Vail on a Sunday afternoon."

The other problem with promoting safety is that it's not very exciting, and the industry wants to sell excitement. Have you ever seen a ski poster featuring a wholesome family cruising serenely down a bunny hill? Or is it more like some gnarly dude soaring and zigzagging along a black-diamond run?

Our ski industry faces the same dilemma as other commercial outdoor recreation.

River outfitters around here want you to believe that the Arkansas is an untamed free-flowing torrent which cascades through hidden wilderness, rather than a very accessible stream whose flow is controlled almost to the drop by the Southeastern Colorado Water Conservancy District. And they also want you to believe that whitewater rafting is a safe family activity.

Likewise, skiing is simultaneously an "out on the edge" adventure in natural powder, and a safe sport with guaranteed opening dates on manufactured snow.

Little wonder that I've never known a ski resort's marketing director who stayed on the job more than a year or two — presenting two contradictory images strains the considerable talents of Bill Clinton and Newt Gingrich, and there just aren't that many people who can do that for a sustained period. For which deficiency, perhaps, we should be grateful.

But we still have the safety-image problem for our vital ski industry — the source of thousands of low-wage no-benefit jobs, the inspiration for hundreds of elegant trophy homes occupied for a fortnight each year, the very reason for expensive plans to expand the capacity of the Interstate 70 corridor.

Now consider the trees along the runs. They're important in an esthetic sense, of course, but in most other respects, they're nothing but trouble.

For appearance' sake, slope-side trees can't be logged, so they're worthless as timber. Given all the commotion nearby, they don't offer much in the way of wildlife habitat, either. Studies at the Fraser Experimental Forest near Winter Park have demonstrated that trees suck up millions of gallons of precious water each year, and that clear-cutting improves water yields, thus providing more to divert and more real-estate development along the Front Range.

And then there's the safety hazard so tragically demonstrated recently. It's safe to predict that a lawsuit will be filed one of these days, alleging that the ski area and the U.S. Forest Service were negligent in allowing trees to grow in areas where people could not be reasonably expected to encounter them.

The solution seems obvious. Replace the real trees with plastic ones which bend or even topple in collisions.

Supply should be no problem — we already have an industry which produces handsome artificial Christmas trees in several natural-looking varieties of fir and spruce.

Removing the real trees and replacing them with plastic trees would provide summer employment in a now-seasonal industry. The supply of firewood and lumber would increase, to the benefit of both the poor who heat with wood and the rich who build new chalets. Plus, the fabricated flora would not consume water, thereby allowing Colorado to continue to grow.

Most important, appearances would be maintained — a Christmas-card picture-perfect slope flanked by evergreens with a light frosting of fresh Colorado champagne powder. Who would even notice that both the snow and the trees, natural as they might appear, were both artificial?

Holiday Greetings

As will be clear from certain of these columns, I'm not fond of holidays. For one thing, I've worked hard over the years to put my daily life into an agreeable routine, and anything that disrupts that routine is by definition disagreeable.

For another, holidays mean deadlines get changed so that The Post's editorial-page editors can have a day off. These changes never involve moving the deadline back — it always gets moved forward.

This can make a timely topic too big a risk — a lot can change in the interval between writing and publication, and the longer that interval is, the greater the chance that a given current issue will change course in some totally unexpected direction.

And so, the holiday itself is often the only prudent topic, and thus, this section.

In case you're curious about my dad, from whom I quoted extensively for a Father's Day column, he's still a lively "maintenance problem" with a bad attitude.

The local paranoia mentioned in the Christmas 1994 column turned out to be quite justified — the state had an undercover informant operating in Salida. Within the month, he got killed in a fight with a local kid, who was then convicted of felony murder. A local pilot, attempting to return the informant's body to his home in Cortez, was killed in a plane crash.

Thus, two lives were ended and another will be spent in prison — and we're supposed to believe the War on Drugs is protecting us.

The Fourth of July is always a good occasion to take another look at that seditious and revolutionary document, the Declaration of Independence, and it's become something of an annual tradition for me. The Fourth is one holiday I'd endorse wholeheartedly if we actually set it aside for the Declaration.

What the Old Man Had to Say
June 13, 1986

SINCE SUNDAY is Father's Day, this is a good time to correct a family problem. Although my parents live in Longmont, my dad's name is the same as mine. On occasion he has been accosted by right-thinking people who want to berate the Ed Quillen who wrote something that offended them.

This must be embarrassing for my father, who's not at all like me. He's a responsible, respectable citizen with a steady job. He's a good Republican and a good Baptist, a teetotaler who does not patronize saloons and other low haunts. His hair is short and neatly trimmed, and he has never grown a beard.

Even so, there are people who cannot tell one Ed Quillen from the other. If my dad has to be confronted by them, then it's only fair that he and they get a chance to argue about his opinions, instead of mine. He has plenty of opinions to argue about.

When I was in college, a new slumlord acquired the apartment house we were living in and announced an immediate rent increase. When I and other tenants protested, the owner said he planned some improvements, financed by the increased rentals, "so it's for your own good." I mentioned this to my dad. "Whenever somebody tells you he's doing something for your own good, make sure you've got your hand over your wallet. It isn't your good he's worried about."

Once I went to the post office with him. In the box was a notice of a certified letter. Instead of going to the counter and signing for the letter, my dad threw the notice into the trash. I wondered why. "Nobody who's your friend ever sends a certified letter," he told me.

Another time he was teaching me to drive. A dog ran in front of us; swerving to miss the dog, I narrowly missed a head-on collision and ended up stuck in a ditch. "Whenever it's a choice between hitting a dog and swerving out of your lane, hit the dog. Otherwise, you run a good chance of getting killed, and I've never met a dog worth dying for."

He had other advice for the road. "When you're driving, keep both hands on the wheel. When you're paying attention to a girl, she deserves both hands. Don't try to devote one hand to the car and the other to the girl, or you'll deserve all the trouble you get into that way."

I quit a boring, dead-end job in 1973. A month later, I was frustrated, angry and broke, because I hadn't been able to find a new job — even another boring, dead-end one. He counseled me. "All your life, you'll either be working or looking for work. Damned if I know which is worse."

After they moved to Longmont, a zoning law came into effect that limited the number of unlicensed cars one might keep in one's yard. This intrusion into his rights as a property owner had an awful effect on him. He couldn't afford new cars that didn't need repairs all the time, so he always kept two or three old Chevys around to provide enough parts to keep one junker on the road. "Laws like this are discrimination, pure and simple. Why don't they quit monkeying around and just come right out and say that they're trying to make it illegal to be poor in Colorado."

My dad is a passionate opponent of all forms of gun control, and I asked him once to explain why. "It isn't the saying that if guns are outlawed, only outlaws will have guns. It's that if guns are outlawed, only cops will have guns. The only reason you can feel somewhat safe inside your own house is private gun ownership. A cop isn't going to kick in your door if he thinks you might be waiting inside with a shotgun. Private gun ownership makes the law respect the law."

When I was just a baby, he worked 10 hours a day in a laundry washroom. It was exhausting toil, but after work every day, he built the house I grew up in. It was made of logs, and he made every cut with a sweat-powered timber saw; my dad couldn't afford a chain saw. I asked recently where he found all that energy. "I don't know. It's just something you can do when you're in your 20s. After you turn 30, you're just a maintenance problem."

I hope he goes on being a maintenance problem for a good, long time.

HOW THEY CELEBRATED THE LAST CHRISTMAS
December 19, 1986

ACROSS THE WORLD, people got the message. They had no choice, because the message appeared simultaneously on every television and radio station, and it was, of course, extensively reported in the newspapers.

Turks beheld Saint Nicholas of Myra delivering the message, as did most other Europeans, although it was presented in France by le Pere Noel and in Italy by La Befana. Russians heard it from Father Frost. Americans saw Santa Claus, who tapped his pipe against the microphone and began to speak.

"Please forgive my intrusion into what must be a busy time for you. And that's the problem.

"This was supposed to be a time of peace and goodwill, of generosity and fellowship — that was my true gift to mankind, no matter what you saw in my sleigh. But what have you done with this gift?

"You celebrate fellowship by crowding into airports and shopping malls, where you are treated like cattle — indeed, I would face criminal charges if I treated my reindeer the way you allow yourselves to be treated. But perhaps you deserve to be handled like animals, because you snarl, snap and trample.

"You honor generosity by brainwashing your children to covet ephemeral trinkets, and you have made the joyful sharing of gifts into a sordid occasion of resentment, guilt and indebtedness. You believe that goodwill can be found in a bottle; too many of your gatherings are debauchery followed by highway carnage. And I need not go into detail about your total incompetence at keeping the peace."

He paused to get his pipe going again, and the world held its breath. "This is it," he said eventually, his voice cracking. "There will never be another Christmas."

A worldwide murmur became an uproar, which quieted as the tired old man continued. "As I am merely a saint, my powers are somewhat limited. But I promise you that henceforth anyone who uses my name or likeness, for any purpose whatsoever, will find himself in court with a restraining order — if my elves don't get to his kneecaps first."

He smoothed his beard and pointed upward from wherever he was sitting. "I also have it from the very highest authorities that they, too, have had enough, and they will take whatever steps are necessary to protect their names and reputations from you. And their powers," he added with a chuckle, "are not limited."

Some people thought this was all an elaborate practical joke, but their laughter stopped when the official White House Christmas Tree appeared on the screen, brilliant against a clear, star-filled sky, out of which emerged a tremendous bolt of lightning. Only a smoking crater remained where the tree had stood.

Then the Denver City and County Building appeared in its gaudy holiday lights, which glowed with unnatural intensity for a few seconds before disappearing in a cloud of smoke. Similar images flashed before the frightened audience until a relieved America saw Santa again.

"You may wonder what to do without a Christmas. But you all possess a few decent impulses and some common sense. Use those gifts."

For the first year or two after the last Christmas, the adjustment was not easy. But it came.

When people thought of friends they hadn't seen for some time, they dispatched a card or note immediately, instead of waiting until December.

When they saw something that they knew a friend or relative would cherish, they purchased it and sent it, at that very moment, whether the impulse struck them in March or September.

When people wanted a social occasion with their co-workers, they held one and comported themselves with decency and good humor. When scattered families found a convenient time to reunite for a few days, they did. And when people felt inspired to attend church, they went.

December 25 became just another day as the Christmas season vanished. It was replaced by small daily infusions of Christmas spirit from those who genuinely felt it, and everyone felt it at least once a year — some in January, some in June, and so forth. It averaged out so that every day, everywhere, there were a few people who were happy because they'd heard from old friends. Others smiled because they had found gifts that someone they knew would appreciate. Some felt renewed by worship, and others were heartened by fellowship.

There were even some genuine efforts at being peaceful, and Saint Nicholas, after 16 centuries of trying, finally felt that he had accomplished some good.

How We'll Celebrate Gripesgiving Day
November 27, 1988

As had become traditional, the Smith family — Fred, Karen and their teen-agers Junior and Sis — went to Fred's parents' home to celebrate the newest national holiday, first proclaimed in 1989.

When they arrived, Grandpa was carving the crow while Grandma brought out a fresh-baked humble pie. As they took their seats, Grandpa poured bitters and raised his glass.

"Here's to another Gripesgiving Day," he announced. "I'll go first."

"You always go first," Fred complained, getting into the holiday spirit. "Here I work my tail off, and most of my paycheck goes to pay taxes and Social Security to keep you old coots going, just so you can march down every election day and vote for any candidate who promises more benefits to you parasites over 65. I sure wish I could just vote myself a pay raise every time I wanted one."

"That's enough, Fred," Grandma interjected. "You know full well that if I hadn't sacrificed for all those years — never getting a new mink, making do with an old Mercedes — we never could have put you through college, and you'd be frying hamburgers today."

"A third-rate college it was," Fred lamented.

Karen interrupted him. "It wouldn't matter anyway for me. Men who just finish high school make more than most women who finish college. What kind of country is this when tree trimmers get paid more than nurses?"

"Tree trimmers work in the cold and wind. They risk falling down or ripping themselves open with chainsaws," Fred countered. "Tell me nurses face risks like that inside warm hospitals."

"It's an outrage, no matter how you try to rationalize it. What are we saying — that taking care of trees is more important than taking care of people?"

"How would you know, Mom?" teen-age Sis interrupted. "The only time I ever remember you taking care of me was when I was so sick that the day-care center wouldn't take me. You thought taking care of people was so important that you hired out it to some minimum-wage drones."

"How dare you insult me like that?" Mom spat. "It wasn't my idea to set up an economy where both parents have to have careers just to buy a simple little house."

"Some house," Fred groaned. "The gold plating is wearing off the fixtures in the third-floor bathroom, the hot tub leaks, the second microwave makes the lights flicker sometimes, and there's not enough room in the garage to fit my Porsche in with your Audi and the Voyager."

"Some career," Karen sighed. "Why, the other day someone asked me about coffee."

"Asked you to make coffee?" Junior wondered, speaking for the first time.

"No, but it was still utterly demeaning that a sexist client visiting our office would even dare to think that I might know where the coffee machine was."

"You know more about coffee machines than you do about what I need," Sis interjected. "I'll just die if I don't get a portable CD player like my friends have. It's mortifying when you just have a crummy VCR that won't do stereo."

"But you've got a Macintosh computer, too, don't forget," Karen responded. "Just wait till I tell them about this at the next meeting of the Support Group for Parents of Gifted Children."

Fred broke in. He glared at Junior. "What's with you, son? Why are you so withdrawn? Do we need to call a therapist?"

"No, Dad," the boy apologized. "In most of the world, people don't have enough to eat and they live in tarpaper shacks, if that. No medical care, limited education, hardly any opportunities. Sure, I suppose things could be better here, but I really am having a hard time finding anything that's worth complaining about."

Both his parents began to sob. His father choked several times before speaking. "Where have we failed? Where did we go wrong? Gripesgiving Day is 100 percent American. It's so American that we used to celebrate it every day. What's wrong with you, boy? Are you some kind of subversive?"

ADDING A HOLIDAY
October 15, 1989

CALENDARS are marvelous devices for spreading confusion. The official celebration of Columbus Day was last Monday. Traditional Columbus Day was Thursday, because on Oct. 12, 1492, the sailor standing watch on the Pinta spied land.

However, they used the Julian calendar then, and it was inaccurate by one day every 128 years. In 1582, Pope Gregory XIII rectified matters by declaring that Oct. 4 would be followed immediately by Oct. 15, thereby synchronizing the calendar with the seasons.

So the real 497th anniversary is yet to come. If our current calendar had been in effect in 1492, then it was on the morning of Oct. 22 that Christopher Columbus landed on San Salvador. He thought he was in the Orient near Japan and India; thus the islands were "Indies" and their inhabitants "Indians."

No matter which Columbus Day you choose, the holiday gets more controversial every year. It used to be one of those unofficial events like Hallowe'en or Arbor Day. The second Monday in October became an official government day off only a few years ago in order to placate a large and vocal lobby of Italian-Americans, who claim Columbus as one of their own, since he grew up in the Italian city of Genoa.

Columbus, however, never thought of himself as Italian, or more properly as a Genoese, since there was no Italy then. In 1476, after a stint as a pirate, he fought for Portugal in a battle against Genoa. He always wrote in Spanish or Latin, never Italian.

So honoring Columbus really doesn't do much to honor Italian-Americans who are proud of their ancestry, since Columbus certainly wasn't proud of his Italian ancestry. The other complication with Columbus Day comes from the descendants of those "Indians" who survived the aftermath of the first Columbus Day.

At a rally Monday in Denver, American Indians called for the abolition of Columbus Day as a national holiday. Several speakers observed that Columbus really deserves to go down in history neither as a misguided discoverer nor as a great seaman, but with brutal tyrants like Hitler, Stalin and Pol Pot.

The speakers charged that Columbus established a colonial system that enslaved or killed 300,000 people in Haiti alone, and 20 million more in the Caribbean and South America.

Russell Means, an Indian activist, received a summons after he poured blood on a statue of Columbus. If Means is guilty of defacing a statue, then the sculptor who omitted the blood is guilty of defacing history.

No matter how many demonstrations are held, Columbus Day will never be eliminated as a national holiday. We don't subtract holidays, we add them, and the trend is to placate ethnic groups by declaring new holidays. Those holidays may be named for one person, but in actual fact, Columbus Day is "the day we honor Italian-Americans," just as Martin Luther King Day is "the day we set aside to honor the contributions and struggles of black Americans."

If Irish-Americans wanted to push the issue, St. Patrick's Day could become an official holiday. Scandinavians have promoted Leif Ericsson Day (Oct. 9). In this part of America, Cinco de Mayo becomes more of a general holiday every year — not because our history books mention much about the Mexican repulsion of French invaders at the battle of Puebla on May 5, 1862, but because we want to celebrate and honor Hispanic contributions.

The Indian activists have a point about Columbus. But their current tactics won't get them anywhere. They should instead start lobbying for a Makhpiya-Luta (Red Cloud) Day or a Goyakla (One Who Yawns, a.k.a. Geronimo) Day or a Tecumseh Day.

But their tribes, unlike ours, didn't bother with confusing written calendars. It is thus impossible to select one leader's birthday and make it a "Native American Day." So my suggestion is Tashunca-uitco (Crazy Horse) Day, to be celebrated on June 25 — the anniversary of the Indian victory at the Battle of Greasy Grass, known to many of us white eyes as "Custer's Last Stand."

YES, VIRGINIA, THERE WAS ONE,
AND HERE'S WHAT HAPPENED TO HIM
December 25, 1994

A FAT WHITE GUY with a grizzled beard and a good start on baldness is no novelty in Salida. For that matter, I can see one every time I look into a mirror.

That's why the stranger didn't look all that strange when he stepped into the saloon on that cold winter afternoon. He was dressed kind of weird, in bright colors as though it were still deer season. We left him to himself, nursing some eggnog at the bar, but when my companions wandered off to shoot pool, he eased over to our table.

"What's with you guys?" he asked. "Why are you so clannish? Why not invite a stranger to your table?"

"You came at a bad time," I explained. "The state and federal guys have been making some undercover busts around here lately, so everybody's kind of leery about talking to strangers."

He nodded, his frame shaking like a bowl full of jelly. "That's how they're improving your community? By making everybody suspicious, almost hostile?"

"Guess so," I said. "Hope you'll understand." After I ordered for both of us, I introduced myself and extended my hand.

He shook back. "Call me Nick," he said.

"Where are you from?"

"Smyrna, to start with. Lately my home base is up in the Arctic. But I used to travel a lot, all over the world, really, especially this time of year."

"Why'd you quit traveling so much?" I was just trying to make conversation.

Nick looked thoughtful as he pulled a pipe from his pocket and began to fill and tamp it. "Is it okay for me to light this thing in here?"

I nodded. "The purity patrol doesn't arrive till evening," I explained. "In the afternoon, they let us relax indoors."

Nick smiled and got the pipe going. He rubbed his shoulder and his lined face showed some pain.

"You hurt yourself?" I asked.

"Well, somebody hurt me. It was in Denver. I was up on the roof, doing my job, and the people downstairs heard noises and called a neighbor. He came running over with what looked like a goose gun — a 10-gauge pump with at least a yard of barrel."

"That's nothing to argue with," I commiserated.

"For sure. I didn't even try. I just took off, but I caught a few pellets before I got out of range. And you know what really galls me?"

I shook my head.

"I catch the tube that night, and it's like this guy that winged me is some kind of big hero. They're even thinking of changing the law so that what he did to me would be all nice and legal."

"Well, people are real skittish about crime these days, and you can't really blame them," I consoled. "Didn't you say you travel a lot?" I wanted to change the topic.

"Used to travel plenty. I fly my own aircraft. Granted, it's kind of offbeat, but it never crashed. Not once. The old government-run Federal Aviation Administration used to cut me some slack, but this new private one is so worried about lawsuits or something that they jerked my certificate of airworthiness."

"Well, I'm sure the benefits of cutting red tape and bureaucracy will outweigh the disadvantages." I ordered another round and wondered why my friends were taking so long at a simple game of eight ball.

"Perhaps so. But that, along with the goose gun, was the last straw. You know, I was always real generous. Little kids, strangers, would come up to me and talk about their dreams, and I'd try to make those dreams come true. I'm a man of some means, so often I really could help."

"And now parents won't let their kids anywhere near you because they're scared you're a kidnapper, molester or murderer?" I asked.

"That's for sure. It hurts, because I really liked children. And then there were the death threats that made me fear to go out in public."

"Denver again?" I wondered aloud.

He nodded. "Don't know what that town has against me. But it's not just Denver. And it's not only parents, either. I just stopped by an orphanage, trying to do some good."

"What happened?"

"Fellow named Newt came out and shook his fist and hollered and threatened to call in an air strike if I didn't leave. He said those kids inside needed to learn some discipline and family values, and getting presents just for being good would hurt their moral character. I knew those kids in there were expecting me, but ..."

"Sometimes discretion is the better part of valor," I soothed. "So what are you planning to do now?"

"Retire. There was a time when the world needed and wanted me, when my skills were valuable to society, but I guess they're obsolete now, and I'm too old to learn a new trade."

We downed our drinks together, and when I brought my head down, he was gone, just like that. Too bad. He seemed like a nice guy.

Since We Don't Really Celebrate Holidays, Let's Eliminate Them
January 15, 1995

Tomorrow is yet another legal holiday. Martin Luther King Day comes only two weeks after the legal version of New Year's Day, three weeks after the legal version of Christmas which came less than five weeks after Thanksgiving, and five weeks before the legal version of a holiday that might be Washington's Birthday, Presidents' Day or Great Americans' Day, depending upon whom you ask.

I have nothing against honoring the Rev. Dr. Martin Luther King Jr. His eloquence, prayer and persistence changed the course of our society, and generally in a better way.

But if I want to honor King and the contributions of African-Americans in general, then I ought to care enough to do it on my own time, just as I occasionally set aside an afternoon or evening for enjoying "The Autobiography of Malcolm X," "Collected Poems of Langston Hughes," or "Robert Johnson: The Complete Recordings."

The problem with the King Holiday is the problem with other holidays.

Like most of my self-employed friends, I've gone to considerable work to arrange my life so that I pretty much enjoy what I do every day.

If we want to do something different, like ski, fish, hike, travel or contemplate the complete betrayal of the principles of the Declaration of Independence by the society that now claims Jefferson's words, we just do it.

We don't need to ask Congress or the Colorado General Assembly for permission to take a day off. We don't insist that every American drop whatever she's doing to join us in a break from routine. We don't demand that banks, post offices and courthouses be closed in order to thwart those who might want to do something productive on those days.

But those who like their daily work do not run our world. The Haters run things. They despise their daily work, and every chance they get they pass laws so that they can escape, however temporarily, their mundane oppressions.

If the Haters couldn't keep adding holidays to the calendar, their anger would build, and eventually they would take steps to solve their problems. They'd strike out on their own, or they'd demand that their workplaces become decent, enjoyable environments.

So a King Day doesn't improve the lot of black Americans, any more than a Labor Day improves the workplace. Eliminating the holidays, so that people would act on their grievances instead of merely pining for the next break, might cause some improvement.

Another problem with modern holidays is that many of them occur on a Monday, by law.

Now, if there's something about observing George Washington's Birthday that makes us better Americans, then why don't we do so on the actual date of Jan. 22, instead of the Third Monday in February?

It seems that midweek holidays are hard on the economy. Wednesday chops the week in two. Tuesday or Thursday, and all the people with any power arrange a four-day weekend, which means that no decisions get made.

But why Monday instead of Friday? My hatred of holidays started when I owned a weekly newspaper that had to come out every Thursday. It was work enough to get the courthouse news when the place was open on a Monday. It became nigh impossible on those weeks with a Monday holiday. Move the holiday to Friday, and I might even have enjoyed the day off.

In the workplace in general, there's a psychological edge if you come in on Monday and think, "If we can get five days' work done in four, we can take Friday off," as opposed to coming in on Tuesday and discovering a pile of extra work with no immediate time-off reward in prospect.

So I suspect the Monday holiday, as opposed to the Friday holiday, was an invention of one of our commercial competitors, probably Japan, to reduce American productivity.

Even these objections to holidays might be ignored if holidays actually accomplished their ostensible purpose.

The root of "holiday" is obvious: "holy day." That is, a day set aside for the sacred. The first holidays were community feasts or fasts when normal operations were suspended so that people might devote themselves to higher and nobler thoughts.

But of the millions who will enjoy a day off with pay tomorrow, how many will contemplate how evaluation by "content of character" has turned into "color of skin" when we were supposed to be evolving toward a color-blind society?

Next month, how many Americans meditate upon George Washington's tribulations in the snows of Valley Forge, leading a band of ill-equipped revolutionaries against the superpower of the day? How many more will frolic in the snows of Aspen or Vail? It's the biggest weekend of the season in an industry based on hedonism.

The same holds for most of our other holidays. They're commercial events. Who thinks about soldiers dying on battlefields when it's the First Weekend of the Summer Season? Or about holding certain rights to be unalienable when it's the Middle of the Summer Season? Or about the Ludlow Massacre when it's the Last Weekend of the Summer Season and the mountains beckon?

So if our holidays are supposed to bind us together as a nation by giving us a common culture, a set of events and heroes whom we all honor, they're a miserable failure.

Most Americans are not out decorating veterans' graves in May, or checking out the conditions at VA hospitals in November, or pondering the Spanish conquest of the Americas in October.

Instead, they're thinking of interesting things they might do on a day off, and never mind the reason they're getting the day off.

It's time to eliminate general holidays. If you've got something to celebrate, you can make your own arrangements. If you're too lazy to do that, then it doesn't mean much to you.

Strange Bedfellows Unite to Fight the Horrors of Hallowe'en
October 31, 1995

After both ends of the political spectrum joined to attack "gangsta rap," I shouldn't have been surprised when two Coloradans, always on opposite sides before, issued an invitation to a joint press conference concerning Hallowe'en.

Sitting before the media were Constance Fundament of Jefferson County, who has attracted national attention with her "back to slates and hornbooks" campaign to improve local schools, and Sunshine Chakra of Boulder County, lately the head of the campaign to prohibit all tobacco possession.

They had formed Coloradans United to Confront Heathenism and Offensive Outfits (CUCHOO). Fundament began by urging trick-or-treaters not to wear witch, goblin and other "costumes that glorify heathen superstition."

Chakra had trouble staying silent as Fundament spoke, but he managed to wait his turn. "The problem with these costumes is that they are profoundly disrespectful. Many women study for years to become Wiccans — gentle healers who have for centuries been defamed as witches — and to allow children to represent themselves as such merely by donning a store-bought, non-biodegradable costume, all in the name of frivolity, is a deep and abiding insult to those who have worked so assiduously to put themselves in touch with the natural rhythms and effusions of Earth."

When it was her turn, Fundament assailed hobo costumes. "As the twig is bent, so the tree grows," she said, "and if we allow children to present themselves as unkempt and unemployed, they may fail to seek management positions with Fortune 500 companies on adulthood."

"This also impacts the self-esteem of the homeless," Chakra added. "Middle-class children who can afford to dress better are making cruel sport of the economically impaired."

Both were vehement in denouncing costumes based on Native American themes. "They were godless pagans," Fundament said. "No one has the right to wear a head dress or breech cloth unless that person has gone on a vision quest and meditated in a sweat lodge. To pretend otherwise is to demean our geospiritual ancestors," Chakra added.

Neither had much good to say about trick-or-treating, either. Chakra led off with a passionate assault on white sugar and empty calories, while Fundament declared "this despicable practice encourages our children to believe that they can get the things they want merely by asking, or even worse, by threatening vandalism if they are not bribed to behave themselves, instead of attaining their desires by the traditional American values of discipline and hard work."

Both said that CUCHOO's goal was to ban Hallowe'en entirely.

Chakra explained that the term is descended from "Hallow e'en" from "All Hallows' Even," or the eve of All Saints' Day on Nov. 1. "The very word is a gratuitous insult to the vast majority of humans who never attain sainthood," he said. "Think of the hurt that an innocent little child must feel when she realizes that, in all likelihood, she will never become a saint. By celebrating saints, we irreparably damage the precious self-esteem of those who are not saints."

In Fundament's eyes, saints are just a smokescreen to obscure wicked origins. "The last day of October was originally a Celtic earth cult festival, and the pioneer European missionaries who brought enlightenment mistakenly believed they could eradicate these revelries by moving All Hallow's Day from May 1 to Nov. 1 in the year 834. That was 1,161 years ago, and you can see how evil persists."

CUCHOO plans to purify similar aspects of American popular culture as soon as Hallowe'en is eliminated.

"Our leadership council has determined that there's something even worse than the H-day," Fundament said, "and that is the infidel nomenclature we casually apply to the days of the week."

Saturday, Sunday and Monday, she observed, come from Saturn, the sun and the moon, which have been "worshipped as deities by idolaters since the expulsion from Eden."

Chakra said, "This mundane weekday mention of that which has been held holy by millions of earnest worshippers is a sacrilege that no decent or humane society should commit."

Wednesday and Thursday derive from Odin's Day and Thor's Day, "which celebrate primitive Teutonic divinities," to which Chakra added that "they were violent warmongers, and an influence even worse for children than GI-Joe™ dolls or toy guns."

They had similar objections to Tuesday, which comes from Tiu's Day. Tiu was the Norse version of Mars, the Roman god of war and namesake of the month of March, and another "blot on the calendar."

Then came Friday, from Freyja's Day. Freyja was the Saxon version of Venus, Roman goddess of love and the root word of "venereal."

"Little wonder that we have so much carnal immorality," Fundament began, to be interrupted by Chakra, who shouted that "We must celebrate love in all forms."

Fundament responded that the planet Venus also was known as Lucifer, and as their discussion heated up, I crept out the door. Perhaps someday CUCHOO will get its act together and cleanse our calendar of paganism and insult, but for the moment, Hallowe'en frivolity seems safe.

WHEN IN THE COURSE OF HUMAN EVENTS ...
July 2, 1996

IT IS JULY 4, 1776, and delegates to the Continental Congress in Philadelphia emerge from the old statehouse, ready to retire after a busy day of pledging their lives, fortunes and sacred honor.

Alas for the 56 men, they've been caught in a time warp. When they step outside, they face a line of TV crews.

"Mr. Henry, Mr. Henry," one correspondent shouts. No one replies. Finally a delegate explains that "Patrick Henry of Virginia was not delegated to this Congress."

"I don't mean Patrick Henry, I mean John Henry — the guy with the signature, as in 'Put your John Henry here.' "

"I am John Hancock of Massachusetts, presiding officer of the Congress," states a man in knee breeches, "and it is my signature that is at the fore, writ large so that King George will not need his spectacles to perceive it."

"You sure your name's not John Henry?" the blow-dried correspondent persists. "They told me to get a stand-up with John Henry, since everybody's heard of him."

Meanwhile, several crews have cornered Benjamin Franklin near a pillar. "Mr. Franklin, is it true that you carried on an affair with some tart, and she had a kid?"

Franklin blinks behind his spectacles. "Of what possible relevance to this proceeding is this tired allegation of wenching and bastardy? Today we have challenged a mighty empire, and unless we all hang together, most assuredly we shall all hang separately."

"That's not a denial, Ben," the interviewer continues. "Do you concede that William Franklin of New Jersey is your illegitimate son?"

"Never hath I denied that," Franklin replies, "but do note that this occurred ere I took Deborah to wife."

"Mr. Franklin," another correspondent shouts. "I just heard that this new Declaration thing has been sent to the printer. Won't that be the firm of Franklin & Hall? Doesn't this represent a conflict of interest? Aren't you just in this to line your pockets?"

"The printer of the Declaration is John Dunlap," Franklin responds. "Please excuse me from your further inquiries, unless they concern the momentous question of the day about our relationship to the British Empire."

"You're trying to stonewall us," comes a chorus. "Don't you believe in the people's right to know?"

Close by, Virginia delegate Thomas Jefferson also answers questions.

"Is it true, Mr. Jefferson, that when Virginia needed you during the French and Indian War in 1760, when you were of age to serve in the militia, you instead attended the College of William and Mary? Can you explain your craven avoidance of military service?"

"The good people of Virginia have trusted me to represent them here," Jefferson replies, "and should they find me wanting in physical courage, they may replace me at their pleasure. Do you inquisitors have more for me?"

"Yes, Mr. Jefferson. You raise tobacco and hemp. Do you realize that your plantation could be confiscated?"

"By whom?" Jefferson asks. "Even King George is not such a tyrant and despot as to tell his subjects what plants they may cultivate." He turns to another reporter.

"Isn't it true, Tom, that you keep slaves?"

"Alas, 'tis so," Jefferson confesses. "In an initial draft of the Declaration we adopted today, I called for the abolition of this execrable commerce which Britain hath commenced upon this continent. But South Carolina would not join our cause unless that proviso was deleted, and as Dr. Franklin hath noted, we must have unity."

"So you're willing to compromise your principles for political expedience," a stand-up commentator proclaims. "And why is it that this so-called Congress lacks diversity? It's all white males."

John Adams speaks up. "Mine own dear Abigail hath written me concerning that very topic, that the fair sex be included in any future polity."

The roar of questions increases, and the alarmed delegates flee back indoors, where it's still 1776. John Hancock takes the gavel and asks for motions from the floor.

Richard Henry Lee of Virginia rises. "Gentlemen, I believe that outside this chamber we saw the future if we should pursue the course which I advocated in my motion of June 7, wherein I advocated that these colonies are, and of right ought to be, free and independent states.

"I beseech the consent of this Congress to withdraw that motion, and substitute instead a motion for adjournment, for I perceive that no good will come of the present course if it means that the essayists of the future will concern themselves with mere vanities and trifles, rather than the great questions of the age."

His motion passed unanimously and the delegates crept out the back doors. The correspondents outside turned their attention to rumors from London that Queen Charlotte had been carrying on an affair with Lord North.

SHAMELESS COMMERCIAL MESSAGE

Back in 1994, Martha and Ed Quillen got back into publishing by launching a small regional monthly magazine, Colorado Central.

It carries articles, essays, humor, book reviews — just about anything that pertains to the customs and culture of the Big Empty in the middle of Colorado.

Of course we think you should subscribe to it. But on the other hand, you probably haven't seen it, and, to be honest, you should reserve your faith for things that really matter, rather than an unseen magazine.

So, we've got a deal for you. Just tell us your name and address, and we'll send you the magazine (we mail it on or near the 20th of each month).

Then we'll send you a bill for $20. If you pay it, you'll get 12 editions of Colorado Central. If you don't, we'll quit sending it.

To get this started, you can drop us a note at the following address. Or you can fax your name and address to 719-539-5345. Or dispatch an email to cozine@chaffee.net.

COLORADO CENTRAL

P.O. Box 946
SALIDA CO 81201